WOMEN AND PANCHAYATI RAJ

WOMEN AND PANCHAYATI RAJ

B.R. Trivedi

CYBER TECH PUBLICATIONS
4264/3, Ansari Road, Daryaganj, New Delhi-110002 (India)
Ph.: 011-23244078. Fax: 011-23280028
E-Mail: cyberpublicationsdelhi@yahoo.com

WOMEN AND PANCHAYATI RAJ

B.R. Trivedi

First Edition 2009

Published by :

G.S. Rawat for **Cyber Tech Publications**
4264/3, Ansari Road, Daryaganj, New Delhi-110002 (India)
Ph.: 011-23244078. Fax: 011-23280028
E-Mail: cyberpublicationsdelhi@yahoo.com

Printed at : **Amit Enterprises**, Maujpur, Delhi, (9810878184)

Preface

The Panchayati Raj was in existence during the Vedic period in ancient India and worked well as the people carried out their personal and official duties based on dharma. After Independence, the Government of India, under the influence of Mahatma Gandhi, was committed to set up Panchayati Raj system to provide real swaraj to the people of rural areas. The dream of decentralization of power in order to empower people at the grassroot level, particularly, to enable rural masses to join the mainstream and claim rightful participation in the process of their own development and governance attained its fulfillment on April 24, 1993. the people of India took over four decades to realize this dream of Mahatma Gandhi. To familiarize a reader with Panchayati Raj institutions and empowerment of women, the book is spread over six chapters. Besides, the detailed bibliography would certainly interest researchers working in this field. The present volume shall provide the necessary base and intellectual stimulus for a more informed debate in working out the future policies and approaches towards democratic decentralization and Panchayati Raj in our country. The book deals with the historical context and examines current issues and would be of much use to research scholars, policy makers, planners, decision-makers, elected members o the Panchayat as well as students in universities and others interested in the concerned subjects.

—Author

CONTENTS

Preface

1. Grassroots Democracy in India 1
2. Women in Panchayati Raj Institutions 31
3. Empowering Women through Panchayats in Rajasthan 67
4. Women and Panchayati Raj 81
5. Gender and Local Governance a New Discourse in Development 106
6. Report of the Steering Committee 155
7. National Policy for the Empowerment of Women 310

Bibliography 331

Index 333

1

GRASSROOTS DEMOCRACY IN INDIA

INTRODUCTION

It has now become clear that, for sustainable economic and social development to take place in any country, it is necessary that people participate in the political process. The process of participation is complex-and it is by no means clear that it is comprehensively inclusive. By this, we mean that it is not possible to assume that all sections of the population take part effectively in the political and democratic processes of society. There are many reasons why people may not participate-from apathy to a sense of helplessness.

In particular, unless specific conditions are met, women face multiple hurdles and find it difficult to participate in the political process that has hitherto been a male bastion. The reasons for this are gender specific. Women are less mobile than men are. They have domestic responsibilities, which puts limits on the time they can spend in such processes. There are historical prejudices. Consistent efforts will have to be made over a period of time to engender the political process and institutions and issues that are critical to this process. This paper explores some aspects of this process in the context of decentralised governance ushered in by the 73rd Constitutional amendment in India in the last five years.

Recognising this limitation where gender is concerned, India has passed laws that make it mandatory for local governments to include women. [These laws do not apply to state and national level legislatures.] One third of the seats in local bodies-gram or village panchayats, municipalities, city corporations and district bodies-are "reserved" for women. This means the contests can only be between women in these constituencies. The first step in enabling women to participate has been taken. This reservation of seats, in the 1993-94 elections, has brought in about 800,000 women into the political process in a single election. They are now just about completing their first term [of five years] in elected office. Elections for the second round will soon have to be held. What has been the experience with this experiment in social engineering?

This paper is organised as follows. Section II presents the overall picture of women in panchayati raj institutions--PRIs. This section also discusses the structure of the system as it has evolved so far, and why this paper is limited to discussing the experience of one state-Karnataka. Section III then discusses some specific experiences of women in PRIs. This brings out in concrete form the field level reality. This is something that may be appreciated intellectually by lawmakers and scholars. But this local reality has to be built into institutions and processes in an essential way if the system is to be made to work as intended. Since these can be sensitive issues, and our intention is to learn from such experience, not cause local turbulence, we are locating all the specific cases we present in the mythical district of Malgudi, immortalised by R.K. Narayan in his novels. Everybody knows Malgudi is in Karnataka! Section IV then tries to identify the barriers or impediments to the full participation of women in the political process.

A MINIMUM OF BACKGROUND

Grassroots democracy has been ushered in by an amendment to the Constitution from the "top". This was not because of a mass movement by the people. This is also true of the 1/3rd reservation for women: it was not because women who were consentised demanded their due share in power, or contested in large numbers to capture seats in these bodies. It happened, and women [as a group] were caught quite unprepared by this development.

For a number of reasons, the Indian State felt that the implementation of development programmes, like the IRDP, for example, would be most effective if local people were involved. The strident debate on Centre-State relations, the poor targeting of poverty alleviation programmes and the like led to the realisation that local involvement-participation-is essential if such programmes are to succeed. This is specially so for beneficiary identification, and to a smaller extent, for decisions on how to spend the limited amount available locally on different local projects. And given the lack of interest in devolving such power in most of the states, coercion through a Constitutional amendment was the chosen route for introducing such decentralisation. The amendment prescribed a three-tier system of local governance for the entire country. This has been effective since 1993.

The Three Tiers of PRIs

These bodies, which are legally local government, have a pyramidal structure. At the base is the gram sabha-the entire body of citizens in a village or "grama". This is the general body that elects the local government and charges it with specific responsibilities. This body is expected to meet at specific times and approve major decisions taken by the elected body. Above this basic unit of democracy, is the gram panchayat or GP, which is the first level elected body, covering a population of around five thousand people. This may include more than one village. It is not uncommon to find several villages coming under one GP. This has implications for women's participation, as women have limited mobility.

At the district level is a zilla panchayat, which is the link with the state government. In between the two is an intermediate body called, in Karnataka, the taluk panchayat, which is expected to play a co-ordinating role among the GPs in its jurisdiction and the ZP in planning and administration. While the levels are common across the country, states have passed laws that are not necessarily similar with respect to roles functions and responsibilities. There is thus much variation and it is essential we learn from this. But that is another question.

In this system, the gram sabha has to play a crucial role-in ensuring downward accountability, transparency and voice to the people. In reality, this is far from being the case. There is even some confusion about the gram sabha-for example, has the electorate of an entire gram panchayat to meet together for the gram sabha, or do smaller habitations have their own gram sabhas in their own area? Are the members of the GPs to be present in all such gram sabhas? If not, what is the mechanism to co-ordinate the decision making and conveying the constituent villages' views upward to the elected body? Who does this, and how is it done?

This is basically an empirical question and the answer will lie in what is happening in the villages. Factors that aid or abet women's participation can be identified in "process" issues like these-when are meetings held? Is the hour and place convenient to women members? Will 2 to 3 elected women's representatives coming in from neighbouring habitations feel free enough to participate in gram sabha meetings? Are all communications [meeting notice, agenda, and minutes of proceedings...] in written form? Who writes them and who has access to read what has been written and recorded? Our impression is that much needs to be done to make gram sabhas effective. This will be crucial to the success of thus entire system. At the moment it is enough if we note these concerns as they clearly place constraints on women's full and effective participation in the system.

The Impetus for PRIs

The word "panchayat" is a traditional one, referring to the five elders in a village who mediated conflict and spoke on behalf of all the residents of a village in pre-modern times. In these traditional bodies, the lower castes-and women-had no representation. The question did not arise!

The word Panchayat has been retained for use after the 73rd amendment to the Constitution. The meaning is now a formal one referring to a body-not of five persons-elected according to law. Further the same word is used for the three tiers of local administration brought in by the 73rd amendment-the highest being the district or zilla panchayat. The lowest is the gram panchayat that may consist of several traditional villages. All citizens of these villages constitute the gram sabha, which then becomes the basic unit of democracy. In between is a co-ordinating level-the taluka panchayat. The powers that these panchayats enjoy are enshrined in the laws enacted by each state, and, in India, there is considerable variation across states. Thus, this traditional word must now be understood in a thoroughly modern context. And this is quite recent. But this does not mean the traditional bodies had disappeared. What influence they wield at an informal level in the rural society, is another matter that merits careful study.

The Constitution provided, [in Part 4, The Directive Principles of State Policy, Article 40] for the setting up of village panchayats. But this is non-justiciable, and there was no pressure on any state to set up such a system. Many saw this article as a concession to Gandhi, rather than as a serious matter to be immediately implemented. The reason for this was the powerful voice of Dr Ambedkar. Drawing on his own experience of rural India as it then was, he argued that local elite and upper castes were so well entrenched that any local self government only meant the continuing exploitation of the downtrodden masses of Indian society. Nehru shared this view. Thus, in addition to affirmative action enshrined in the Constitution, the distribution of powers was deliberately made to favour the Union as against the local, even state governments. The Union, being far away from the squalid battles of rural India, and being looked after by an educated and urban strata of society, would, it was felt, be more just-or at least more impartial-in its dealings with the downtrodden. Historical experience would tend, we suspect, to justify this early expectation. But is this still true after 50 years of gradual change? Has not the power of the upper castes in the rural areas declined? To what extent have things changed for the SC/STs--for the better?

The Union in those early days took up what was called the Community Development Programme. This was meant for all round social and economic development, and it was an important ministry headed for long by S.K. Dey. It was this programme that brought in such functionaries as the Village Level Worker and the Block Development Officer. After the 1960s this programme declined, as centrifugal forces led to the gradual dominance of the Union. Finally, the Ministry of Community Development ceased to exist. That philosophy became a thing of the past. But the bureaucracy it created remained. Whether this helps the new PRIs is still an open question. This is not the place to trace the experience of this ambitious programme. Suffice it to say that, when it was being reviewed, the Balwant Rai Mehta Committee in the late 1960s came up with the idea of local governments, which was given the traditional name of panchayat. Later, in another context, the Ashok Mehta Committee in the late 1970s too made recommendations for the setting up of local governments. As we shall see, these had an important impact many years down the line. It is from the Union's experience of development programmes that the idea/need for local governments came to be pushed. It has been a top-level initiative for local development and decentralised administration. And, we might add, it continues to be so.

Given the overall centralising trends in the Indian polity, the States too developed an authoritarian system of governance. States almost became subservient to the Union. Art 356 was used to keep a firm check on the behaviour of state governments. This ensured that strong hierarchical systems developed. All this was further strengthened during the Emergency. The states behaved in the same dominating way with lower tiers of governance-or, more correctly, administration. Strong line departments of the state governments took over development programmes. This is true, perhaps in varying degrees, of all the states. Indian democracy lost the grass roots link: it became a top down system. At the same time the bureaucracy grew in influence. Women were suddenly brought into this system as one dimension of this complex process-and it defines the context in which they have to function.

Yet, and this is the Indian paradox, several state governments conducted their own experiments with local self-government. This is the result of the shift in power from the traditional upper castes to the OBCs or intermediate castes-certainly in states like Tamil Nadu and Karnataka. The changes that occurred over the last 50 years of planned development also resulted in pressures from below, to which political forces have had to respond. How this impacted on the SCs and STs that Ambedkar was concerned about is another question. Caste and class are not overlapping categories. Grabbing political power from the brahmin and other upper castes does not mean that SC/STs will automatically be empowered-and the same applies to women as well. An interesting point missed out in all debates on reservations is that there are women in all castes, class and religions!

PRIs in Other States

This brief review of experience will be incomplete without some reference to the realty in the different states. This is a subject that has been extensively studied by many, in particular the Institute of Social Sciences, the National Institute of Rural Development and the Institute of Social Studies Trust. We can just note some major points that emerge from our general reading, meant only to give a flavour for further discussions in this conference.

It is only a few states that have experience over several electoral cycles with panchayati raj. For one thing, after the 73rd amendment, it is only now that the second round of election has become due. Thus, when we speak of such experience, it is that of states which experimented with PRIs before this amendment. Among them, West Bengal, Karnataka, Andhra Pradesh, Gujarat and Maharastra are the major ones. Kerala has much to offer in recent years, especially in involving people in the planning process. But Kerala is exceptional in several ways-for example, in the high levels of literacy, in the history of political mobilisation, etc. In Kerala, the role of the party is critical, and there is apparently an overlap between party functioning and patriarchal attitudes. A recent study has shown that, in this state with high literacy, women who have held positions in the PRIs are not keen on contesting again. But it is still a new experiment.

West Bengal has gone through several cycles of elections since 1978, when this system was introduced. A major reason for success here was the commitment of the Left Front government to these bodies. It has been argued that their strength comes from the fact that the cadres of these parties have now entrenched themselves in the PRI institutions. This is the charge made by the breakaway faction of the Congress, the Trinamool Congress led by Mamta Banerji. Be that as it may, the fact remains that these bodies have taken root, and work at the local level in this state is done through these bodies-and there has been an improvement over the centralised administration of the past. But this has also a flip side. For one thing, it has not meant that corruption has been eliminated-there are charges of much corruption. For another, NGOs have little space in West Bengal. They work in a hostile environment where PRIs are pitted against them. This can have a political base, but it is the reality. Overall though, West Bengal scores high on implementing Panchayati raj. About the role of women in PRIs, it is more difficult to say-but we would be inclined to hypothesise that the situation is better than most other states.

Andhra Pradesh is another state that took to PRIs in the 1980s, when N.T. Rama Rao was the Chief Minister. Here also the system started with hope. 9% of the seats were reserved for women but not the chairman positions. But the most important struggle that Andhra is known for-the anti-arrack agitation-came, not from women in the PRIs, but from women in the literacy programme in Nellore district. As a result of increasing literacy, and analysis stemming from the praxis methodology of Paulo Freire, women began to organise against the evils of drinking alcohol, and pushed for a policy of prohibition. This was, however, hijacked by the Telugu Desam Party, which rode on this slogan to power in AP. Once the state took over the demand of these women they became curiously disempowered. Prohibition became the hotbed of corruption. Women got trapped into a situation in which they had no control. Their organisation broke up. Little remains of the excitement of the literacy campaign days today.

Also, in more recent development, while the PRI system continues to exist, NTR's successor, Chandrababu Naidu, taking a leaf out of South Korean experience, introduced the Janmabhoomi programme for rural development. This is a programme run efficiently from the Chief Minister's office, by creating a bureaucratic edifice that is clearly accountable to him. The programme calls for contributions from local people for taking up projects that are of importance to them. This is done by selecting projects through discussions with the people in well organised meetings, attended by all the concerned officials, who have with them the authority to take decisions. Clear guidelines have been given for the patter of financing-how much will be matched in funds by the state government and for what purpose. Often shramdaan-free labour-is called for. The programme explicitly seeks to involve women in this process-in deciding upon what is to be done, how, and in monitoring the work. By all accounts, the programme has made a big difference to the implementation of projects in rural Andhra Pradesh. Even critics of the programme agree that it has made a big difference. Corruption has not been eliminated, but the percentages, we are told, are smaller. However, more work is being done, and so volumes make up for the difference.

The interesting thing about this programme is that it has many of the good points that are used for justifying local governance. But it achieves this end by marginalising the elected system of PRIs. That this is true is seen from the fact that elected Pradhans have recently gone on a fast in front of the Chief Minister's house.

What is the lesson from Andhra Pradesh? Good work can be done outside of PRIs. But PRIs are a value we stand for-and so the managerial techniques of Janmabhoomi need to be welded into the PRIs. How this can be done is still an open question.

Madhya Pradesh is another interesting case. The Chief Minister realised its potential and decided to gamble his political career on it. He had two advantages. None of the major parties in MP were looking at decentralised governance-their attention was fixed firmly on urban areas and large contracts. He left these issues to his Cabinet. Two, the 73rd amendment had just been passed, elections had been held, and a large number of local elected representatives were looking for work and responsibility.

The state had just brought out the first state level Human Development Report in 1995. Among the finding was the paradox that, in a state where every village had a school, literacy levels were abysmally low. So were health and other social indicators. The Chief Minister made these his priority-he set up the Rajiv Gandhi Missions, which were co-ordinated from his office.

Putting together the expertise in his office with the energies of the local representatives, a Lok Sampark Abhiyan was organised. Each elected representative, accompanied by the local schoolteacher, conducted a survey of education and other conditions in his/her constituency. The Mission Office provided the technical support. As a result, each representative developed a good idea of what his/her constituency needed, and priorities were set which would be met through the Rajiv Gandhi Missions.

The finding for education was interesting. It was true that each revenue village had a school. But in MP, a revenue village consisted of several habitations-sometimes four or five, called tolas, which would be quite remote from it. Children in these tolas did not have access to school. Hence the low literacy was more due to problems of access than anything else.

The response was the Education Guarantee Scheme. Consider a village which had 40 children [25 in tribal areas] who wanted to go to school. If the panchayat met, decided to offer space where the school could be run, and to identify a "guruji" from the panchayat-or a neighbouring one-who had finished 12th standard, then the government undertook to set up a school within 90 days. In this time, the guruji would be trained in pedagogy, and materials would be provided. The power to sanction the school was vested in the janpad panchayat. Funds were transferred directly to the panchayat, which would supervise the functioning of the school. Within 2 years, over 20,000 such schools were set up-access to school is no longer a problem in MP.

Madhya Pradesh has made use of the panchayat system in an innovative way to meet social sector demands. Several of the Rajiv Gandhi Missions-all implemented through the PRIs-have done well, on an independent reckoning. Today, perhaps, it has the most progressive PRI system in the country. But here too, the support of the Chief Minister has been critical. It is not power that has been demanded, but power that has been given. For all that, it is a positive development that must be built upon.

PRIs in Karnataka

Karnataka has been something of an exception when it comes to decentralisation and panchayati raj. For various extraneous reasons, the state legislature passed a law in 1983 setting up a system of panchayati raj. That system was a two tier one-of the zilla parishad at the district level and the mandal panchayat for a cluster of villages at the local level. Already at that time the progressive step of reserving 25% of the seats for women had been taken. This system went through one electoral cycle before it was abandoned. But this experience was important to those who drafted the 73rd amendment. And after the amendment, Karnataka brought in a new law, and that too has just about completed one electoral round. Elections are due sometime after February 1999.

As a result of this historical background, women in Karnataka have gained valuable political experience. Between the two rounds of [different] local government systems, thousands have stood for elections. Hundreds have held elective office because of reservations of important positions. Since the reservations were in favour of the hitherto oppressed sections of the population. Women from the poorest sections have gained this experience. Most are not literate, yet have held office. Such an opportunity is bound to have had an impact, not only on the women themselves, but also on the whole of rural society. It would be useful to try and understand the nature of this change-even if this is rather early to do so.

In local parlance, the word "member" is used for the President of the GP. The other members-men or women--are known as "numbers". This is how they refer to themselves in rural Karnataka.

The question of oppressed castes is an old one in India-often called the anti-brahmin movement. In Karnataka, the Miller Commission [in 1918] was of the opinion that, except for Brahmins and Christians, everyone else was backward in Mysore. Policies were made on this basis-and in all fairness, they led to improvements in the situation of many castes. Many who till then had little exposure to modern education and professions moved into them. This however, directly benefited the men of these castes. Women probably benefited indirectly. The anti-brahmin movement of the time did bring about change, and a shift in power equations.

In this background, political power moved from the upper castes-largely brahmins-to what are today variously called socially and culturally backward castes [SCBs], or other backward castes [OBCs]. It is not clear that it benefited the SCs and STs as much. For one thing, SC/ST reservation is more recent, stemming as it does from the Constitution. For another, they fall below the OBCs in the caste hierarchy. It is far from clear that they were the beneficiaries of the anti-brahmin movements in the South. There is antagonism between them and the OBCs. Whether the ascendancy of the OBCs to political power has helped them has to be seen. The hostility of the Bahujan Samaj Party to both the upper caste Congress and BJP on the one hand, and the "mandal" Janata Dal and its offshoots on the other, suggests that this is a complex matter. We have an anti-brahmin movement still, but are the brahmins still the major exploiters? Have other castes now taken over the dominant role that the brahmins previously had? Who is the target of the anti-brahmin movement today-brahmins. Or those who behave like the brahmins of old? There is much that needs to be clarified. We leave it there.

While there is some overlap between caste and class, it is far from complete. Some of the backward caste people were not poor in an economic sense. More accurately, there were affluent groups among them. And, among the upper castes, including brahmins, there were those who were below the poverty line. But they were not traditionally exploited, and their exposure to, and access to, education, was always much better. This is not true of the SCs and STs, who had limited productive assets, could only sell their physical labour. They were systematically exploited, denied access to opportunities of education, facilities like drinking water etc. But then, this is well known.

The reservation for backward groups then had two distinct meanings. When used by the Union of India [under the inspiration of thinkers like Dr B.R. Ambedkar], it referred to today's Scheduled Caste and Scheduled Tribe categories. These are definitely the most deprived of Indian society. But when state level authorities use the term, it refers to the OBCs-the intermediate castes. While many who belong to these castes are poor, they are not necessarily the most wretched of the earth. The legislation reflected this duality. Because of the Constitutional requirement, there has been a reservation for the SCs and STs. But in addition there has been a reservation for the OBCs. If one looks at the figures in the panchayati raj system, this comes out clearly. In the current system, where the reservation for women is one-third, in a three-tier system, the reservation is as follows:

In 5,640 GPs in the state, there are a total of 80,627 seats. Of these 17,906 are reserved for SCs; 7,575 for STs; and 26,828 for BCs. The open seats number 28,306. Many who contest on the open seats are OBCs.

While the SCs and STs undoubtedly enjoy representation on a scale unheard of in the past, the largest group is the OBC group-it is this, which today wields effective power. And in recent years, caste has been gaining in importance in political matters. Caste and class are often used interchangeably. And there are so many classifications we have to deal with: advanced, backward, forward, dominant, scheduled, dalit Christian...

To the extent that there is an overlap between caste and gender, the representation given to women has done little to change the caste hold on power. For example, in a given situation, do women align themselves with their caste or along gender lines? Experience has shown that it is often on caste lines. Thus, while the representation of women in these bodies is a welcome move, it is not reasonable to expect that it will change the caste balance of power in favour of the most disadvantaged groups. This matter requires more careful analysis. This paper is only a preliminary effort.

In the context of a drinking water problem, an upper caste woman member took up the cause of harijans when the pipe leading to their basti was broken. She was asked why she was bothered when she had water-it was, after all, "their" problem, not "ours". The issue has been discussed in the gramsat training tapes.

What has been the impact on women of two different kinds of panchayati raj system? We have a longer time span to study. We have a state in which progressive legislation led to a backlash-and more restrictive new legislation. We have what many would call a "PRI friendly state". What is possible and what has been achieved in Karnataka will probably tell of what is the most we can expect. If other states achieve as much, we would probably have made the best use of this system. How much of the experience is of a generic nature and which should hold in essence in any Indian state is a separate question. This paper, then, draws its lessons mainly from Karnataka.

In the rural areas, Karnataka began experimenting with panchayats in 1960-and this was based on the experience of Princely Mysore. Other states, like Gujarat and West Bengal too have valuable experience to learn from. It is also true that in some other states, there has been little positive change.

Some case studies may help us to understand issues that may have a more general validity. Karnataka is a middle ranking state, and the district we will use to illustrate our points, Malgudi, is a middle-ranking district, typical in essence. The focus is on gender issues: other factors are frozen under the "ceteris paribus" assumption. How far one can generalise is a matter we will leave open at this time.

After the 1960 experiment with decentralisation, the next major change in Karnataka was a new law passed in 1983-and implemented from 1987. This had a two-tier system of Zilla Parishads and Mandal Panchayats, created on the basis of population size. A notable feature of this system was that it gave the President of the Zilla Panchayat the status of a Minister of State. It vested in him the control of the senior officer [of about 15 years experience in the IAS] who was posted as the Chief Secretary of the district. This gave the zilla parishad importance in the eyes of both the public and the civil servants. It became an important political forum.

This experiment was aborted for several reasons to do with state politics. But this experience was important in giving shape to the 73rd amendment to the Constitution. Ironically, the same party that was busy demolishing it in the state passed this amendment, which drew much inspiration from the 1983 Karnataka Act, in the Lok Sabha. We mention this only to show that, for all the stated agreement on these issues, there is in many quarters hostility to local self-government. This fact must be factored in if any new policies meant to strengthen the system are to succeed.

The Karnataka Act which followed the 73rd amendment is less liberal to local stakeholders than the 1983 one. It has brought about obvious changes. In Karnataka, for example, although the reservation for women is 1/3rd, as in the rest of the country. At the gram panchayat level well over 40% of the elected representatives are women. Many are into politics for the first time. If they lack in experience, they also have not been spoiled by past practices. Many are young, and look forward to a long career in politics. The prospects for participation by women in framing and implementing social sector programmes are therefore bright. A start has been made. This has now to be taken forward and the question is How can this best be done?

It is therefore possible to learn from the Karnataka experience. In Shimoga district, there is even an all women panchayat in one grama. The conditions under which this came about are peculiar. Reports have it that the inspiration for this came from an influential local man. We understand that these women are not enthusiastic about contesting for elections again. Since we have not yet personally studied it, we do no more than mention this oddity here. There are many such cases that have yet to be carefully studied. We are not as far advanced as we should be in our research and documentation in this field-a lot more has to be done.

Experiences from Malgudi

As may be expected, the experience of women in panchayati raj has been varied. Many are surrogates for husbands and fathers who could not contest because of the reservation. Some were put in place by the wealthy and powerful, for their malleability-a kind of puppet to serve the vested interest while appearing to be an elected representative. This has led to many problems that have been extensively discussed in the literature and form the basis for an excellent film, sponsored by UNICEF, called Shansodhan.

There have also been many efforts to train the women who have been elected. Interestingly enough, the state government has undertaken some of these. In Karnataka, the Department of Women and Child Development co-operated with professionals in what has come to be known as the Gramsat Programme. This had two parts. The first was an interactive session, using satellite technology to link the different district headquarters to Bangalore. This session used material generated through meetings of women elected to gram panchayats. The impact was immediately visible, and even today, its role in giving these women self-confidence to face a big challenge cannot be underestimated. As a part of this programme, these women were taken to visit the Vidhana Soudha, the seat of the state government, and to the Legislative Assembly. They were awed by the Council chamber. They saw where the Speaker sat and conducted the proceedings. They saw where the Chief Minister and the Leader of the Opposition sat for the debates.

Later, we found this was an immensely empowering experience. In meetings in their GPs, they often ended an argument, especially with men, with-"What do you know? Have you seen the Vidhana Soudha? I have!".

The second part was training material developed as an extension of the first, including issues of concern to women-nutrition, water, primary education, basic health services, immunisations, common property resources, etc, which were used in training programmes across the state. The objective here was two fold-to raise certain questions in their minds on these issues and also to provide them with some basic information that would enable them to play their roles in the GPs. The impact of this so far as we know, has yet to be assessed.

Yet, it must not be forgotten that this experiment in local self-government is being undertaken in a society that is predominantly illiterate. Many of the people elected, especially those in the reserved categories are very poor. In attending meetings of the GP, they often have to give up a day's wages. To use terms popularised by Amartya Sen, the entitlements of the actors in this great drama of democracy are way below what they should be. As a result, their capabilities to play these roles are low as these are in uncharted territory.

All the training programmes referred to above can only mitigate this to a small extent. These are people who have not been supported by society so far to play any formal leadership roles or achieve their full functionings. Yet they have embarked on this great experiment. To expect too much would be unfair on our part; not to recognise what they have achieved, despite all these constraints, would be boorish. We have to make haste slowly.

We present below some field level experiences of women in panchayati raj. These are cases of which we have direct knowledge having observed them in the course of our work. They relate to a restricted area, yet, we feel they throw up questions that have a general validity for many parts of India. It is these matters that we feel can be usefully discussed. To facilitate this, we raise a few issues after each case is presented.

Case 1

Haleuru gram panchayat is located between Malgudi, the district headquarters, and Balgudi, the taluk HQ-it is 17 km from each on the main highway. The total population is over 4000. There are 490 houses and 580 families. The GP is divided into 7 wards, and has 8 members. Two positions are reserved for SCs and one for STs. Out of the 8, 4-four-are women.

When the elections to the GP were held in 1993, there was considerable discussion in the village. Under the guidance of the elders of the village, it was decided that only one candidates' name would be proposed for each post. So each member was declared elected without a contest.

After the election, the post of GP President was reserved for an ST woman. Smt Gangamma Jayakar, the only eligible candidate, thus became the President. She has passed her 4th standard.

The other members who did not mind her being an `ordinary member', could not accept her in the role of the President of the GP. They asked her to resign, so that one of the others could take over as President. This she was not willing to do. The others refused to co-operate with her.

She sought the advice of the officials at the taluk and zilla levels. She was told that she need not resign: the post was hers by right. She was also told that the quorum for meetings was 3 members, and that she and two other members could take decisions. With the help of the two SC members, she conducted the meetings. When the others protested against this, as advised by the officials she went to the High Court in Bangalore, which ruled in her favour. After that, the three members have been conducting meetings for the village. The others attend every third meeting, sign the register and leave (just to retain their membership]. They refuse to co-operate in the running of the panchayat so long as she remains President. She can be a "number", but not a "member"! These members also argue with the GP secretary, who therefore seeks an excuse to ask for a transfer. The present Secretary is the third one in this term. Gangamma is not happy with him.

Ms Jayakar feels that she could have achieved a lot more if the others co-operated. As it is, in getting works like gutters dug, she has effectively to work alone. But she is proud that she could get a bus stand constructed. She could do all this because of the support of officials at the TP and ZP levels.

Several questions arise. Does a mere reservation for women bring in social change? What is the relation between caste and class? Here, reservation has brought to prominence a person who would never have attained such a position under "normal" conditions. Would a man have fared differently in this situation? Can officials make the difference to the functioning of local governments to this extent? If so, under what conditions will they play a positive role, as in this case?

Case 2

There has been a public protest, early in January 1999, by the women members of the Malgudi zilla panchayat. Located in the capital of the state, this should be a "model" of sorts. It is. The women, who we noticed in the course of our visits, always sat in one group on one side of the chamber, have now said there is no point reserving seats for them if there is no intention of the ZP listening to what they have to say. They have pointed out that the current President is a woman. Yet when Ms Ganga Bai was present in the chamber and presiding over the meeting, the Vice President, a man, was answering the questions that were being raised. The President was not allowed to answer! They have pointed out that when the President in the house, the Vice President cannot usurp her powers and functions.

We tried very hard to interview Ms Ganga Bai. She has been elected from a remote part of Malgudi-a very backward area with poor roads, no electricity and little drinking water. We had to walk a long way to get to her place. When we got there we were told she did not live there; she has been living for long in Malgudi. We could not find her in Malgudi either. The phone number given to us as a contact number turned out to be that of an STD booth that did not know her. Yet, one day, she became the President of the zilla panchayat.

It is not surprising this matter has come to the fore. It is surprising it has taken so long to do so. And we do not know how the issue will be resolved. It clearly shows the situation in which women have to work after getting elected.

The Chief Executive Officer of this ZP is also a woman-an IAS officer. But she seems to have no difficulty in doing her job. We have seen her differing on many matters with the earlier President, a powerful male politician.

What questions does this protest raise? Ms Ganga Bai is clearly a "dummy" member, there because a male relative could not contest due to the reservation for women. What is she to do? In a traditional society, it is difficult for men to accept women in positions of authority. These is not only a loss of face, but of power that has been exercised without gender controls till now. What kind of orientation do men need in this situation? Has this question been addressed in any way in training them? And if it is ignored then what will be the consequences for women? Also, why is it the CEO does not seem to face such problems? Does belonging to the IAS give her a special status? Or is it the fact that she is highly educated? If so, is this a gender question at all?

Case 3

Is Gangavva Bai President of Hosahalli Gram Panchayat? The question is not an idle one.

Hosahalli gram panchayat is located in Malgudi district, about 55 Km from the district HQ. It is on the main road to Bhimeshwar, about 10 Km from Balgudi-the taluk HQ. In 1991 it had a population of 10,991, of which 707 were SC and 365 ST. The area grows chilly, and the village has 100 small farmers, 498 medium farmers and 410 large farmers. The GP consists of Hosahalli village and Nayahalli hamlet. It is a relatively prosperous village, with a railway station and 6 primary schools. 80% of the houses have tap water facility.

Elections for the gram panchayat, which has 28 members, were held in 1993. 9 seats are reserved for women. The post of

President was reserved for an SC woman-and Jamunavva became the President. She had the support of two other members who were also SCs. The rest of the panchayat members did not like the fact that her associate-a man who they said was her lover-began to dictate events in the panchayat. They moved a no confidence motion against Jamunavva and she was voted out of office in 1995. The presidency, however, was reserved for an SC woman, and the other woman, who supported Jamunavva, refused to accept the Presidency. Since she was an SC, and a friend of Jamunavva, the others also did not really want her as President.

Now comes the astounding part. All the other members [except Jamunavva and her friend] resigned, and the panchayat got dissolved. For one year this state of affairs continued. An administrator was appointed to look after routine matters.

When no work could be done, the elders in the village decided to act. New elections were scheduled, and a new panchayat was elected without contest. They took the officials into confidence, and effectively "selected" 27 members to the GP-on the 16th of July 1997. Most of them were people who had lost the election in 1993. This group elected Gangavva, who is an SC, "selected" into the panchayat, President. Since then, panchayat matters have been running smoothly-the panchayat's tax collection is about 3 lakhs!

Is this a situation we purists can be happy with? Was this situation due to gender effects, or not? What was the basis of objection-that it was Jamunavva's lover who was dictating terms? Would it have been acceptable if her husband was doing so?! Are reservations for women alone enough to bring in democratic change in our society? And, if the local people have accepted this situation, and it is performing well, then is opposition on merely ethical grounds correct in a democracy?

Case 4

Ms Gangamma Jayker has just completed her 20-month term as President of the Malgudi zilla panchayat. She now plans to contest the election to the Legislative Assembly of Karnataka when elections come around later in 1999.

Gangamma is a product of reservations in the PRI system. She comes from a small village called Haleuru in Malgudi taluk, and belongs to the SC category. Her childhood story is typical [in several respects] to women born into that strata of society. She was married at the age of 10 had a son at 13, and struggled to get a primary education-walking 7Km to go to school. She was the only girl from the area going to school. She completed her primary education, and attended school till the 8th standard.

Being educated she felt she should do something for the women in her village, and started a mahila mandal. Growing to strength of 100 members this mandal was successful in accessing govt loans meant for poor women-like sewing machines under TRYSEM. This was the beginning of her political career.

When the PRI institutions were set up in 1987, the mandal became her base, and she was elected to the mandal panchayat-the second tier in the earlier Karnataka system. She completed her five-year term, and learned a great deal about the functioning of local government in the process. She established good links with politicians from the area-in particular the local MLA, X.Y. Patel, who later became a minister in the J.H. Patel ministry in Karnataka.

These panchayats were abolished by the Bangarappa government, and later, after the 73rd amendment, when elections were held for the new gram panchayats in 1993, she was elected once again-and offered the presidency of the GP. She did not accept this. She wanted to fight elections to the zilla panchayat and did so by resigning from the GP when elections were called. In the ZP, the post of President was reserved for a woman from the SC category-and she fought for this position. With the support of X.Y. Patel, who was powerful in Bangalore, she won the position. Although she had the usual problems, she completed her term, and at the end of it, she brought out a pamphlet on her achievements.

In Gangamma's view, the earlier two-tier system was better than the current three-tier system. It is a matter of local autonomy, she says. In the current system, there is greater delay built in.

Gangamma Jayker is an example of the new politician emerging from the PRI system in Karnataka. Women like her would have found it impossible to make a mark in the system without the reservations. Yet, she argues that this is only a first step. Without educational improvements, women will find it difficult to work the system. Gangamma shows the system of reservations for women and for depressed sections of society working at its best.

How many such cases are there? Do cases that show genuine growth of new political players, like Gangamma, outnumber the cases of "proxy" members and so on? Under what conditions will such reservations lead to positive results, especially where women are concerned? How will established politicians react to the emergence of politicians like Gangamma? We do not know.

Case 5

Gangamma Jayaker is a sarpanch. She had been active in her village, and, after the panchayat elections, had been elected sarpanch. She is very keen on promoting education. An educated person herself, she has been running literacy classes for women in her village-and continues to do even after her election. On hearing of the government program for girl's education, she got the details of the scheme, and followed the procedures to get a school opened in her village. When she heard that we were visiting schools in the area, she made sure that we visited her school

Her activities did not go unnoticed in the village. She was going against age-old traditions and customs. Some of the panchs got together, and got her defeated in a no-confidence motion. She was forced out of office. She was not discouraged. She fought back, organised, made her political deals, and got re-elected sarpanch when the post came up for re-election. She is the kind of person from whom the political leaders of the future will emerge. While there are people like her around, there is little doubt that panchayati raj will succeed-and not be male dominated either! People like her can be relied upon to develop their areas responsibly.

How many persons like Gangamma Jayakar are there in our rural areas? How many of them are capable of fighting as she did? What gave her the confidence, and strength to fight as she did? Would it be very surprising if many of them did not relish such fights and opted for "softer" solutions? What can we do so that the system supports the Gangamma Jayakers?

Case 6

Ms Gangamma and Ms Jamunavva were elected President and Vice President of Malgudi District panchayat, defeating Shri Honappa and Shri Siddappa respectively, when elections became due after the earlier incumbents had completed their 20-month term of office. Is this a cause for celebration by women?

Ms Gangamma was elected from Haleouru constituency in Balgudi taluk on a party A ticket. Ms Jamunavva was elected from Hosaouru in Malgudi taluk on a party B ticket.

Four hours prior to the election for the ZP President and Vice President, Ms Gangamma joined party B along with 5 "rebel" members of party A. A former President of the ZP, Shri Ayaram, who had joined party C after being expelled from party A some time ago, accompanied her in this. He too joined party B. As a result of this re-alignment, party B's strength in the ZP rose to 11 from 4 previously.

In the election, Ms Gangamma and Ms Jamunavva, as party B's candidates, secured 11 votes against 8 for the party A's candidates.

Ms Gangamma is 45 years old and is a graduate. She has worked in literacy programmes and organised women in different ways in Balgudi taluk. She said she joined her new party to end political uncertainly and to work with others for the development of the district.

Ms Gangamma has shown considerable political dexterity. The realignment of party loyalty of a few persons has changed the fortunes of major political parties in the district. Few men could match these political skills. But has this in anyway improved the status of women in Malgudi? Has this in anyway improved political ethics? Has Ms Gangamma stuck a blow for gender, or for personal gain? If women behave in this manner, what benefits does reservation bring?

These cases, of which we have direct knowledge, raise a number of issues for discussion. We are not clear about the direct positive gender impact from them. Except for the fact that women are fully into the political process, what specific gains have women made in Malgudi?

IN LIEU OF A CONCLUSION

What can we say then about the factors that influence the effective participation of women in the new panchayati raj institutions? We will try to put all this together.

One, the grinding poverty in which most of the people live makes abstract notions of democracy and ethics rather distant concepts. Exploitation of different sorts is a reality. Corruption is a matter of routine, where payment of a bribe is at best seen as a minor nuisance to getting something, never mind that it is a right, done. It is into this situation that local self-government has been introduced from the top. If one goes by the spirit of the Balwant Rai Mehta Committee report, nothing loftier than an efficient local tier of development administration was intended. This is what the higher level would like to see. It is important to remind ourselves of this basic truth.

Added to this is the fact that the women who have come in under caste reservation have come in `with their social and economic disadvantages'-mostly non-literate, with little productive assets, largely dependent on wage labour and into a rural society that has fixed places for various castes and gender. These cannot be changed by a wave of the constitutional amendment wand!

What can we reasonably expect of this system? Are we expecting too much?

Two, while people have a clear sense of survival, they are prepared to cope in a feudal type system in which direct action does not work. Rural reality is complex-being freed from bondage has often not meant freedom as many expected it to. Experience has taught them to go slow, to approach their goal indirectly. They have to decide if attending PR meetings is sometimes worth missing their daily wage. This is even more so in the case of women, who have to worry about crying babies and hungry husbands.

This is how they see the new system of PRIs. Thus, it is unrealistic to expect much in terms of their response. It has first to be demonstrated that the system is indeed here to stay. In West Bengal, it is only after one or two rounds of elections had been held that the system settled down as a permanent part of the rural countryside. In Karnataka, the constant tinkering with the system has meant that people are still cautious about this system. No one is sure it will not be overturned tomorrow! Why then should anyone take a risk?

Three, the new system co-exists with traditional institutions. The elders wield power in a way the Constitution may not have foreseen. If the PRIs are to succeed in their main goals, then they must work in harmony with these traditional institutions, not confront them head-on. This is easier said than done.

The traditional institutions have not given space for women. The pros and cons of this are beyond the scope of this paper. It is enough to note that many of the factors that hindered women in the earlier systems continue to exist and operate in rural areas-and legal changes cannot change them.

Four, giving women positions in the panchayats is good in itself. But it would be naïve to believe that it would address social injustice or issues of poverty. Women have class and caste identities, not just a gender identity. In fact gender as a phenomenon hardly ever appears in a pure form. It is almost always alloyed with caste, class and religious factors. In matters where there is a clash between gender and caste or class, we cannot expect women to align themselves with other women, going against their caste or class loyalties.

Some women have developed political ambitions too, especially when it is seen as a quick means for upward mobility. And political survival will be difficult if they "betray" class and caste interests. This is why the reservation of the posts of President to the SC/ST category is so resented. They can be members of the panchayat, but not its President or Vice President. And if they are in such posts then a conflict between their different roles is inevitable. Different individuals will cope in different ways. The problem is in society, not in the panchayat that only reflects social reality.

Five, it is essential that the panchayat system be stable. In Karnataka, the state began well in the 1980s. But since then the spirit of local democracy has taken several steps backward. The state Act passed after the 73rd amendment is far less progressive than the earlier one. Given that both were imposed from the top, the withdrawal can be seen as a response of politicians at the higher level to the backlash on the ground-from politicians and the civil servants.

But the continuing tinkering with this Act has done little to convince people that the system is here to stay. In this situation, women in particular will choose to play safe. What is the point of risking one's local position with powerful people if the system itself is likely to undergo changes? The experience of West Bengal provides a strong contrast to Karnataka.

Six, the power enjoyed, and exercised by line departments of the state government, will have to be reduced. Today, it is they who decide major matters. And officials, who belong to these departments, treat district postings-and panchayat authorities-as minor nuisances.

This administration is quite gender insensitive. It is just not enough that there are women in the civil service-the service has to be sensitised. While an effort has been made in Karnataka to reduce diarchy in administration by giving the Chief Executive Officer a co-ordinating role in the ZP, much more needs to be done. Capabilities have to be developed at this level. It is only when ZPs develop their own [gender sensitive] expertise that they can begin to chart their own path. Important in this will be co-ordination amongst themselves.

For example, they could get together to form an Inter-District Council on the lines of the Inter-State Council. It is important that, in such a body, the Chief Minister remains one among equals, not a superior. This kind of body does not exist at all at the moment. Much needs to be done.

Seven, what is the relationship between NGOs and PRIs? NGOs work in the social sector, and have strong links at the grassroots. They do not have a very positive experience of government at this level.

In fact, many of them came on the scene because government was unable to deliver the goods. There are NGOs that resent the emergence of PRIs because they now have to vacate space for these new bodies. There are some who argue that panchayats are NGOs. There are NGOs that see PRIs as rivals and competitors for implementing government programmes and believe they are superior because they are not "political".

NGOs have been involved in training those elected to PRIs. But there are also other NGOs that have welcomed the emergence of these local governments. It will be essential to reduce the hostility of some of these NGOs to PRIs in the coming years. How is this to be done? The involvement of NGOs with the grass-roots democracy arises out of their activities in the following areas-

1. Organisation of the disadvantaged sections of rural society- e.g. the dalits, minorities, landless, SC/STs, agricultural/ plantation labour, labour of the unorganised sectors etc. It is these sections that have been provided a 'space' in the PRIs under the reservation policy.
2. In addition to organising, most NGOs run training programmes-leadership development, capacity building, group dynamics and management and so on. Some of the NGOs have organised training specifically for PRI members (E.g.-SEARCH & UMA in Karnataka, FRCH in Maharastra, CINI in West Bengal, YIP in Andhra Pradesh...to name a few).
3. The most valuable area of contribution of NGOs to engendering the PRIs has been in the organising of women (whatever sector the NGO works with-health, IGPs, SHGs, housing, water & sanitation, education, watershed...) The opportunities provided in small groups dealing with the above issues has been a kind of 'testing ground' for women to enter a larger arena, having been empowered in the smaller arena. Further, it has also been reported that women in PRIs who have been supported and nurtured by NGOs and those who have been involved in larger people's movements have gained a more 'assertive' stance which gives them an edge over other women in the PRI process. The best examples of this can be seen the 'Right to Information' movement in Rajasthan and the Anti-Arrack movement in Andhra Pradesh.

Inspite of these very positive aspects, many NGOs seem vary of getting directly or closely involved with the PRIs. An often heard comment is 'we are working in development; politics is not our cup of tea'! But, if PRIs, especially GPs, are the forum where development and politics has to be wedded, it is difficult to see how NGOs can keep non-aligned in the process.

Perhaps some of them are bound by donor conditionalities or wise enough to avoid working against the 'establishment'... But, sooner or later NGOs will get entangled in the politics of power transfer in the PRIs; the clearer their perspective on gender, the greater will be their contribution to the process.

Eight, what has been the impact of PRIs on women individually? Why is it that so many of them say they do not wish to contest elections again, in spite of the fact that it has given them power and status? Is it that they have only male role models that they do not wish to follow? Is it that this experience has taught them they cannot change the system without joining it, in all its corruption? This needs deeper probing.

The experiences of women in the PRIs has been so varied, across the three levels of the PRIs and the different states that except for some 'tautological' statements little can be said.

We need to distinguish between women who hail from families with political background and those who can be termed 'first generation political aspirants'-women who drifted into PRIs due to the 73rd amendment. Even though the amendment made the 'space' for both these to enter the PRIs, the alacrity with which they take to the new role will vary.

The point to be noted is that hitherto, space for women to participate in institutions like the PRI which are in the 'public sphere' were negligible.

Consequently, the early entrants have had only 'male role models' of political leadership.(Some of us will recall the paradoxical statement made on Mrs. Gandhi being 'the only one wearing the pants in the parliament!). Thus, we have had women in a double blind-to be seen as effective, they have to take to masculine ways and when they do that they cease representing women's interests!

From everywhere, an often-heard comment is that many of these women would not like to contest in the next round of elections! Why is that so? Is it a pointer to their 'unsuitability' to assume leadership? Or an inability to cope with multiple and conflicting role demands? Or Is it time we ask ourselves what is it about PRIs (and politics) that makes it unpalatable to half of humanity, even when it can determine the quality of life?

Nine, What is the constituency for panchayati raj? Is it women as a gender? Is it the local electorate? We have seen that the changes that have so far been brought about have come from the "top"-the union of India, for a number of reasons. At the local level, there is a great deal of opposition-from the bureaucracy, from the established politician like the MLA.

If they have little interest in PRIs, then who, other than a small number from the urban elite-like us-is interested in promoting the cause of PRIs-and of women within them. Is it not a coincidence that researchers, women's groups and international organisations are more excited about the PRI experiment than the politicians? How else can we explain the backward steps that Karnataka has been taking? And if the system provokes such opposition, then what can we do to support women within that system? It is a difficult problem.

Ten, there is an ethical problem for people like us. We have reported in this paper from our direct knowledge of the field. All are real situations. We have spoken of situations that would call for official action if the "authorities" were aware of the identities of those we are talking of.

But this would mean administrative and legal intervention in local situations, resulting not from local events, but from our observation of them. What is our goal-to learn from what we have seen, or to [inadvertently] intervene, and cause changes of a type over which we have no control, and in which there will be few winners and many losers? We of course will be far away from the local havoc. Clarity is needed in this matter. We would not like to cause trouble for those who have trusted us with information, with their confidence. This matter merits discussion too.

In conclusion, for fundamental changes in society, much more than PRIs are required; but that does not mean PRIs are not important. That the PRIs as they are now are limited does not mean that they cannot be improved. PRIs as grassroots democratic governance institutions are a necessary, but not sufficient condition in the transformation to a better social order. And in that transformation, enabling women's participation through reservations is a first and important step.

In this process of social transformation, there may be some negative unintended consequences-sub-optimal utilisation of resources, weakening of other bodies of governance...not all these will automatically mean empowerment of women or engendering of the PRIs.

Much more will be needed if gender justice is to become the norm. And it will take time. We must not be impatient. But it is important to support this fledgling experiment in every way we can-if we believe in democracy at the grassroots.

2

WOMEN IN PANCHAYATI RAJ INSTITUTIONS

The Father of the Nation, Mahatma Gandhi observed:

.If an ancestral treasure lying buried in a corner of the house unknown to the members of the family were suddenly discovered, what a celebration it would occasion. Similarly, women.s marvellous power is lying dormant. If the women of Asia wake up they will dazzle the world..

The 73rd Constitutional Amendment Act, which becomes part of the Constitution on 24th April 1993, has brought about a silent revolution in the country. Together with the 74th Amendments it facilitated the entry of about one million women into public life.

Conferences on Panchayati Raj and political, social and economic empowerment of women are held each year by Institute of Social Sciences (ISS) Elected representatives of Panchayati Raj Institutions (PRIs) and members of NGOs, prominent academicians, social workers, government officials and media persons representing the states of India participate in these important events.

The ISS 1995 conference discussed the problems facing the panchayats with a special focus on the problems of women members and office bearers in particular. There was absolute unanimity among the participants on the steps to be taken for strengthening the system in such a way that women can play their designated role in building self-reliant prosperous villages and through this a vibrant and strong India. Some of the recommendations pertaining to measures to be taken to empower women elected representatives recommended by the conference are enumerated below.

(a) In order to enable the members and office bearers of panchayats, particularly women, to carry out their functions efficiently and effectively, suitable awareness.generation, education and training programmes should be organised. The methodology and contents of training should be practical and oriented to solving problems. Considerable experience and knowledge is available at the local levels. They must be fully tapped. Local NGOs, social activists, and women office bearers and members themselves should be actively associated in imparting training. There is great need for awareness generation in the community particularly in underdeveloped regions. NGO.s and grassroot workers should take the lead in this matter and organise awareness campaigns on a large scale.

(b) Effective campaigns to eradicate social evils like dowry, child marriage, early marriage and untouchability must be launched.

(c) Information sharing is an essential component if the Panchayati Raj system is to succeed. People at large should know what is happening. Various measures have to be taken to introduce appropriate measures to reach out information in an understandable manner even to illiterate elected women members of panchayats.

(d) The gram panchayat must meet regularly as stipulated under rules and orders.

(e) Among the multifarious functions entrusted to panchayats education of women, specially the girl child, should receive top priority.

(f) Funds should be made available to panchayats through tax assignments and sharing of taxes and grants.

(g) Panchayat should try to raise internal resources to become self-reliant which would help them to function in a free and autonomous manner.

(h) Women members should be inducted in standing committees including those for planning, finance and vigilance. Panchayati Raj bodies should function in such a way that they do not tend to become another bureaucracy. They must develop and retain the character of subgoverning institutions committed to public good with compassion and sharing and should develop participatory character in approach.

(i) NGOs and other autonomous organisations have a crucial role in women.s development, particularly in areas of education, health and capacity building.

(j) Men also have to be sensitized to women.s legitimate rights.

(k) Eliminate middleman and exploitating organisations and empower women to get the fruits of their labour through strong marketing networks.

(l) Make all efforts to achieve political empowerment of women so as to become effective partners in the decision-making process, thereby leading towards achieving decentralised planning. Through this process visible changes will take place in the patriarchal, caste ridden, hierarchical society into more egalitarian and just society through making women elected representative as agents of change.

A typical Indian village is fragmented by caste, party politics and social hierarchies and our aim is that village communities, consisting of both women and men to be brought together by principle of unity that must go beyond each one of them. This society has to endeavour itself through time. It gathers up the past and prepare for the future by means of panchayat community in which each member is an heir and possesses certain talents that enrich their identity and whose fruits must develop. Each individual owes loyalty to the communities which he or she is a part of and respect those in authority who have charge of the common good. This philosophy has to be inculcated in the mind of every individual to understand their responsibility and contribution to the panchayat and the community. Every member of the gram sabha have to be empowered to understand the philosophy of common good and support all causes and action for the common good.

Participation of the greatest number in the panchayat community on issues relating to economic and social goals, to revitalising traditional cultural and recreational activities, traditional crafts and skills to various professions and matters relating to political affairs would result in better prosperity. This type of socialisation also expresses the natural tendencies for human beings to associate with one another for attaining objectives that exceed individual capabilities. This develops qualities of persons, especially the sense of initiative responsibility and helps guarantee his rights.

Empowerment is an essential ingredient to bringing out originality and individual initiative for serving the common cause of the village communities.

POLITICAL AND SOCIAL EMPOWERMENT

The Constitution of India recognizes the political rights of women without any discrimination, distinction or qualification, to participate in the decision-making process at all levels. After five decades of strides in democracy and development, women.s participation and their role in public life has not made the desired headway. The field reality is that women.s constitutional right in decision-making at all levels, whether national or local is still marginal.

The Lok Sabha general elections between 1989.1999 clearly showed that voting by women has declined. In the 1989 general elections approximately 71 per cent of men voted in contrast only 43 per cent of the women voted and in 1991 elections 52 per cent of men voted when there were 47 per cent women who voted. It would not be far from truth to state that no serious effort appears to have been made to mobilise women as an important political constituency by any political party.

Statistics indicate that the proportion of women contestants in parliamentary constituencies has not increased significantly over the years. Political parties seem reluctant to field women candidates. In the 1993 Lok Sabha there were only 35 women members in the house of 543 members and in the Rajya Sabha 28 women in the house of 245. The records of subsequent parliaments, also indicate similar trends.

Generally speaking, the Indian society and its dominant culture over the centuries have downgraded the status of women, socially and economically depriving them of opportunities for development, participation and management. Women, who form the majority of country.s illiterate, are underpaid or unpaid servants of society and family with no chance of expressing free opinions of their own. They are also objects of oppression or subjects of welfare. They are often relegated to the background and marginalised.

The process of empowerment will open a new vista of human resource development to them and bring them in the mainstream of social and economic development. The task that faces the government and society in setting right this inequality in sharing of power in a diverse and complex country with many religions and linguistic variations is how to overcome the attitudinal, institutional, cultural and social restrictions that have grown over the centuries.

Women's progress has been painfully slow and even today they remain the poorest of the poor. In the emerging new economic order and liberalized world order the women who have lower level skills will get further marginalised. Almost 90 per cent women in employment work in the unorganised sectors and therefore outside the purview of protection. The provisions of the 73rd Constitutional Amendments and the Panchayati Raj Acts would give opportunities for their socio-political advancement. Guided and well-planned empowerment thus, can make them overcome the inferior status in the family and society and emerge as capable equal partners of men. Such equal participation will lead to a qualitative change not merely in women.s lives but in the functioning of public institutions and nature of politics in our democracy.

AWARENESS

Knowledge is power. Deprivation of knowledge is reflection of their lack of awareness of various issues, agencies, procedures, schemes, projects and methods of management. Information on these and access to such information therefore becomes critical in their empowerment. The corner stone of the strategy to help women empower themselves is to facilitate various processes of action through which awareness can be generated. This will evolve dissemination of information and training in handling and using media appropriately. The identification of the training process and training needs of persons involved at different levels of Panchayati Raj and selection of training institutions is a major theme of empowerment.

POLITICAL EDUCATION

(a) Those women who have already entered panchayats through elections need to be politically educated and informed regarding the concepts and relevance of Panchayati Raj institutions, the functioning of state machinery, the Indian Constitution, the nature of Indian democracy and the policies and programmes for women and other weaker sections of the society.

(b) Women in the community who are by definition members of gram sabha who participate in election by way of contesting or voting would need training for campaigning in election or questioning the candidate. Political education can be imparted on the basis of concrete information, information on social issues, the current political development and trends, legislation, developmental schemes and other topics. Policy information and political mobilisation are mutually strengthening and would result in positive people.s movement for implementing many social-economic reforms which have had a tardy progress. Political training should aim at tapping their hidden potential and it should seek to build political awareness on the basis of collectively common interest and community development.

(c) Role of Catalytic Organisation Political action groups, the National Service Volunteers and woman study groups, agricultural extension institutions as well as agricultural colleges and universities, and social work departments can be mobilised as link organisation to play the role of catalyst. These institutions can provide necessary inputs for political education. Further, women.s self-help groups, social activists, Mahila Mandals and grassroots level NGOs add positive vigour to the process. Networking and effective linkages open up new vistas.

ECONOMIC EMPOWERMENT OF WOMEN IN PANCHAYAT

The constitutionally mandated panchayats were visualised as institutions of self-governance. States would devolve power to the PRIs and give them resources and responsibilities so that they emerge as institutions of self-governance instead of remaining as agencies for developmental administration only. As the process of devolution is slow, it requires pressure from women.s groups to force state governments to act fast and issue notifications to make it possible and practically brought to the field. Empowerment of women in political terms is a must to ensure this process.

The empowerment of powerless sections of society. women, Scheduled Caste/Scheduled Tribes (SC/STs). does not happen by merely giving them representation in the PRIs. The 73rd Constitution Amendment promises that through a representative democracy, that is, by giving representation to socially and economically disadvantaged sections, PRIs will gradually be transformed from merely representative to participatory bodies. This, in fact, was implied in the provision of 1/3 representation to women. It envisages a shift from meeting the developmental needs of the people to enabling them to undertake developmental planning and bring about a change in development perspective. Democratic decentralisation presupposes that people not only have control over the resources but also have a perspective as to how to plan and allocate the resources at the local level.

DEVOLUTION OF POWERS BY STATE GOVERNMENTS A MUST FOR EMPOWERMENT

The 11th Schedule of the amendment of the Constitution specifies 29 areas of responsibility covering all aspects of village life, which states may transfer to panchayats along with sufficient resources and decision making authority. As mentioned, many states are yet to establish and accomplish this important task. Out of the 11th Schedule some of the areas that women members bear primary responsibility for are noted below:

(1) Agriculture, including agriculture extension
(2) Minor irrigation, water management and watershed management
(3) Animal husbandry, diary and poultry
(4) Fisheries
(5) Social forestry and farm forestry
(6) Minor forest produce. MFP
(7) Drinking water
(8) Fuel and fodder
(9) Poverty alleviation programmes
(10) Education, including primary and secondary schools
(11) Adult and non-formal education
(12) Health and sanitation, including hospitals and primary health centres (PHCs)
(13) Family welfare
(14) Women and child development,
(15) Social welfare, including welfare of the handicapped and mentally retarded, and
(16) Maintenance of community assets.

These indicate that there is an urgent need for State governments to issue notifications specifying devolution of administrative and financial powers to the panchayats.

SIDA'S COMMITMENT TO WOMEN EMPOWERMENT THROUGH ACTION PROGRAMMES AND RESEARCH IN RAJASTHAN: 1996

In 1996, with Sida support, ISS selected Rajasthan to launch an experimental project to take initiatives for action to empower elected women representatives of panchayats after the panchayat elections in 1995. What really motivated ISS is the basic recommendation given by the Conference on Panchayati Raj and political, social and economical empowerment of women held in April 1995. For India to build up a broad-based, solid foundation for economic and social progress it must uproot the last vestiges of feudalism and instill democratic values and practices. The people who live in the villages of India must become authors of their own lives and become sensitive to the needs of women, and women must be respected and supported in the process of development.

7.2 Initially ISS selected three districts representing three distinct geographical regions of state (Alwar, Pali and Rajsamand). Each district is different in terms of agricultural patterns, socioeconomic development and history of people.s participation in the freedom struggle. Annexe 2, give details of zilla parishads, panchayat samitis and gram panchayats in the whole state. This also gives the total number of zilla parishads, panchayat samitis and gram panchayats selected for studies. The number of cases chosen for studies in the three districts were 3 zilla parishads with six women from them, 6 panchayat samitis with 18 women from them and 16 gram panchayats with 48 women from them.

SECOND STAGE OF PROGRAMME (JANUARY 1997 TO DECEMBER 2000)

Based on the experiences gathered in Rajasthan and the positive results observed, the Swedish International Development Agency (Sida) supported a three-year programme:.Empowerment of Women through Panchayats in Rajasthan and Orissa., beginning January 1997. The areas identified for implementation of this programme are three districts of Rajasthan (Alwar, Kota, Pali) and three districts of Orissa (Jagatsinghpur, Nuapada, Rayagada).

The long-term objectives of this innovative project and action plan is to work towards political empowerment of women, that is, to prepare them fully to become effective partners in the decision making process, thereby leading towards the envisaged decentralised planning process. The second objective is to bring about change in the patriarchal, caste-ridden hierarchical society into a more egalitarian and just society through making elected women representatives as.agents of change.. Further, efforts should be made to generate a development process that is more gender-friendly, and finally, to strengthen the third tier of village level institutions including the Gram Sabhas, which are the lifeline of panchayat system.

Short Term Objectives

- to examine the nature and extent of women.s participation in Panchayati Raj institutions in the light of their social background factors. class, caste, age, education, marital status
- and to identify the factors (both within the public and private sphere) which may hinder their participation in the political process and democratic institutions at different levels.
- to closely identify concerns and priorities raised by women in meetings and analyse the treatment meted out to them within the gender dynamics and background of the elected women representatives.
- to articulate, give expression to and find solutions to the problems and conflicts which women members might be facing in their work.
- to help them to take up issues with higher authorities.
- to instill confidence among women members by providing opportunities to meet their peers, share experiences and learn about their political rights and powers.
- to monitor performance of women panchayat members and to codify the lessons learnt for wider dissemination for the benefit of women in other districts in the same state as well as in other states.

Study Areas of the Project

The status of women in Rajasthan is very low, and this is reflected in zero female literacy rates in some villages, higher incidence of female infanticide, low female sex ratio and patriarchal society. In Rajasthan, the districts selected for the study are Alwar, Kota and Pali, which also represent divergent problems, caste, low female literacy and patriarchal society. On the other hand, in Orissa, the status of women is relatively high. However, a majority of the tribal population lives in abject poverty and ignorance, incapable of receiving the fruits of growth percolating down to them. The districts identified for the project (Jagatsinghpur, Nuapara, Rayagada) also represented varying sections of ethnic populations at different levels of socioeconomic development.

Among the non-tribal population in both States, the benefits of development reach women the last; where they do reach they reach slowly and haltingly. The development process for the past fifty years, both in Rajasthan and the coastal areas of Orissa, has created a middle class income population, but there is need for empowerment of women in these communities.

The panchayat elections in Rajasthan were conducted in February 1995 and after the expiry of the term, elections were held again in 2000. The project study was made for the panchayats elected for the term 1995.2000, even though the project could be started only in 1996.98. The newly elected members are being contacted by ISS. On the other hand, in Orissa, panchayat elections were held in January 1997 and they will in all likelihood continue in office till 2002. So the project districts in Orissa had the opportunity to study women who were freshly elected.

(a) Keeping the above parameters in mind, the ISS planned a programme of action in the six districts for the three years, i.e. 1998, 1999, 2000. The work related to monitoring the performance of elected women representatives in Panchayats was taken up in the initial programme. Questionnaires on women.s participation in PRIs were prepared and distributed among the investigators. After compilation of data a thorough analysis was made and results were used for further intervention.

(b) A detailed paper on the social background of the women panchayat members who are within the project was prepared and published as a source material for using during the training programme. These directories were found to be quite valuable and the women members regarded them as valuable possessions.

c) For the members of panchayats, a one-day training programme was organised. About 30 elected members, both men and women, from two panchayats underwent training simultaneously. This was done with a view that men also will be sensitised through their participation so that they can get a clear understanding of the role of women in Panchayats and in society.

The content and methods of the training undertaken by the ISS can be given as follows:

i) Interactive discussions instead of structural lectures;

ii) Role-plays.

iii) Simple learning materials in Hindi and Oriya were prepared and distributed and used extensively with required photographs and illustrations;

iv) Case studies of success and failures of women in panchayats were explained. There was reporting about the initiative taken by various members of panchayats who received training during the first stage of the project;

v) Rajasthan and Orissa Panchayat Acts were prepared in simple Oriya and Hindi as background materials and explained to the members in the interactive sessions;

vi) Video film shows were a strong and integral part of the training programme. Video film shows on women.s empowerment and thereafter discussions were significant impact on the minds of the people, especially those who are illiterate world benefited maximum with this exercise. The ISS organised regular video shows to impress upon the Panchayat members about their role and the requirements of empowerment.

d) The directory of the women members under study (one page for each member with a passport size photograph, her address, and other important details) was prepared and distributed. This step provided information to the people in the Panchayats and other parts of the State about the elected members. It has enhanced women.s status and boosted their self-esteem in the society.

e) Appropriate banners carrying messages such as.Women.s Political Empowerment is through Panchayats. were displayed in the village streets, market places and other common public areas. Appropriate wall writings in the selected villages, blocks with an objective of creating the much needed atmosphere and awareness about panchayats and women.s participation in it, were encouraged.

f) Two-day conferences at the inter-village panchayat, inter-block panchayat and district and state levels were organised. The conferences focussed on issues such as the importance of grassroots level democracy, role of local government and development of society, women.s participation in decision-making and many other relevant topics. Such programmes held in the panchayats boosted the morale of panchayat members, especially women, which otherwise got sidelined by vested interests.

g) Case studies and profile of women members were prepared. This included their struggle for success, difficulties in achieving their aspirations and their suggestions for rectification of the system.

The Institute was responsive to situations that arose from time to time. This approach facilitated maximisation of benefits to the target group as envisaged in the programme. The Institute is making an effort to make these districts into model districts from the point of functioning of the panchayats. The grant given by Sida was utilised in the broad framework of investing in people for creating much-needed social capital as well as institutions in order to build a society where women and men are equal partners.

PURPOSE AND SCOPE OF EVALUATION

The constitutionally mandated panchayat bodies were visualised as institutions of self-governance, and state governments are to devolve administrative and financial powers to the PRIs and give them resources so that these bodies reach the level of taking care of their affairs themselves. This process of devolution is slow but could be made faster if the elected members, specially the women, are empowered, and that empowerment of women in political terms is a must to ensure this process. It is also to be evaluated about a positive shift from meeting only the development needs of the people to enabling them to undertake development planning and bring about a change in development perceptive. How far the intervention through the activities and programmes of action brought out these changes.

The evaluation also envisages the nature and extent of women.s participation in Panchayati Raj institutions in the light of their social background and factors such as class, caste, age, education, marital status and other identifiable factors, which hinder their participation in the political process, and democratic institutions.

Regional variances, differential economic development, availability of infrastructure and education levels indicate different priorities and issues for different areas and villages. The community and members of the panchayats have their own perceptions about their needs in terms of social and economic development. How far ISS interventions have made them (women) raise these issues at the panchayat level including the gram sabhas are to seen. Were there appreciable changes on the treatment meted out to suggestions and firm recommendation of women members? When the women members are brought to level of confidence which enables them to articulate and select suitable solutions to the problems and issues that they raise for the benefit of the common good, there is great need to prepare them for taking up various issues to the higher authorities including the zilla parishad, and in the governmental level to the BDO and collector.

Exchange of ideas with women members of other panchayats and sharing of experiences and learning about the progress made by them is a very important aspect of the objectives of the interventions. All these interventions would add to enhanced functional efficiency and completion of projects and programmes in the panchayat for imparting social justice. These achievements made by the women members through their own initiative and efforts are codified for larger exchange and wider dissemination for the benefit of women in other districts.

THEMATIC LEVEL-GRASSROOT LEVEL INTENSIVE CONTACT

The relevance of empowerment of women through the programme intervention adopted and introduced by ISS is well-focussed taking into consideration how far these composite exercises introduced by ISS have given progressive shape to the overall objectives of the programmes.

(a) The first task of the programme was to make initial informal contact with the elected representatives important members of village and communities and express the intent of ISS on what exactly they were planning to introduce into the Panchayati Raj system. This was a difficult task which ISS could establish through a group of dedicated local level youth, both boys and girls, the more among them being girls. These investigators were motivated and trained with the specific tasks of interventions from time to time. A majority of the elected women ward members of the panchayats were illiterate only 10% of them had completed Class 10 and 70% attended school up to Class 5, the remaining had not received any formal education. Initially, very frequent visits were made by the investigators, block level coordinators and district level cordinators to ascertain the eagerness and willingness of these women members to take up the planned empowerment programme. During the course of field visits for evaluation it was strongly expressed by the village elders and the members of the civil society that elected members of the panchayat were very keen to get acquire knowledge about various aspects of the panchayat programme and its effective functioning. In the absence of any organised programme of this nature initiated by the government or any other body these women came very close to ISS field staff and started to open up and express their difficulties and grievances to get the required help and assistance. The transparency of the communication between these women and the investigators and coordinators was one of the most important composition of empowerment. Once the initial ice is broken the village communities come forward to support the investigators in their work of providing elected members with more information and training.

(b) Thereafter, workshops were organised in which 32 to 40 representatives participated and various subjects were introduced such as highlights of the Constitutional Amendment Act, powers of the panchayats, duties of the elected members, responsibilities of gram panchayats and conduct of Gram Sabha meetings. After this, periodical visits were made to oversee the performance of the elected members in discharging their duties as envisaged under the Act. Initially there were difficulties, but by gradual motivation and encouragement many of them shed their shyness and came out openly to express how they intended to solve the problems of the village community. After a period of three months, training programmes were organised with specific subjects introduced to them in a simple manner so that during these interactive sessions they could clarify their doubts about various aspects of their functioning. Local government officials from the development departments, prominent members of NGOs, college teachers dealing with social sciences also gave their valuable time and made efforts to be associated with these programmes. The most important and striking result of this is that the women members learn the art of effective articulation to make their suggestions and recommendations clearly and logically to the authorities. They felt very enthused when they acquired the skill of taking interview with senior block development officials to represent the case of the village in development.

(c) The above interventions made it possible to introduce to these members the importance of holding periodical Gram sabhas with well regulated agenda points and also explain to the members of other village the progress made in various socio-economic activities. Gram sabhas were at first attended very thinly; with the efforts of the investigators and active members the attendance grew in strength and the quality of participation improved. Many of these women members expressed their happiness that well coordinated and orchestrated gram sabha meetings brought out meaningful and useful suggestions for the composite planned development of the village. The minutes of these meetings were recorded with the help of investigators and sent to the panchayat meetings for their consideration and support. These efforts brought about an indirect pressure on the authorities of panchayat hierarchy to clear sanctions for the projects. Some of the panchayat women sarpanches were keen to take up these issues with the Block Development Officers for getting their genuine needs met. All these improvements were possible with the continuous efforts of the field staff working for the project. After a period of one year a district level convention was organised in which about 250 women representatives participated. This gave them the opportunity to exchange ideas and share information on the progress made in their respective panchayats. After this convention field level activities were intensified through field visits and maintaining of close contact by the field staff.

Observations of the field study on the impact of the programmatic interventions can be summarised as follows:

a) In the light of social background factors. caste, age, education level and other factors. the interventions by the ISS brought all these women representatives under one umbrella. Caste and class barriers narrowed down. Parda system, and shyness among village women started disappearing. They acquired courage to express their views both in formal and informal gatherings.

b) The women started showing keen interest to learn more about panchayat administration and community development.

c) These changes amongst the women brought respectability for them in the community.

d) With the help of the field staff they started taking initiatives to solve problems in the community.

e) The women acquired the confidence to share their experiences and also learn from their peers.

f) The women were encouraged to meet higher authorities of the government and represent their problems before them.

g) There is a wind of change in the panchayats as these women are acting as.agents of change..

h) In the course of discussions they complained that the panchayats are not provided with adequate funds from the state government to meet their development needs.

i) They are getting slowly sensitised to the issues concerning social evils; they need more support to equip them for awareness and programme interventions in this area.

j) Great eagerness is demonstrated by the women to accomplish social justice for the marginalised and underprivileged.

k) A majority of them pleaded that they need more intervention for improving their awareness and functional capabilities.

l) They have started organising women.s groups for income generating activities and thrift societies and need more support.

m) Initiatives are required for raising income from the Panchayat.s common assets, MFP sale, etc.

n) The secretaries to the panchayats have started co-operating better with woman sarpanches. This has improved the administration of Panchayats.

o) Block level officers are looking at the quality of change in the study area and then to expand the programme to other areas.

Periodicity and extent of the Gram Sabha meetings and improved participation of women voters in these meetings added a new dimension to the participatory approach of PRI. Minutes were prepared and sent up to Gram Sabhas. Gram Panchayat is acquiring the status of a neutral body to take care of the problems of the villages without any prejudice and extraneous considerations. This will improve the happiness and satisfaction of the Gram Panchayats as a whole.

Even though ISS had made some arrangements to include male representatives in some of their programmes, it was observed that there is a need for introducing programmes for sensitising male members of the villages on gender issues and impressing upon them that women play as important a role as men in all activities of the community and that their potential must be used for development participation and management. This thematic change can be easily incorporated by ISS in their programmes without diluting the theme.empowerment of women for social change..

Knowledge is power and its application brings about positive changes in the society. Awareness creation is an important area which requires emphasis for future interventions in the programme. Twenty-nine specific areas of responsibility covering all aspects of village life shown in the Amendments requires detailed introduction with such schemes under various Ministries and Departments. This will have to be prepared in detail by way of modules and effectively introduced to the panchayat. ISS will have to prepare necessary material for it as well as prepare the trainers.

THEMATIC CAPACITY OF THE ISS AND FIELD STAFF

Field Staff as a friend and philosopher ISS was founded in 1985 as a registered society to study contemporary social, political and economic issues, and problems that confront the country, in an inter-disciplinary perspective and make its findings and recommendations to the members of the decision-making organisations at various levels.

ISS has a highly qualified, motivated and experienced Director who is supported by research faculty consisting of senior fellows and senior research officers to add to its academic and research standard. Institute also seeks to build a large community of concerned scholars and activists engaged in ushering in a humane and just society. Recently the Institute has been permanently located in a building of its own in the prestigious institutional area of Vasant Kunj. The Institute provides high quality facilities for top class output. The Institute is capable of introducing the thematic of social relevance in an appropriate manner and gradually develop it as the programme progresses in spread and depth. So far the direction given by the ISS has had dramatic impact in the initial introduction of the theme.Empowerment of Women in the Panchayat.. in the most backward blocks of the underdeveloped districts. ISS has got the inherent capability to adopt and incorporate shifts for strengthening the programme and enlarging the scope. ISS Headquarters have assigned responsibility to two senior research officers to coordinate field programmes and report to the director. Dr. Ramesh C. Nayak is in charge of Rajasthan and Dr. Ms. Bidyut Mohanty is in charge of Orissa. Detailed discussion and interviews with these officers have left positive impressions of their capabilities, methodology and application for having taken this programme to an effective level and demonstrated visible results in the field. They are a great asset to the programme.

At the state level according to the availability of retired senior personnel from the government or NGOs state coordinators were assigned. In Orissa Shri Nirakar Beura was inducted into the project as State Co-ordinator since its inception in 1997. His experience, commitment and vision was demonstrated through the results which have reached into the far-flung areas of Rayagada and Nuapara districts. He was in constant touch with grassroot level workers, community elders, members of civic society and local government staff engaged in the developmental activities of the state. Since January 1999, Shri K.K. Patnaik, former Director (Panchayats) and Rural Development has been Regional Co-ordinator of ISS in Bhubaneshwar with his vast experience in the Department of Panchayats and Rural Development, he will be a great asset for the project. In Rajasthan the responsibility was given to Shri Kaushik the regional youth co-ordinator of Nehru Yuva Kendra Sanghatan. With his vast experience in working with youth and association with Mahilla Mandals and youth clubs, he could easily establish rapport with women members. Similarly, the contribution of the 6 district coordinators block coordinators and filed investigators have contributed immensely to the success of the project.

Block co-ordinators and district co-ordinators as well as village level investigators were all motivated to the level needed to accomplish the tasks assigned to them. Their responsibility is given below.

The job of the State Co-ordinator is:

1. To assist project co-ordinator in preparing literature for training.
2. To assist the project co-ordinator in organising workshops, state level conference, and training programmes.

3. To assist in preparing wall posters and cloth banners on.Women.s Empowerment through Panchayats..
4. Supervising the training and research work of district co-ordinators.
5. To report to the project co-ordinator every month.

District Co-ordinators

Each district is in charge of a district co-ordinator. These district co-ordinators are recruited from the respective districts. They are familiar with local needs and aspirations of the PRI members.

Their job is:

1. To coordinate research and training programmes at the district level.
2. To supervise the work of block co-ordinators.
3. To forward every months progress report to the state co-ordinator and project co-ordinator.

Job of Block Co-ordinator

The block co-ordinators are in charge of the block; their job is:

1. To co-ordinate research work and training progammes at block level.
2. To supervise the work of field investigators.
3. To accurately report every month.s progress to the district coordinator.
4. Organising Training and Awareness Programmes at Gram Panchayat level.
5. To assist in organising gram sabha meetings effectively.

Field Investigators

Field Investigators will work in the Gram Panchayat/village level under the guidance of block coordinators. These investigators will be recruited from the village level.

1. To report success and failure stories of Gram Panchayats and the women panchayat members to block/district coordinators

2. To suggest innovative ideas to the project co-ordinator regarding training/awareness programmes.
3. To motivate women to attend Gram Sabha meetings.
4. To assist block/district co-ordinators in organizing village level workshops, cultural and sports activities.

Apart from this, volunteers from among mainly retired technicians, bureaucrats, school teachers, and other such professionals can support the programme at the village level. They are paid only travel expenses. Being local they can be an asset to the project, when the project staff face problems.

During the course of field visits the field staff accompanied the consultant. Periodical discussions were made with them which give an insight into their commitment and interest in undertaking the task. Some of the female investigators and block co-ordinators who come from modest village backgrounds acquired quite good standard in their performance of the tasks assigned to them by associating with the project. In the light of the suggestions included in this report for thematic shift, appropriate refresher programmes will have to be arranged for these field staff. Advanced thematic changes need introduction of new techniques.

Training for the Elected Women Members

- Training is non-residential and for the day only.
- The medium of communication is the local language/ dialect.
- The master trainers are project staff and active women panchayat members,
- ISS provides all literature on panchayats to master trainers.
- All participants are provided with reading materials on Panchayats prepared by ISS in Hindi/Oriya.
- The emphasis is more on group discussions rather than on classroom teachings.
- Cultural programmes and sports activities for women are organised to motivate them for effective participation.
- All members are personally invited by field investigators to these programmes.

- The training date and course content are announced before hand.
- Loud speakers, banners, posters are used for gram sabha meetings.

Activities

i. National Conference on Women.s Political Empowerment held on 24.26 April annually at New Delhi and since two years at state and district levels in study areas.
ii. State Level Conference
iii. Block level conference
iv. Regional workshops on women.s participation
v. Cultural programmes and sports activities
vi. Awareness camps for women on panchayats/gram sabhas
vii. Training programmes
viii. Exchange programmes

The details of all the activities are to be fully reported.

SUSTAINABILITY OF THE INTERVENTIONS, BOTH STRUCTURALLY AND THEMATICALLY

The people who live in the villages must become authors of their lives and sensitive to the special needs of women and give support in the process of development. The main objective of the programme is to work towards the political empowerment of women, that is, to prepare them fully to become effective partners in the decision-making process, thereby leading towards a gradual decentralised planning process. Women empowerment will bring about change in the patriarchal, caste-ridden hierarchical society, making it into a more egalitarian and just society, through elected women representatives as agents of this change. To make the programme more effective and practical, there is need for slight shift in the thematics and there by structural adjustment in the existing staffing. This includes networking and involvement of civil society numbers in the process. Indeed, there will be sure necessity for enhanced financial allotment to meet the required changes in the programmes and the emoluments of the staff. The enhanced grants will be utilised in the broad framework of investing in people for creating vibrant social capital and responsive institutions to build a society where women and men are equal partners.

The sustainability of the programme cannot be organised by the people themselves as this involves resources such as finance, competent organisational backup and effective interlinking with governmental organisations working in the field. The support from international bodies, multinational and bi-lateral organisations would be necessary for a decade to cover the backward areas and establish credible standards of developed human resources among the elected members. When such models are placed on the ground, government will be induced to incorporate budget provisions for the purpose of empowerment of the elected members in the neglected areas. Sida should consider extending long-term support for this programme to establish workable models of the empowerment of women through Panchayati Raj.

It was observed that the interventions made by ISS have shaken up district administrations to evolve systems for organising gram sabhas; some of the BDOs have sought assistance from the ISS staff and are scrutinizing the thematics introduced by ISS for improving the conduct of gram sabhas. The emerging interest and sincere efforts from the government side would bring rapid changes to the progressive path of sustainability. Well-prepared and people-friendly models laid on the ground would inspire organisations and bodies to support these efforts.

OBSERVATIONS AT THE FIELD LEVEL

In order to economise on the administrative cost the field offices are established and run in a cost effective and austere way. In many places the district level co-ordinators and block level co-ordinators share the premises of the collaborating agencies. As indicated earlier, through modest training, motivation and the good standard of activities undertaken by them networking was made possible for them with other members of the village community, government agencies and other NGOs; these have added to their capacities for achieving good results. Further, structured refresher training with reserved thematics and added incentives by way of enhanced honoraria to meet the increasing costs of subsistence and travel will result in better implementation.

There is a need for covering all the women elected representatives in the block/panchayats under study. Special attention should be given to women who are panchayat members working under male sarpanches. Men should also be included in the training programme for sensitising them about the importance of the participation of women members in the Panchayati Raj administration. This can be worked out by the ISS.

The potential impact of the training programme and interventions was visible in the study area. Women.s participation in the gram panchayat meeting and suggestions and decisions have brought about substantial efficiency in the running of the programmes, completion of programmes, and extension of social justice to the needy. It is observed that the level of articulation and identification issues requires more guidance. This can be attained only through continuous training programmes and exposure to the areas of responsibility assigned to them as per the 11th Schedule.

The project structure and the leadership operating it is very effective-proper guidelines are issued periodical field visits and interactive sections held and motivational approaches held out to staffs. The consultant participated in three interactive sections with staff and observed the effectiveness of their perception and field work. These processes along with proper guidance have build up confidence among the staff. The staff at the field level is largely women who are very sensitive to the needs of women PRI members. Periodical travel of the representatives to the block, district, state, and New Delhi accompanied by volunteers have added a new dimension of confidence in them.

Project management was done through clear-cut guidance, field visits and inspections and reports received from lower functionaries to the state level co-ordinators. This gave the required information for monitoring the programme and the progress made in the identifiable goals. Perhaps it will be necessary to make detail planning regarding time-bound activities for the modified programmes.

RECOMMENDATIONS

There is a need for greater awareness generations in the panchayat community for which more NGOs and grassroot workers should be networked. The vision must be to develop PRIs to develop and to retain the character of the sub-governing institutions committed to public good with compassion and sharing with participatory character and approach. We have to make panchayats in to arbingers of an egalitarian and just society through making women elected representative into agents of change. Equal participation will lead to better functioning of public institutions and transform nature of politics in our democracy.

There is a need for slight shift in the strategy as far as the coverage is concerned.

a) As indicated earlier, male members to be brought under the scheme, incorporating them at appropriate levels.

b) Greater thrust to be given in equipping ward members and sarpanches for the administrative and developmental role they have to perform.

c) Introduce more traditional, cultural folk and sports competition to bring about cohesion among the village groups, especially the youth.

d) Prepare modules containing material narrated in simple regional languages as resource/ training materials.

e) Awareness has to be built up through interactive discussions and distribution of simple understandable materials.

f) Evaluation of standard of performance of panchayat through local colleges and universities.

g) Intensify awareness campaigns in the colleges and schools about empowerment of women and ISS/Sida activities in this area.

h) In order to equip field staff organise training programmes at appropriate level at the initiative of ISS.

i) In order to bring about quick results in political empowerment, net-working should be done with the local NGOs, women study centre, Mahila Mandals, grassroots level workers, etc. The universities and colleges in the locations can play very effective roles.

j) Generation of self-employment through rural income-generating activities to supplement the income and also to occupy them profitably should be a priority area in the strategy.

Model programmes can be encouraged through the project staff.

The vision approach adopted by ISS need not be renewed because of the fact that the programme itself is revolving round a vision of.Women elected representatives as agents of change,. women as capable, equal partners of men, an opportunity to develop hidden potential of women for serving the community, and finally to restore rights and equality enshrined in the Constitution. The vision is to take women to reach to the higher echelons of democratic institutions at state and national level.

I) The immediate goals are to make women PRIs to be able to articulate their aspirations, issues of importance to village communities, and also to make them aware of developmental programmes. They must equip themselves with the knowledge of their rights and equalities.

II) Prepare elected gram panchayat members to know their duties, prepare them to effectively discharge their duties.

III) Sensitisation to the eradication of social evils.

IV) Implement the theme that.education is basic. for strengthening democracy and ushering in development.

V) Introduction of modern science and technology into village life.

VI) Communities, specially male members, should acknowledge the role of women in the community.

VII) Inculcate dignity of the human being and equality as the basic value of the society.

As mentioned earlier in the paragraph on thematic capacity of ISS and performance level of human resources available, there is no doubt that with required support and direction, ISS would be able to prepare the existing field staff to handle the shifts in strategies and introduce elements of upgradation to equip all concerned to reach the goals of the mission. The following suggestions are given in this regard.

- Taking into consideration the output of programme co-ordinators and the added responsibilities which will be thrust upon them, there is a need for upward revision of their emoluments. ISS could decide this upward revision and charge it to the project.
- Each of the programme coordinators may be given part-time secretariat service in preparation and compilation of reports.
- At present, state level co-ordinators are working on part-time basis and this arrangement may continue. They are managed well and motivated by the ISS headquarters. Taking into consideration the added responsibility which would be entrusted on them, there will be need to enhance honoraria paid to them.
- Most important and significant field staff management pertains to the motivation level and training of field staff so as to envisage better output through them at the field level. There is a need for an enhancement of honoraria and travel expenses on par with other voluntary organisations working in the field. These training programmes and upgradation of capability would make the field staff more committed and motivated. ISS has ample capacity to take up to this task.

Financial management of any programme is very vital for the successful achievement of the goals. Swedish International Development Agency was liberal in releasing grants for the programmes which started in 1996, thereafter in the second stage 1997.2000. Annexe. 3 give percentage break-up of the programme (Budget heads). It can be observed from the budget heads that for the period 1996.1997, the following are the details.

i) salary for the programme coordinator and field investigator;

ii) travel for field work;

iii) questionnaire, books, stationary, infrastructure facility, work consultation.

iv) and meeting and overheads.

But for the subsequent period 1998.2000, training programme budget head was added along with literature, background materials and stationery. An additional head for reports and publication was also added. The major expenditure was for salaries for programme coordinator and honoraria for field staff which consumed on an average 35 per cent, travel and field visits 15 per cent training progamme expenditure 12.5 per cent, meetings and workshop and consultations varied between 25 per cent to 30 per cent, literature and background materials and stationary 5 per cent, reports and publications 2 per cent, and an average overhead expenditure between 5 to 7.5 per cent.

For the period January 1998 to March 2000 consisting of 27 months, the total expenditure is about Rs. 43 lakhs. This indicates average project cost for each state per annum works out to be an average of Rs. 10 lakhs. Under the restructured and enhanced programme content there is a need to raise this financial allocation to Rs. 15 lakh average for each state covering about 25 panchayats. This would mean that for a block period of 2 years the allocation would come about Rs. 60 lakhs to cover both states. The proposed budget heads suggested:

1. Salaries for programme co-ordinators and field staff honoraria = 35 per cent
2. Travel and field visits = 15 per cent
3. Meetings, consultations and exchange visits = 17 per cent
4. Preparation of back ground materials and stationary = 5 per cent
5. Reports and publications and media = 5 per cent
6. Overhead including publicity = 5 per cent
7. Training programme including material = 18 per cent.

Details of minor heads will have to be prepared by ISS. It would be necessary to work out details of expenditure on training programmes meetings and consultations and rationalise it by using facilities available in the districts and other austere measures.

Empowerment of women in the Indian context is to bring about gender equality. Thematic approach to structural planning of the entire programme address the question related to gender equality. When 1/3 of the sarpanches in block are prepared well to manage the affairs of the gram panchayat and take decisions as per rules and regulations, chairing the meeting is one of the achievements reaching towards gender equality. Male ward members in the villages patiently listening to their female sarpanches will definitely bring about gender equality. ISS has very thoughtfully structured their approaches to remove the hurdles in a most gentle way by using interactive sessions, group discussions and other community actions. During the course of the visits in Rajasthan it was a pleasant surprise to listen to the achievements and experiences narrated by the former sarpanches and upa-sarpanches. They were full of confidence and hope about the full gender equality. Some of them have not attended formal schools, but the interventions through this programme have brought out their inner talents which changed their personalities and made them ready to serve the community. Some of them have sufficient calibre to be assigned as trainers for the future generation of elected members.

INFORMING ABOUT THE PROGRAMME

State government functionaries, having observed the success of periodical gram sabhas and the methodology adopted by field staff, have come to conclusion that at least the state government should make efforts to ensure conduct of effective gram sabha meetings. In Orissa, as per the government orders, block development officers are organising gram sabha meetings. They have approached ISS for the co-operation of then field staff. As and when the news of effective implementation of panchayat programmes through empowered and trained women members spreads, more requests will come to adopt similar practices. To quote an example, the woman sarpanch of panchayat Smt. Sulochana Das of Palosda Jagatsinghpur district was awarded the best performance certificate in Orissa for completion of all tasks. This can be achieved through proper reporting and media publicity. There is a need to hold periodical media conferences at state level and for coordinators and ISS to bring about public awareness at the national level to highlight the vision, mission and goal. ISS should also endorse their research publications to other states for replication of their model.

ACTIVITIES IN THE LOG FRAME

In order to facilitate a well co-ordinated approach to programmes and completion of given task within the time frame, a log frame has been prepared for the second phase of the programme. The items of the activities enumerated in the log frame has to be expanded taking suggestions and recommendation incorporated in the earlier paras of the report. Periodical reporting at various stages and its analysis will give direction for taking corrective measures while senior staff make inspections in the field. These would also help generate confidence among the communities regarding the utility of the entire mission. Even though the requirement of publicity exercises has not been spelled out in the log frame, would have to be adopted and included in the second phase.

• Activities for 2000.2002

1. To organise state/district/block level conventions to create awareness among women representatives.
2. Organising women representatives. visits to panchayats institutions of other states districts, and panchayats to get a first hand experience of the working of panchayat institutions.
3. To organise workshops on problems faced by women PRI members in completing various development programmes.
4. To organise Women's Empowerment Celebrations programme in New Delhi and other locations from 2001.03 April.
5. To organise awareness campaigns on Women's Empowerment is through Panchayats..
6. Preparation for field contacts, recruitment of staff for the new panchayats to be covered in Rajasthan.
7. Preparation of literature for Training of Trainers (TOT) and PRI members training programme.

8. Rapport with village/panchayat and NGOs in study area.
9. Mobilising people for active participation in gram sabha meetings.
10. Training of trainers.
11. Training for elected PRI members in different phases.
12. Conduct of model panchayat meetings.
13. Networking with government officials, NGOs, youth Clubs, Mahila Mandals, and civil societies.
14. Organising gram panchayat/block/district level sports, folk song competition and cultural programmes relating to women.s empowerment.
15. Appraisal of progress in empowerment by the members themselves. once in six months.
16. Awareness programmes on gender issues, social evils and supporting women.s participation in grassroot politics.
17. Introduction of social development programmes and specific intervention as needed for the area.
18. Collection of socio-economic data on women.s participation in PRIs and publication of research documents.
19. Publication of directory of newly elected women PRI members.
20. Leadership training for potential women candidates in Orissa.
21. Election study in Orissa (in 2002-3) as done in Rajasthan panchayat elections 2000.

METHODOLOGY

The methodology applied to carry out the assignment of consultancy was carried out through a variety of activities as suggested in the terms of reference:

- Field visits with required preparation and planning.
- Focussed group discussions with elected women representatives.
- A meeting with individual former sarpanches and ward members. this was done in Rajasthan only.

- Individual discussions with the current office bearers of the panchayats.
- Intensive interaction with village elders, present male sarpanches, college professors and lecturers of the colleges engaged in social science academics and members of other NGO groups operating in the area.
- In each of the blocks sufficient time was utilised to deliberate with block development officers, panchayat officers and others connected social development programmes to ascertain their observations about the intervention and government.s plans to introduce these programmes in more areas under their charge. Intensive discussions were held with ISS staff in its headquarters in Delhi and field staff at their respective offices and very detailed discussions were held with field investigators about their work towards achieving project goals.
- The consultant had to take resource to secondary sources such as local media reporting, reports submitted by district level co-ordinators state level co-ordinators, and finally, documentation made by the ISS headquarters including a large number of useful and illustrative photographs giving empirical evidence depicting the intensity of the programme and the enthusiasm it evokes.
- The consultant took the initiative to visit two panchayats each in control blocks where the study has not been undertaken and interacted with sarpanches and members. This gave an idea about the differences that exist in panchayats where interventions were not made.

The time framework given for the evaluation could not be adhered to nor could reports be submitted as stipulated because of the need for intensive travels in the interior areas of Orissa and the intervening holidays for puja.

The programme of field visits as per Annexe 4 was taken up after detailed discussion with ISS staff in the ISS headquarters who conveyed detailed instructions to field the staff about the programme and the need for intimating all concerned about the visits and requests for sparing valuable time of the personalities involved in our programmes. The consultant was accompanied by the respective project co-ordinators during the visits to the interior villages. Their presence at various levels of meetings and discussions with various sections of actors in support of programme for empowerment was useful. Annexe. gives details of various activities in the field.

QUICK OBSERVATIONS ON FIELD VISITS

I. ISS headquarters and field staff worked as a well-knit team with clear-cut line of command, understanding, and communication regarding achievements and bottlenecks from time to time. Co-ordinated and orchestrated approach has won the confidence and respect of the village community. This fundamental strength would enable ISS to easily adopt the shifts recommended in the strategy. Intensification of programmes with additional contents will be conceived with required rapidity.

II. Favourable response from village elders, NGO volunteers working in the area make operational capacity of ISS better.

III. There is an urgent need for synchronised awareness generation programme all-round. This was the fundamental request from all quarters.

IV. ISS must take up issues with the state government for gradual but prompt devolution of funds to reach panchayats. All our efforts for empowerment will become meaningless if parallel efforts are not made by state, centre and district administration to bring about the required degree of opportunity change to make gram panchayat emerge as institutions of self-governance.

V. It was observed that majority of the women members desired to keep politics away while deciding socio-economic development proposals of the panchayats. This is a positive influence of the programme for empowerment.

VI. Many of the former women members in Rajasthan who have gone through the training programme for three years have acquired the required potential to assist ISS as resource personnel.

VII. It was found that many members desired to introduce social developmental programmes into the ambit of the project.

VIII. There is a need for emphasising community action for better hygiene and sanitation in the villages.

IX. In some of the affluent agricultural areas of Rajasthan, the panchayats in the study area have initiated establishment of private schools for better all-round education. Large number of girl children in uniforms attend.

X. Vision, mission and goals achieved need to be intensively covered in the local national print media and electronic media. At the time of state and national level conventions state government, central government should support the good work of ISS and Sida to be known to the people.

CONCLUSION

73rd Constitution Amendment Act was legislated to give full opportunity for grassroots democracy to be strengthened with an added special right for women.s participation in all the activities. As the field reality is that women.s participation in decision-making at all levels, whether national or local, is still marginal, this calls for concerted and committed efforts with initial support from agencies such as committed NGOs to assist them in their efforts. Empowerment is an essential ingredient to uphold the dignity of individuals and bring out originality and initiative for working for the common good. The vision, mission and goals of the Women.s Empowerment through Panchayati Raj project are laudable and appropriate for ushering in democratic decentralised developmental initiatives in the rural areas of India.

SUMMARY

The main objective of the project was.Empowering Women through Panchayats in Rajasthan and Orissa.. Three districts from each state were selected for the study. The participation of women in Panchayat and Gram Sabha meetings were monitored and evaluated by the ISS project staff. The experiences from these districts shows, even men PRI members are not aware of the powers and functions of Panchayats. In the second stage of the programme both men and women members to be included under study. Since the literacy level is very low in these districts except Jagatsinghpur district in Orissa in comparison to the state average there is a need for more awareness generation programmes for both PRI members and village people. Thus awareness generation programmes on powers and functions of panchayats, campaign against social evils and on going developmental works of government agencies will be great help to these PRI members. The network with local level NGOs working on similar developmental issues be taken to widen the base of ISS work these districts. The training of PRI members should be given and on continuous phases. Since, the majority of Zilla Parishad and Panchayat Samiti members are comparatively better educated and can manage their work for themselves emphasis should be on gram panchayat members. The number of gram panchayats both men and women headed under study should be increased to 25 in each district.

The new strategy for the programmes recommended are:

1. The men PRI members to be brought under the programme.
2. Awareness programmes both for PRI members and villagers to be intensified.
3. Along with video shows on success stories of panchayats, sports and cultural activities should be included in the training programmes for PRI members.
4. Training of Trainers (TOTs) to the included in the programme activities.
5. Networking with local NGOs, Women.s Association and grassroots level organisations should be part of the activities.
6. ISS should prepare training modules in simple regional languages both for field level staff and PRI members.
7. In order to facilitate better management and control there is need to strengthen staff of Project Coordinators.
8. The salaries and honorarium of the project staff need to be revised.

3

EMPOWERING WOMEN THROUGH PANCHAYATS IN RAJASTHAN

The 73rd Constitutional Amendment (1992) is an important landmark in the history of women.s participation at the grassroot level. For the first time 33 percent seats were reserved for women. Rajasthan was the second state to hold panchayat elections in 1994 after implementation of 73rd Amendment.

In 1994 panchayat elections 38791 women were elected in PRIs of Rajasthan. Since the majority of these women elected were first timer and illiterate it was a great challenge for them to perform their functions. Also the local customs and traditions did not support women.s active participation in politics and development work. After the panchayat elections were held newspapers reported women were treated with indifference by their male colleagues in the meetings. The bureaucracy did not treat them with dignity. In many instances they were used as proxy women and their male family members conducted panchayat meetings.

Also the elected panchayat members faced violence and rape if they dare to come out alone to attend meetings. The working conditions were not congenial. Women were frustrated to wok in the panchayat which has been vitiated with corruption, violence and petty mindedness. Even dalit women who were agricultural laboures before panchayat elections had to stop their wage labour after being elected as panch/sarpanch. Atrocities against dalit women members increased. There were instances from Rajasthan where dalit women sarpanches were not allowed to sit on chair in front of their upper caste male colleagues at Gram Panchayat meeting. There were many cases where no confidence motions were brought and passed by two third majority by their male colleagues to remove from their post. The worst victims were OBC and dalit women.

Data from Alwar and Pali district of Rajasthan shows 61 no confidence motions were brought for hearing between 1996-98. ISS with a finance support from SIDA started the work in Rajasthan for the project in March 1996. To begin with relevant literature was reviewed, sample district were selected, interview schedules were prepared and pilot testing of the questionnaires were done. The project was launched in Alwar, Pali and Rajsamand districts on 2nd October (Gandhi Jayanti Day) to monitor and evaluate the performance of women PRI members. These districts represent three diverse socio-economic and cultural regions of the state. The main objective of the project was to understand women.s participation at grassroot level. In these districts with the support of the local NGOs, Youth Education Society in Pali and Rajsamand and Nehru Yuva Kendra (NYK) in Alwar we started monitoring the panchayat meetings.

Alwar

Alwar is situated in the eastern part of Rajasthan. It is 148 kms away from the state capital Jaipur. It is one of the biggest district of the state. It has 14 panchayat samitis and 478 gram panchayats. Both agriculturally and industrially it is one of the developed district. The major crops of the district are wheat, onion, pulses, oilseeds, cottons and sugarcane. Majority of its people are SCs, STs, OBCs and Meo Muslims. The district constitute part of Mewat region which has its distinct linguistic and cultural identity in Rajasthan.

Pali

Pali district is situated in western part of Rajasthan. It is 286 kms away from Jaipur. The district is situated in the semi-arid zone of Rajasthan. Both industrially and agriculturally it is one of the developed district. Majority of its people are Rajputs, STs and SCs. The Rajputs ruled over Rajasthan for centuries. They are main land owning caste in Pali. The district has 10 panchayat samitis and 320 gram panchayats. The district is part of Marwar region of the state. It has its own distinct linguistic and cultural identity. This region has produced many prominent enterpreneurs in India.

Rajsamand

Rajsamand is situated in Southern part of Rajsthan. It came into existence in 1991. It was carved out of the erstwhile district of Udaipur. The district is 376 kms away from Jaipur. Majority of its people are OBCs, Rajputs, STs, and SCs. The district is backward in terms of agricultural development and infrastructure. Since 1980s the district has been main centre for.right to information. launched by Mazdur Kissan Shakti Sangathan (MKSS). The MKSS has been highlighting corruption at grassroot level and organising protest rally and public hearings at panchayat level. The district has 7 panchayat samitis (PSs) and 205 Gram Panchayats (GPs). The district is part of Mewar region of Rajsthan. This region has separate linguistic and cultural identity in Rajasthan. The three districts discussed above represent three distinct geographical region of the state. Each district is different in terms of its agricultural patterns, socio-economic development and the history of its women's participation in politics.

Thus these districts are representative sample of Rajasthan to understand the performance of elected women representatives in local bodies. We selected 2 panchayat samitis and 4 gram panchayats from each district under study. All total we selected 72 elected women panchayat members under our programme. We recruited three district coordinators and 17 research investigators to assist the project coordinator in monitoring and evaluation work. Our project staff visited the GP, PS and ZP selected under study. They selected the basic information on these PRIs. We organised workshops at district headquarter and invited these elected panchayat members to attend these programmes. The women were enthusiastic about our programme. With their support and active participation we started our Ist phase of project work in 1996.

In the initial stage of the project our objective was monitoring the panchayat meeetings. When our project staff visited panchayats meetings the panchayat officials were suspicious of our activities. Even the male members suspected our intention when we invited women PRI members to attend women.s Empowerment Day Celebrations at New Delhi from 24.26 April 1997. We realised that the women panchayat members are not informed about the date and venue of the panchayat meetings.

Though the Rajasthan Panchayat Act says that a prior seven days notice to be given to all elected panchayat members. Even the women sarpanches complained the government officials from Engineering, Electricity, Irrigation department never consult them.

Where as they consult secretary and male members. Their self esteem was very low.

Even if the women attend panchayat meetings their participation was not satisfactory. They lacked about the procedures and proceeding of the meetings. Even they attend these meeting they leave in between or earlier than their male colleagues ISS project staff in charge of Rajasthan decided to train these women members.

In the mean time the male members demanded they should be included in all these activities otherwise they will not allow their women colleagues to attend these programmes. Youth Education Society.s (YES) Work in Rajasand and Pali district was not satisfactory. The Research Investigators did not attend the panchayat meetings regularly. We decided to cancel our contract with YES. Also we decided to take Kota district instead of Rajsamand. The reason was NGOs like Seva Mandir, Astha and MKSS were very active on Rajsamand district. Kota district situated in South-Eastern part of Rajasthan is a separate linguistic and cultural zone.

This district along with Bundi, Jhalawar and Baran is known as Hadoti region of Rajasthan. In this region NGO activities were negligible in comparison to other zones. Thus we decided to take Kota district. Also we decided to publish a directory of women PRI members selected under our study. School level slogan and painting competitions on womens empowerment were organised in these districts. Our field project staff had no idea on panchayat Acts powers and functions given to PRIs. Many panchayats had no Secretary and gramsevak. In Rajasthan one secretary is in charge of two to three panchayats. The workload for the secretary was too much.

They could not give the time required for each panchayat. The women sarpanches who are illiterate and could just sign their names were in disadvantage to function in panchayats. Many of them even signed cheques and panchayat proceedings without knowing what is written on it. The secretaries took advantage of this situation. The first phase of training programme started in 1997. The training camps were organised at village panchayat level. We invited both women and men PRI members to these camps.

Our experience shows, the women never reach in time. We found that since they had no idea of these training programmes earlier they hesitate to attend women from agricultural labour hosueholds feel that they lose their daily wages if they attend such programmes. Women elected members from ZP did not attend this programme.

They think they are higher in status to GP and PS members. They thought these training programme are for GP members. The PRIs women members are hetrogeneous group on basis of their age, caste, education, and socio-economic background. Younger women in rural Rajasthan have to cook and take care of their children and family members. Even they have to take permission of their father-in-laws brother-in-laws and husbands to attend these programmes.

Their elders thought it is meaningless to attend these training programmes. When the project coordinator met one woman sarpanch in Pali district and invited her to the training programme. She replied.If I make papad I will earn Rs.150 a day. Why should I waste my time in a training camp.. The project coordinator asked her,.why you wasted your money and energy in panchayat election. You could have invested in papad making.

Also the project coordinator asked her to make arrangement for a training camp. We will show a video film on panchayat. She agreed to our proposal and motivated other women to attend it. In another training camp in Pali not a single women turn of for the programme. We found that women have to prepare their lunch and do many household works. We invited local BDO, retired bureaucrats, school teachers, NGOs as resource persons. The women members perceived `trainers. as people who would solve their routine problems immediately. And when we specified our objectives they lose interest.

In the second phase of the training programme their attendance increased. They realized this project is for their benefit and they should attend it. By this time they had already attended our District/State/National Level conferences. We had established our rapport with these women. These women had already attended training programmes given by various departments of the state government. They could realised our training programmes were interactive and gender sensitive in comparison to state government sponsored training programmes which were mainly lectures by government officials. Since the majority of the women are illiterate it was a great challenge for us to train them. We simplified the PRI Act and gave them simple instruction. From our monitoring and evaluation study we had realized these women are signing cheques and official proceeding without asking the secretaries. We trained them to ask the Secretary before signing any paper. Also to sign in front of any educated and co-operating male colleague. After attending our training programme these women started asking the secretaries before signing any paper. The secretaries realised now these women will never allow them to work smoothly.

(i) XI Schedule to the Constitution of India

(ii) Total number of women PRI members selected for study.

(iii) Financial statements indicating expenditure in the years 1997, 1998, 1999, upto March 2000.

(iv) Itinerary of field visits of the Consultant.

(v) List of ISS field staff working in the project areas

(vi) Details of the persons interviewed during field visits to Rajasthan and Orissa

(vii) Experience from the field. A report by Dr. Ramesh C. Nayak, Rajasthan Co-ordinator.

(viii) Socio-economic profile of the districts under study.

(ix) Specimen copies of field reports from investigator, Block co-ordinators, and State Co-ordinators.

(x) Newspaper clippings and articles published related to the project.

(xi) Pictorial description of the project activities.

Rajasthan at a Glance

1 Area 3,42,239 sq.kms.

2 Population 440.06 lakhs

3 Density of population 129

4 Sex Ratio (Females per 1000 males) 910

5 Literacy rate (Population aged 7 years and above) 38.55

6 Percentage of female literacy 20.44

7 Number of Villages 39810

8 Number of Zilla Parishad 32

9 Number of Panchayat Samitis 237

10 Number of Gram Panchayats 9185

11 Percentage of SCs 17.29

12 Percentage of STs 12.44

13 Average population in a Gram Panchayat 3750

14 Average villages in a Gram Panchayat 4.13

15 Total number of Lok Sabha seats 25

16 Total number of MLA seats 2000

Number of elected members in PRIs of Rajasthan 1994-2000

Sl.No.	Category	Zilla Parishad	Panchayat Samiti	Gram Panchayat
1	General	216	1145	57057
2	SCs	177	943	17904
3	STs	154	804	15616
4	OBCs	119	625	13137
5	Women	331	1740	33566
	Total	997	5257	137280

Chairpersons of the PRIs in Rajasthan 1994-2000

Sl.No.	Category	Zilla Parishad	Panchayat Samiti	Gram Panchayat
1	General	5	45	1941
2	SCs	6	41	1643
3	STs	5	36	1477
4	OBCs	5	35	1060
5	Women	10	80	3064
	Total	31	237	9185

List of Project Staff Working in Rajasthan

Dr. Ramesh C. Nayak Project Co-ordinator

Mr. S.P. Kaushik State Co-ordinator

Alwar

Ms. Renu Agarwal District Co-ordinator

Mr. Naveen K. Yadav Block Co-ordinator, Umren

Mr. Abhinandan Sharma Block Co-ordinator, Thanagaji

Mr. Binod Meena Field Investigator

Ms. Maitri Vashistha Field Investigator

Kota

Mr. Satyanarayan Suman District Co-ordinator

Mr. Brujbhusan Sharma Block Co-ordinator, Ladpura

Ms. Jaya Trivedi Block Co-ordinator, Sultanpur

Ms. Anita Field Investigator

Ms. Dimple Sharma Field Investigator

Pali

Ms. Kamala Jawahar Consultant

Dr. N.M. Purohit District Co-ordinator

Dr. M.S. Inda Block Co-ordinator, Bali

Ms. Hemalata Mehata Block Co-ordinator, Marwarh Junction

Ms. Vinita Vyas Field Investigator

Ms. Ranjana Field Investigator

List of Project Staff working in Orissa

Dr. Bidyut Mohanty Project Co-ordinator

Mr. K.K. Patnaik ISS Regional Co-ordinator, Eastern Region

Mr. Nirakar Beura State Co-ordinator

Jagatsinghpur

Mr. Amarnath Parida District Co-ordinator, Jagatsinghpur

Ms. Jolly Pattnaik Block Co-ordinator, Kujanga, Jagatsinghpur

Ms. Banaprabha

Ms. Meera Dash

Ms. Anjali Pradhan

Ms. Ratnamanjari Mohapatra Field Investigator

Ms. Binita Rout

Ms. Sukanti Behera

Mr. Abhiram Samal

Mr. Gyanranjan Mohanty

Rayagada

Dr. Padma Ch. Mishra District Co-ordinator, Rayagada

Mr. Sudarsan Rath Block Co-ordinator, Bissam Cuttack, Rayagada

Mr. Santosh Kr. Naik

Mr. Sankar Melaka

Ms. Babita Gouda

Ms. M. Rabanama Field Investigator

Ms. K. Asha Kumari

Ms. Pramita Satpathy

Mr. Pramod Padhi

Nuapara

Mr. Saroj Samal District Co-ordinator, Nuapara

Ms. Sangita Pattnaik Block Co-ordinator, Khariar, Nuapara

Ms. Neelima Nial

Ms. Geetanjali Majhi

Mr. Rabindra Kumar

Mr. Ramchandra Sabar Field Investigator

Ms. Basantamanjari Barik

Ms. Bimanta Patel

Ms. Sudhangini Panigrahi

Ms. Kabyarani Sahoo

Number of Women PRI members selected for study in Rajasthan

S.No.	Panchayat	Alwar	Kota	Pali	Total
1	Zilla Parishad	4	4	4	12
2	Panchayat Samiti	6	8	4	18
3	Gram Panchayat	40	45	35	120
	Total	50	57	43	150

Number of Women PRI members selected for study in Orissa

S.No.	Panchayat	Jagatsinghpur	Nuapara	Rayagada	Total
1	Zilla Parishad	9	5	8	22
2	Panchayat Samiti	17	14	12	43
3	Gram Panchayat	74	54	42	170
	Total	100	73	62	235

Details of the persons interviewed by D.K. Manavalan, Consultant during field visits to Rajasthan

Rajasthan

Ms. Rekha Meena

Sarpanch, Bhogaru Gram Panchayat, Alwar

Ms. Mandodari Devi

Former Chairperson, Umren Panchayat Samiti, Alwar

Ms. Dakha Devi Banjara

Former Ward Panch, Bamambas Kankar Gram Panchayat, Alwar

Ms. Asha Devi

Former Sarpanch, Bhangdoli Gram Panchayat, Alwar

Ms. Shimburi Devi

Up-sarpanch, Bhangdoli Gram Panchayat, Alwar

Ms. Lila Devi

Former Up-sarpanch, Bhogaru Gram Panchayat, Alwar

Ms. Kisan Pyari

Former Ward Panch, Bhogaru Gram Panchayat, Alwar

Ms. Anandi Devi

Former Sarpanch, Kasaba Dehra Gram Panchayat, Alwar

Smt. Ladama Devi

Former Ward Panch, Kasaba Dehra Gram Panchayat, Alwar

Ms. Sushila Devi

Former Ward Panch, Kasaba Dehra Gram Panchayat, Alwar

Ms. Santosh Kumari

Member, Kota Zilla Parishad, Kota

Ms. Sugna Bai

Former Ward Panch, Naya Nohara Gram Panchayat, Kota

Ms. Nainiki Bai

Former Member, Sultanpur Panchayat Samiti, Kota

Ms. Ramanathi Bai

Former Sarpanch, Jalimpura Gram Panchayat, Kota

Ms. Ram Kanwar

Member, Ladpura Panchayat Samiti, Kota

Mr. Rajdheshyam Mimorta

Former Sarpanch, Sogaria Gram Panchayat, Kota
Ms. Lalita Bai
Former Sarpanch, Naya Nohara Gram Panchayat, Kota
Ms. Dwaraka Bai Bagadia
Former Sarpanch, Nimoda Gram Panchayat, Kota
Ms. Radha Rathod
Former Ward Member, Sogaria Gram Panchayat, Kota
Ms. Parbati Bai
Former Ward Member, Sorgaria Gram Panchayat, Kota
Block Development Officer
Sultanpur Panchayat Samiti, Kota
Mr. S.P. Kaushik
Youth Coordinator, Nehru Yuva Kendra, Alwar
Mr. Satyanarayan Suman
District Coordinator, Kota
Mr. B.B. Sharma
Block Coordinator, Ladpura Panchayat Samiti, Kota
Mrs. Jaya Trivedi
Block Coordinator, Sultanpura Panchayat Samiti, Kota
Mr. Abhinandan Sharma
Block Coordinator, Thanagji Panchayat Samiti Alwar
Mr. Naveen Kumar Yadav
Block Coordinator, Umren Panchayat Samiti, Alwar
Secretary, Sogaria Gram Panchayat, Kota

Orissa

Ms. Meena Rani Benera
Sarpanch, Gandikipur Gram Panchayat, Jagatsinghpur
Ms. Sandhya Rani Senapati
Sarpanch, Sabhamul Gram Panchayat, Jagatsinghpur
Ms. Jayanti Mishra

Sarpanch, Chatikona Gram Panchayat, Rayagada

Ms. Kamala Jakasia

Sarpanch, Jhigdi Gram Panchayat, Rayagada

Ms. Kulunji Ulka

Chairperson, Bissam Cuttack Panchayat Samiti, Rayagada

Ms. Nishika Sabitri

Sarpanch, Kotapeta Gram Panchayat, Rayagada

Ms. Surama Pradhan

Sarpanch, Pitamahal Gram Panchayat, Rayagada

Ms. Jakaka Pushpanjali

Member, Rayagada Panchayat Samiti, Rayagada

Ms. Chandrama Shabar

Ward Member, Duajhar Gram Panchayat, Nuapara

Ms. Mamita Pod

Ward Member, Duajhar Gram Panchayat, Nuapara

Ms. Sabita Jhankar

Ward Member, Nehna Gram Panchayat, Nuapara

Ms. Prabhati Panda

Naib-Sarpanch, Komna Gram Panchayat, Nuapara

Ms. Tulsi Pod

Ward Member, Komna Gram Panchayat, Nuapara

Ms. Sebati Nag

Naib-Sarpanch, Tikrapada Gram Panchayat, Nuapara

Ms. Taruni Raut

Ms. Radha Tandi

Ms. Gomati Sunani Ward Member, Tikrapada Panchayat, Nuapara

Ms. Ahalya Dalpati

Ms. Shasmita Jagat

Member, Nuapara Zilla Parishad, Nuapara

Block Development Officer, Komna
Panchayat Samiti, Nuapara

Secretary, Jigdi Gram Panchayat, Rayagada

Secretary, Chatikona Gram Panchayat, Rayagada

Dr. Dusmant Kumar Mohanty
Lecturer in Rayagada College

Dr. Henry and Mrs. Henry in Bissam Cuttack Christian Hospital Rayagada

Mr. Karunakar Patnaik

ISS Regional Co-ordinator, Eastern Region, Bhubaneswar

Mr. Nirakar Beura, State Coordinator

Mr. Amarnath Parida, District Co-ordinator, Jagatsinghpur

Ms. Jolly Patnaik, Block Co-ordiantor, Jagatsinghpur

Dr. P.C. Mishra, District Co-ordinator, Rayagada

Dr. Sudarsan Rath, Block Co-ordinator, Rayagada

Mr. Ranjit Swain, District Co-ordinator, Nuapada

Ms. Sangita Patnaik, Block Co-ordinator, Nuapada

4

WOMEN AND PANCHAYATI RAJ

Through the experience of the Indian Panchayat Raj Institutions (PRI) 1 million women have actively entered political life in India. The 73rd and 74th Constitutional Amendment Acts, which guarantee that all local elected bodies reserve one-third of their seats for women, have spearheaded an unprecedented social experiment which is playing itself out in more than 500,000 villages that are home to more than 600 million people. Since the creation of the quota system, local women-the vast majority of them illiterate and poor-have come to occupy as much as 43% of the seats, spurring the election of increasing numbers of women at the district, provincial and national levels. Since the onset of PRI, the percentages of women in various levels of political activity have risen from 4-5% to 25-40%.

According to Indian writer and activist Devaki Jain, "the positive discrimination of PRI has initiated a momentum of change. Women's entry into local government in such large numbers, often more than the required 33.3 %, and their success in campaigning, including the defeat of male candidates, has shattered the myth that women are not interested in politics, and have no time to go to meetings or to undertake all the other work that is required in political party processes...PRI reminds us of a central truth: power is not something people give away. It has to be negotiated, and sometimes wrested from the powerful."

Contrary to fears that the elected women would be rubber stamp leaders, the success stories that have arisen from PRI are impressive. A government-financed study, based on field work in 180 villages in the states of Uttar Pradesh, Rajasthan and Madhya

Pradesh, and coordinated by the Center for Women's Development Studies in New Delhi, has found that a full two-thirds of elected women leaders are actively engaged in learning the ropes and exercising power. Says Noeleen Heyzer, executive director of UNIFEM, "This is one of the best innovations in grass-roots democracy in the world."

Women leaders in the Panchayati Raj are transforming local governance by sensitizing the State to issues of poverty, inequality and gender injustice. Through the PRI, they are tackling issues that had previously gone virtually unacknowledged, including water, alcohol abuse, education, health and domestic violence. According to Sudha Murali, UNICEF Communications Officer in Andhra Pradesh, women are seeing this power as a chance for a real change for them and for their children and are using it to demand basic facilities like primary schools and health care centres.

The PRI has also brought about significant transformations in the lives of women themselves, who have become empowered, and have gained self-confidence, political awareness and affirmation of their own identity. The panchayat villages have become political training grounds to women, many of them illiterate, who are now leaders in the village panchayats. Says Sudha Pillai, joint secretary in India's Ministry for Rural Development, "It has given something to people who were absolute nobodies and had no way of making it on their own. Power has become the source of their growth."

By asserting control over resources and officials and by challenging men, women are discovering a personal and collective power that was previously unimaginable. This includes women who are not themselves panchayat leaders, but who have been inspired by the work of their sisters; "We will not bear it," says one woman. Once we acquire some position and power, we will fight it out...The fact that the Panchayats will have a minimum number of women [will be used] for mobilizing women at large." It is this critical mass of unified and empowered women which will push forward policies that enforce gender equity into the future.

An observation by Deepak Tiwari in This Week, India's No.1 Weekly News Magazine, displays the promising future made possible by the PRI. He notes, "'Learning politics' is the latest fad for young village girls, who dream of joining the growing band of women panchayat representatives, 164,060 at last count, in the state."

EMPOWERING THE POOR THROUGH PANCHAYATI RAJ

In the history of Panchayati Raj, April 23, 1993 is a landmark day. As on this day the institution of Panchayati Raj was accorded constitutional status through the Constitution (Seventy-third Amendment) Act, 1992, thereby seeking to transform Mahatma Gandhi's dream of Gram Swaraj into reality. The UPA government has made Panchayati Raj as one of the pivots of the Common Minimum Programme. A full fledged Ministry status was accorded to Panchayati Raj with the two key functions of economic development and social justice.

Panchayati Raj (local self-governance) holds the key to garibi hatao (alleviation of poverty). This can come about only if the institutions of Panchayati Raj are strengthened at the grassroot level. The Government has identified 16 major dimensions to this whole process adding two more rural business hubs and IT enabled e-governance, as also 100 different steps that need to be taken to strengthen this process. It's a movement from empowerment to entitlement and then on to enrichment, according to the Minister of Panchayati Raj, Shri Mani Shankar Aiyar.

A fresh national impetus has been given to the devolution of powers, responsibilities and finances through the Seven Round Tables of State Ministers of Panchayati Raj which arrived by consensus, at 150 recommendations pertaining to 18 dimensions of Panchayati Raj.

Women Power

Women hold a key place in making Panchayati Raj effective. It is clear that women have been able to enlarge their representation beyond a minimum 33.33 per cent prescribed by the Constitution. In Karnataka 45 per cent of the elected offices are occupied by women and in Uttar Pradesh 54 per cent of the Zilla Panchayat Pradhans are women. Similarly in Tamil Nadu 36 per cent of the chairpersons of gram panchayats are women. In promoting the larger social objectives through PRIs, States have been sensitized to issues of gender empowerment so that unintended consequences of such policies do not diminish the role of women in Panchayati Raj.

The Centre has the responsibility for implementing in letter and spirit, the provisions of the Constitution relating to Panchayats and Nagarpalikas. Efforts are being made towards evolving the Local Self Government institutions in States and Union Territories as a role model. Considerable progress has been made in this regard in Damn and Diu and Nagar Haveli.

The Indian voter is one and indivisible. The principle of parity between parliamentary and assembly elections, on the one hand and panchayat elections, on the other, must therefore be maintained, especially as it is noticed that peoples participation in panchayat elections is substantial and generally equal to or higher than in parliamentary/assembly elections. While all matters relating to panchayat elections have been vested by the Constitution in State legislatures/governments, there is a need to work towards commonality, if not uniformity, in election procedures and provisions.

Strong PRIs in Karnataka

In the southern part, Karnataka shines as an example in implementing and strengthening PRIs. Karnataka has initiated implementation of 77 of the 106 recommendations of the Round Tables. The amendments made to the Karnataka Panchayat Raj Act in October 2003 and the subsequent steps taken to strengthen the Grama Sabha; create and empower Ward Sabhas; complete Activity Mapping; and rationalize and simplify schemes entrusted to the Panchayats are examples to be emulated countrywide. The monitoring of the actualization of devolution by the Legislative Committees is a significant step in the strengthening of Panchayats in the State.

The entrustment of schemes by the State Governments to Panchayats in the current year's budget is a giant step forward in matching the functional transfer with funds. Through this process, the Panchayats now handle in excess of Rs. 3,500 crore of Plan funds per year.

West Bengal Shows The Way

West Bengal has been at the forefront of the empowerment of Panchayats from 1973 onwards. In 1994, it enacted its State Panchayat Legislation to conform to the 73rd Amendment to the Constitution, so as to establish Panchayats as institutions of local self-Government in the letter and spirit of Part IX of the Constitution. The steps taken in this State to institutionalise peoples' participation through Panchayati Raj, stand testimony to its sustained commitment towards Panchayati Raj.

The panchayat system appears to provide a systematic training ground for the people who will take top leadership positions in the country in the future. Women are making impressive strides in this quest for leadership. It appears that the leadership of the ordinary people is being established in West Bengal. Through the panchayat system, the voiceless seemed to have gained the voice.

With commitment to democratic decentralization, these bodies are on their way to becoming truly self-governing institutions.

INTRODUCTION

The success story I bring to you is from India. It is a story about 330,000 women who have entered the arena of formal politics. This number will soon rise to more than 1 million women. These are women who have been elected to local councils by the processes of classical democracy: universal adult franchise; political party campaigns in a multi-party system; and mandatory elections every five years. As elected members of local government, the power these women have is real. This includes the power to decide both the direction and pace of local development and also to administer and monitor the implementation of those decisions.

Significantly, the remit of these local councils mirrors the themes of the World Summit for Social Development, held in Copenhagen in 1995: poverty eradication (usually economic programmes targeted towards the poor); social security programmes such as welfare for children, the old and the disabled; and the social sectors of education, health, women and development. The success story of the women of India is that they are beginning to translate these global themes into policies and programmes at the local level. The story begins with a law passed in 1983 in the southern state of Karnataka. This law included a clause that 25 percent of the seats in local councils would be reserved for women. The elections to these councils were held in 1987. On 1 May 1987, the Janata Dal (the party that won the elections) called a convention of all the 56,000 elected representatives, of whom 25 percent were women. It was a wonderful sight to see 14,000 women in the audience, shining bright, 80 percent of whom were participating in politics for the first time, thrilled with their victory at the hustings. Even those who had passed the law, and advocated for its positive discrimination in the interests of gender equity, were stunned.

By 1995, the presence of women in local government had increased by many multiples, as the whole nation had introduced this political/ administrative change to reserve seats in local councils for women through the 73rd and 74th amendments to the Constitution. In India, we call this new system the Panchayat Raj Institutions system (PRI). The women whom PRI has brought into politics are now governing, in the formal sense of the word. They are the government for their area, be it one village, or a larger area such as 100 villages or a district.

The entire process of restructuring the national political and administrative system started as recently as January 1994. It is, therefore, too early to assess how far women's entry into formal structures of government as a result of PRI has changed the direction and practices of development, especially in relation to sensitive packages of social and economic security, the reduction of inequality, the safeguarding of livelihoods and the environment, and the reduction of domestic violence and other forms of oppression of and discrimination against women; in other words, all the elements of a feminist agenda for social and economic progress.

The 73rd Amendment to the Constitution of India

This Amendment, dated 24 April 1993, directed all state legislature to amend their respective Panchayat legislation to conform to the Constitution Amendment, within one year. All the states complied and adopted new Panchayat legislation by 23 April 1994. By April 1995 all the states were expected to complete decisions on new Panchayats-and those who delayed ran the risk of losing central government assistance, as announced by the Prime Minister.

Why?

The Constitution of India was adopted in 1950. It had envisaged (Article 40) that "the State shall take steps to organise village Panchayats and endow them with such powers and authority as may be necessary to enable them to function as units of self-government."

This provision of the Constitution was primarily advisory. In the following four decades, some sporadic and indifferent steps were taken by some of the state governments to organise Panchayats; but they were invariably denied any meaningful powers and authority and, worst of all, the elections were seldom held at 5-year intervals as required. This deplorable state of affairs was an affront to the Constitution (Article 40) and there was growing demand in the country for a definite constitutional mandate to secure periodical and regular elections to Panchayats just as in the case of Parliament and State Assemblies.

The features of the Act in brief are:

o Panchayats shall have a uniform five-year term and elections to constitute new bodies shall be completed before the expiry of the term. In the event of dissolution, elections will be compulsorily held within six months.

o In all the Panchayats, seats shall be reserved for Scheduled Castes(SCs) and Scheduled Tribes(STs) in proportion to their population and one-third of the total number of seats will be reserved for women. One-third of the offices of chairpersons of Panchayats at all levels shall also be reserved for women.

o Offices of the chairpersons of the Panchayats shall be reserved in favour of SCs and STs in proportion to their population in the State.

o The Gram Sabha will be a body comprising all the adult members registered as voters in the Panchayat area.

It is too early to assess how far women's leadership of local development has facilitated a more just and peaceful society.

Nevertheless, we have some indications of women's impact on the administration and on their male colleagues' attitudes towards women's priorities and women's capabilities, which this paper will discuss. To make this assessment as quantifiable as possible, we must address both the national and the state level. As the PRI process came into effect nationally only in 1993, the information on impact is still not adequate, although there is some preliminary and anecdotal evidence on which to draw. A more detailed assessment may be made at the state level, and this paper will discuss the evidence from the state of Karnataka, which is one of the two states that has experienced a full 5-year term of this new administrative and political regime (1987-1992), with about 14,000 women in the development councils. With this in mind, I have prepared this paper to:

- bring to you the voices of the women concerned, in assessing the impact of the constitutional change;
- draw from this experience some inferences regarding the characteristics of women's leadership at the grassroots;
- comment on the outcome, especially the indications of success;
- argue the case for political restructuring, for a widening of representation, as a key to sustainable development with equity;
- identify some interventions, by both international agencies and the global movements committed to the elimination of inequality and poverty, which could strengthen grassroots women leaders; and
- relate my own involvement in this story, not as evidence of personal achievement, but rather to indicate the role of an individual in collective action.

Transforming the State from Within

PRI is a success story. But the measures of this success must be somewhat different from the indicators that are commonly used to identify success stories. Examples of such commonly used indicators include the capability (vision, insight, commitment) of organisations of women, or NGOs, to establish movements which generate ideas and prototypes for people-led development activities (e.g. the Green Belt Movement in Kenya and the Sewa Movement in India), or the success of organised advocacy and pressure groups, such as the "Support Stockings" in Sweden and the National Women's Coalition of South Africa, in transforming political representation by putting direct pressure on the State from outside.

But in this story, the success of PRI lies in the possibility of women transforming the State from within. I argue that this new arrangement provides the first step to converting grassroots leadership into State leadership, which many feel is the key to ushering in equitable, people-led development. What appears to be happening is that as women enter the structures of governance in large numbers, they are changing these structures so that they reflect more closely the concerns of women.

This is different from the usual process by which a small number of grassroots representatives are elected and can easily be isolated and forced to make compromises. The sheer number of women that PRI has brought into the political system has made a difference. But the difference is also qualitative, because these women are bringing their experience in governance of civic society into governance of the State. In this way, they are making the State sensitive to issues of poverty, inequality and gender injustice.

Measuring and assessing these qualitative changes is not easy, however. Furthermore, the immeasurable is sometimes invaluable. Thus, while much in this document is subjective and preliminary in character, it gives a strong indication of positive outcomes for gender-equitable governance, and is very suggestive of areas for future research.

Who are these women?

The women who have entered politics through PRI are from local areas, representing various backgrounds; rich and poor, dominant and oppressed social classes, educated and illiterate, working and not-working. In a survey of elected women in Karnataka between 1987-89, the following picture emerged (Shashikala et al 1989):

Age: They were usually young women, 25-45 years old (more than 50 percent were 25-35 years old, while 75 percent were below 45 years of age). The explanation given is that older women still feel a reluctance to go into public office. Elected men, on the other hand, were usually of an older age-group. It was noted that experience in political work was an advantage for all candidates, from which men were more often able to benefit.

Political Experience: 20 percent of the women, compared to 80 percent of the men, had previous political experience.

Caste: The pattern of caste representation was the same as before the constitutional change. 60 percent of the elected representatives, whether men or women, were from the dominant castes. However, a reservation for the "downtrodden" castes and minorities added a margin of representation for these groups.

Education: Most of the women elected were illiterate. Here too the variations were striking between men and women, with 20 percent of men being professionally-educated compared to 5 percent of women.

Occupation: The majority of women declared themselves as homemakers. However, we know that this is a broad category which includes heavy work, including income-generating activity.

Positive discrimination works

The percentages of women at various levels of political activity has shifted dramatically as a result of this constitutional change, from 4-5 percent before PRI to 25-40 percent after PRI. At the local level, the numbers of women representatives have increased from no more than 6 in each assembly, usually less than 1 percent in these bodies and that too as nominated or co-opted members, to a total of 330,000 and a presence sometimes in excess of the mandatory one third, the highest proportion being 43 percent. In other words, in some cases women have moved out of reserved constituencies.

Could these women have entered these elected bodies in such large numbers, without the reservation of seats, and the considerable pressure it put on the parties to field women candidates? There is evidence to suggest that women would not have entered these councils in these numbers were it not for this constitutional mandate. It was the pressure of national law, combined with the political imperative of winning elections, that changed political parties' perception of women's limited capacity for public office.

In this regard, it is interesting to note the genesis of the constitutional mandate. The legislative action which enacted the reservation of seats for women did not result from any significant campaign by the women's movement, nor from an unusually gender-sensitive leadership of a political party. There may have been some pressure from the women's wing of the Janata Dal party, in which there was a history of demanding more places for women in the allocation of constituencies for the central parliament.

But this was less significant than the fact that, at that time, the leadership of the Janata Dal party was projecting an image of being "people-led" and progressive and whose political philosophy (which could be deemed an amalgam of democratic socialism and Gandhian philosophy) regarded the issues of justice between the genders as a part of their broader concept of justice. By contrast, in west Bengal, where decentralised government was also introduced at the same time, the political party in power (namely, the Marxist CPI(M) party) did not make this special accommodation for women in the first phase. In other words, PRI cannot simply be equated with progressive politics, as there was not a special place for gender within a Marxist political analysis of the class struggle.

Thus the story I am telling is a complex one. Its plot-line is not a conventional tale of excluded women fighting to gain entry into bastions of male power. Women's entry in large numbers into local government arose from a mixture of political opportunism and an ethical sensibility that regarded the implications of gender as integral, rather than peripheral, to the creation of a more just society. Critically, it arose from the actions of both women and men.

Nor should the effects of the PRI system be described simplistically. Increasing the representation of women has not automatically led to a more gendered analysis of the issues confronting local government. Nor has it necessarily raised the profile of women's needs and interests in the policy agenda, particularly as surveys indicate that most of the women were elected because of the status of their husbands, fathers or sons and that such women often act as proxies for men's views at the councils, being advised by their male relatives. However, as one woman elected through PRI has noted:

> It is true we came through our men the first time and are often proxies for them, but we know what it is about and will come on our own next time.

Thus, the positive discrimination of PRI has initiated a momentum of change. Women's entry into local government in such large numbers, often more than the required 33.3 percent, and their success in campaigning, including the defeat of male candidates, has shattered the myth that women are not interested in politics, and have no time to go to meetings or to undertake all the other work that is required in political party processes.

PRI has also highlighted the intersection between gender interests and social class, for its reservation of seats has enabled poor and marginalised women to demonstrate their deep political consciousness and interest in obtaining power. For them, politics and elections are very practical routes out of poverty and instruments of social change. The next two sections will explore the ways in which PRI is beginning to transform both women and the system of governance itself.

The History of Women's Inclusion in Political Representation in India

1946 There were 16 women out of 150 members in the Constituent Assembly.

1957 When Panchayat Raj was first introduced, the concept was to co-opt two women "who are interested in work among women and children" (Balwantrai Mehta Committee Report).

1961 Maharashtra Zilla Parishad and Panchayat Samiti Act of 1961 provided for the "nomination of one or two women" to the Panchayat bodies "in case women were not elected".

1973 West Bengal Panchayat Act, also provided for co-opting 2 women.

1976 The Report of the Committee on the Status of Women (CSWI) demanded representation of women in Panchayat as well as the establishment of "All-Women Panchayat at village level".

1978 In Maharashtra Panchayat, only 6 women were elected although 314 were nominated. In most parts of India, women were brought into Panchayat only through co-option.

1983 As many as 25 percent of seats were reserved for women in the Karnataka Zilla Parishads, Taluk Panchayat Samitis, Mandal Panchayat and Nyaya Panchayat Act of 1983. Elections under this Act were delayed for various reasons and could only be held in 1987. Some 14,000 women were elected out of 30,000 candidates who contested.

1988 Elections were held in Uttar Pradesh for 74,000 village Sabhas, the first elections for 22 years. There was provision made for the co-option of only one woman.

In Panchayat elections, less than one percent of women came through elections.

1991 Orissa Panchayat Samiti provided for "not less than one third of the total number of seats to be reserved for women". Elections were held in 1992 and over 22,000 women were elected. In Kerala Districts Councils elections, while 30 percent seats were reserved for women, 35 percent seats were won by women.

1993 About 71,000 women candidates contested elections and with 33 percent seat reservation, 24,900 women came in through the ballot box.

1994 In Madhya Pradesh 150,500 women were elected to village, block and zilla Panchayats.

33 percent of seats were reserved for women in village Panchayat and women captured 43 percent of the seats.

PRI: TRANSFORMING WOMEN

Women's experience of PRI has transformed many of them. The elements of this transformation include empowerment, self-confidence, political awareness and affirmation of identity.

Empowering women

Women have gained a sense of empowerment by asserting control over resources, officials and, most of all, by challenging men (Jain 1980; Anveshi 1993). Men and their habits, long outside the realm of female influence, seem to be a major concern of elected women. For example, Deviramma, a 50-year-old woman from the "Golla", or cowherd community, kept cattle and sold curd until recently. Today, she is president of the Yeliyur Gram Panchayat, one of the 5,611 Gram Panchayats constituted in December 1993 under the Karnataka Panchayat Raj Act 1993. As quoted by Rai et al (1995), she states:

If we are outspoken, they-the men-call us brazen and dub us shameless. But now we don't care because we know we have access to people who will have to hear us. The day we have our Gram Panchayat meeting, the men and the people at home mock us-that's when we bring out books and show them what we know.

Nevertheless, Deviramma reports that: "Our secretary, who is a male, doesn't let us talk at the meetings", a complaint that she has already made to the Deputy Commissioner. Similarly, 50-year-old Sibamma has now become an articulate Scheduled Caste member of the Brahamasandra Gram Panchayat. She says (Rai et al 1995):

The men have always ridiculed us, and perceived us as incapable of the management of public affairs. We now make up one third of the councils. This adds to our sense of strength. We must be 50 percent or more. We must overpower them with our numbers.

Women are also aware that their strength comes not only from their numbers but also from their knowledge and skills, for example literacy. Thus, women see training as an important part of their empowerment. Many NGOs have seized on this as a fundamental issue and have begun to focus on the training of women. Clearly this is necessary, but the danger of too narrow a focus is to suggest that it is only women who need training. What the presence of women politicians has done is to invert the conventional hierarchies as to who are the teachers and who are the taught. Such women are making it clear that it is the male extension officers who need training, and not just the female representatives. This is an important message for donors and other funders of training, who have tended to assume in the past that the objects of their support must be women.

Women's empowerment challenges traditional ideas of male authority and supremacy. It is unsurprising, then, that PRI has been opposed by some men. Ratanprabha Chive (Ratna) is the sarpanch(head) of the seven halets(hamlets) that comprise the Ghera Purandar Panchayat. Ratna was beaten up as soon as she assumed office by her rival who could not accept the fact that a female had outwitted him (Rai et al 1995). Today Ratna puts forward proposals in this male-dominated office and poses questions when she is unsatisfied. She says:

Whenever there is any tension in the villages, they come to me and I have learnt how to sort out the problem. Many people have realised that it is indeed a waste of time to make a complaint to the police chowki(station).

She has launched programmes for adult education, digging wells for drinking water and repairing school buildings. She seems to have tackled the political and bureaucratic system which is complicated for a women who has studied only up to Standard 7 (the public education system runs from Standard 1-12). As Ratna says:

It is not the education that matters so much here. It is the grit and determination, which a woman has in plenty.

Self-confidence gained through belonging to local organisations seems critical to enabling women to step out of unequal relationships (Antrobus 1985; ISST 1992). This sense of freedom is even more profound when the group to which women belong is the PRI. This freedom is carried into the very activity of politics by these women. There is a visible difference, a sense of excitement, in the women of rural India.

We are better representatives than men, as we can always be found at home in the kitchen or in the nearby fields. Men wander about, they are either in the town or the beer shops.

Nagamma was an elected member, from a reserved constituency, but she won against a male Scheduled Caste member, which was a very unusual occurance in the Panchayat Raj elections. The villagers in the area who were interviewed during this study were unanimous in their view that this woman was the most effective among all the female elected members of the mandal, a view which was also shared by the Pradhan(the head of the village).

Not all men have opposed PRI and the changes it has brought. Kultikori, a big village in West Bengal, elected an all-woman Panchayat in 1993. When it was time to decide on party candidates for the May 1993 elections, all the members of the male-dominated body stepped down.

They asked their party, the CPI(M), to field the young women of the Ganatantrik Mahila Samiti (the women's wing of the party) who had done remarkable work in eradicating illiteracy in the village. The CPI(M) fielded women candidates in all 11 seats of the Panchayat, and they won (Rai et al 1995).

Understanding Politics

PRI has given many women a greater understanding of the workings of politics, in particular the importance of political parties. Vijayalakshmi was a Congress-I member of the Mandal, a homemaker, of Munnuru village. She wanted party politics to operate in the elections to Mandals because the party bureaucracy (at the State level) usually controls its members in the Mandals. Without the party, no one else would be able to control them.

The party functionaries and the leaders are well-informed of the activities of the Mandal members, and they take some care to see that they function in such a way as not to jeopardise the outcome of elections, which, since 1993, means that female members must be respected.

Kamalamma is a Scheduled Caste member and belonged to the Janata Party. She used to roll beedis to earn some money, and remained at home most of the time. She says that the influence of the political parties is such that now persons from deprived groups have a better chance of being elected members. Earlier, only persons with money and of the upper castes could be elected to any position of importance.

Affirming Identity

On the other hand, some women's involvement in PRI has helped them affirm their identity as women with particular and shared experiences. A woman at a Panchayat meeting in Karnataka stated (SSF 92):

When we meet we work together as women, for our lobby. We don't take much notice of our party identities.

Such women seem to be drawn to an identity above caste or party. This self-perception arises from two sources: from women's own sense of their shared experience and from attitudes and imagery imposed on them by the men. The men see these new political actors as women not as party colleagues. Party politics, a necessary condition for classical democracy, is competitive, but the women bring a non-competitive or cooperative ethic as they are drawn to work together across party lines and seem to have similar interests. Gender can supersede class and party lines. Women have opened up the possibility for politics to have not only new faces but a new quality.

Women Changing Governance

PRI has helped to change local government beyond simply increasing the numerical presence of women. There is now a minority of women who are in politics because of their leadership qualities or feminist consciousness, for example, the women who were formerly part of the Sanghas of the Mahila Samakhya Programme, an awareness-raising, group-based programme. Visible changes in the articulation of ideas and leadership qualities exhibited by this minority were noted in the survey between 1987, the first year, and 1990 (ISS 1994). The difference women are making to local government is becoming evident in different priorities and different values (Jain L.C. 1994).

Changing Priorities

Some of the ways in which women, through PRI, are changing governance are evident in the issues they choose to tackle; water, alcohol abuse, education, health and domestic violence. For example, forty teams of women in Sonbhadra (Uttar Pradesh) area had carried out systematic yatra, or processions, covering ten villages each, or 400 villages in all, to explain the salient features of the 73rd Amendment and the place given in it to women. In the discussions that took place during these yatras, women voiced clear priorities. For nearly 90 percent of the women, the top priority was water. They expressed a need for clean water for fields, for their cattle and for their families. They said life was unbearable and cultivation impossible without developing the water resources of the area. Even as they were determined to prevent the outflow of water from their areas, they were equally determined to prevent the inflow of liquor into their area.

We have been ruined by liquor. We are being ruined day after day. The day's wages are drunk by the men-folk. There is no money for groceries, hence no cooking.

Alochana, a centre for documentation and research of women in Pune, found that only two of the nine members in Bittargaon could sign their names. However, in this village which has a 16,000 population, Alochana found out that the women have "learnt to keep accounts from the local school teachers and the gram sevaks(rural workers). They have put an end to gambling and have come down heavily on liquor dens." The policy they adopted was to "shut the door on every drunken husband." Any protest made by them or children is met by physical assault.

We will not bear it. Once we acquire some position and power, we will fight it out. We know that it is not going to be easy because this battle will be carried out in each home. But the fact that the Panchayats will have a minimum number of women we will use that strength for mobilising women at large and keep liquor out, as a priority.

Women are also taking action against child marriage and child domestic labour, whilst promoting girl-child education, as is evident from the many success stories from Nellore, the heart of the successful anti-arrack struggle (Rohde 1994; Anveshi 1993).

We want education for our children. There are schools and teachers who draw their salaries regularly. They mark the attendance of non-existence students in their registers. But they scarcely come to the schools. With this sorry state of affairs, how can you have education for your children? We are going to tell those teachers: either teach or go. As with education, women have used their elected authority to address quality health care as a critical issue. In Maharashtra, the Indian School of Political Economy organised 60 workshops at Pune under the project of "Leadership Training for Rural Women". The chief conclusion of these workshops was that family planning, drinking water, schools and bio-gas plants are the priorities of women, rather than the TV set or temple (Mahipal 1994). Women, too, have brought domestic violence onto the agendas of political campaigns. In these and other ways, the issues women choose differ from conventional political platforms, which are usually caste/ethnic/religion-based.

But not only do women choose different issues, they appear to choose less corrupt practices as well. Kogendranath Mohato, Panchayat secretary of Kultikori, says:

> The men I had worked under formerly passed on their expenses in cigarettes and paan (bread) to the panchayats. But the didis (sisters) here are not only clean on this score, they are more dedicated.

Women value proximity, whether it be to a drinking water source, a fuel source, a creche, a health centre, a court of justice or an office of administration. Poor women have to walk to access these facilities, which is exhausting and consumes valuable time. Moreover, when there is an attack, a rape, a burning, a witch hunt or other violence against a woman, seeking redress from Councils, which are located far away, may not be feasible. But if these Councils and the people in them are near, the chances of redress and effective action are greater.

The decentralisation of government structures has, however, been regarded with suspicion and anxiety by progressive groups. Decentralisation can exacerbate lack of local resources and perpetuate regional disparities. It has often been misused by central government to offload social security provision. It has also been misused politically by dictators or single authority regimes to control from the centre through decentralised mechanisms.

But the enormous expansion of women's representation in decentralised government structures has highlighted the advantages of proximity, namely the redress of grievance and (most important of all) the ability to mobilise struggle at a local level where it is most meaningful, for example, the anti-arrack movement. Thus women are helping to radicalise local government. If the critique of macro-economic policies is about equity, then what better response can there be but to put political power in the hands of those most inequitably treated, namely women? In this sense, PRI may be conceived as a macro-political adjustment whose effects are felt at the micro-level.

Women are beginning to change not only the issues and values of governance but are also adopting different methods to those of men. They do not let official protocol stand in their way. Narayanan (1993) recounts the story of one Panchayat official, Suman.

According to them (the officials) the area was not a catchment area and hence not suitable to construct a tank. They could not think anything beyond that. But Suman wanted to keep up her promise to the electorate of reviving the old tank. She mobilised necessary resources through other sources, and was able to fulfil her promise. After a good monsoon, the tank was flooded with water much against the scientific thinking of the bureaucracy.

The Obstacles to Transformation

Many obstacles to the realisation of PRI's transformative potential remain. Scepticism about decentralisation persists in many quarters. There continues to be a resistance to really devolving power and funds from centres of (male) power to the periphery. Women still face considerable handicaps to their involvement in politics; for example, inadequate education, the burden of reproductive and productive roles, a lack of self-confidence and the opposition of entrenched cultural and religious views.

There are also administrative obstacles to be overcome. The current administration framework has a departmentally-administered sectoral funding pattern which conflicts with the women-led, area-derived programmes arising from PRI. There is a need to cut through the existing system of development finance to find more flexible approaches capable of responding to the new priorities that are being expressed. United Nations and other donor agency funding for central government inadvertently supports this regressive national budgeting process (Jain 1994b, 1995a).

Sustaining the Transformation

PRI is beginning to transform the processes and priorities of local government in India as well as the women who have been brought into politics. But sustaining this transformation is a significant challenge, given the inertia and resistance of patriarchal institutions and values. Those women elected through PRI need specific kinds of support which go beyond technical training. They need support to build solidarity amongst women, through strengthening links between women's organisations and elected bodies. They need information about innovative organisations which enhance women's lives such as health providers, credit institutions and so on. Many women's NGOs are already providing these kinds of support to women representatives (Jain 1994a).

There is, however, a major gap in this woman-to-woman support which needs attention by the world-wide women's movement and local feminist groups. This is the need to build feminist consciousness, and strengthen women's sense of common identity, by articulating the elements of a feminist consciousness and presenting it as the special quality of women's leadership. These qualities of women in leadership are becoming well-known, especially as they continue to emerge from the collective struggles of poor women (Jain 1995b, 1995c). Such qualities include: avoiding conflict, pre-empting injustice, responding to issues of basic needs for the family, learning through doing, consulting, sharing, caring, undoing hierarchies and rebuilding informality. The question remains as to whether it is possible to assist women both to recognise these qualities as being valuable and unique and to identify with such qualities as being constitutive of the way they see themselves.

The emphasis from the women's movement today is to demand more opportunity for women to lead, to demand more power for women (translated, for example, into demands for fixed percentages in all decision-making bodies, or legal and educational programmes for women's empowerment). But there has been insufficient elaboration of what that leadership has to offer which distinguishes it from men's leadership and which commends it as something special (Jain 1992). Such an elaboration through feminist discourse and action is essential for this revolution to deliver the promise it holds.

PRI has created an opportunity to take forwards this feminist discourse and action in order to elaborate the qualities and benefits of feminist leadership in local governance. If they are to seize this opportunity and not only take power but also transform the values and priorities of India's political and cultural space, women must raise their own consciousness of the quality and content of feminist leadership.

An Agenda for Action

How can women raise their own consciousness and sustain the transformations of PRI? The support of the women's movement in India is critical. Many sections of the movement were initially sceptical about the real value of this "revolution". However, as they have become more familiar with these elected women, they have been overwhelmed by the vitality and the enthusiasm of the women and are now offering both moral and material support. This process is of central importance, and must be continued and reinforced.

There is also a need for a more enabling environment, which would allow PRI to become a process for the empowerment of women, not to mention other social groups who have been left out of participation in representative governance. Such an environment would include legal frameworks and services as well as packages of technical support.

Multi-lateral and bi-lateral development assistance also needs to be re-thought. UN agencies, for example, are often obstacles to efforts to shift power structures from the civil service to the citizens. The procedures of donor bureaucracies require the continued presence of central government and central machineries for negotiation and accountability.

Their division into subject sectors also inhibits the establishment of integrated support services such as social development services, to be designed and accessed by women at the local level. Ironically, it is development assistance agencies which often provide vigorous examples of patriarchal obstruction to people-led development. Finally, careful research is required to substantiate the claims made by supporters of the PRI movement.

CONCLUSION

Deep poverty is a social and political phenomenon as much as an economic problem and thus requires political and social change, particularly within the sites of power. The quest for equity cannot come about without wider representation of all groups, especially those currently denied access to power, and the presentation of all points of view in the process of decision-making. Revision of the current administrative and political structures, and their rules, is necessary in order to facilitate this broader representation and its translation into political power for those who are currently marginalised.

PRI reminds us of a central truth; power is not something people give away. It has to be negotiated, and sometimes wrested from the powerful. Enshrining political change within the law has forced both the pace and direction of such change. Democratic politics is, in reality, the interplay of vested interests and PRI's great achievement has been to mandate a vested, and mutual interest, between women and the political process. The lesson of PRI is clear: if the wisdom of grassroots organisations, especially the courage and clarity of women, is to become policy, it will not be through the art of intellectual persuasion but by the arrangements made within a political system for their voice to have power.

Bringing women into power is thus not only a matter of equity, of correcting an unjust and unrepresentative system. The World Summit for Social Development, Copenhagen 1995, addressed itself to the removal of poverty, the achievement of full employment and social integration. Many believe that these questions cannot be effectively addressed without the kind of democratisation of the representative process that has been discussed in this paper. Political restructuring is key to economic growth with justice. PRI is also demonstrating that transforming local councils into representative bodies means they are likely to be more environmentally protective, as the new members have a greater stake in their local natural resources.

PRI in India offers an opportunity to women to change the face of political leadership. But we still have to ensure that these are spaces where women can go to negotiate for power. Other questions that arise at a conceptual level are:

- Is this model a valuable method of restructuring the State?
- Does local government with special reservation to ensure the participation of "subordinated" groups as discussed here, bring a form of convergence between the State and civil society?
- In our discussion of alternative economic models, do institutional arrangements provide the safeguard for economic equity by changing power structures?
- At the level of discussion on macro-economic policy, especially structural adjustment programmes, does local self-government of this kind provide the necessary challenge to the imposition of economic policies which reinforce inequity and exploitation?

But I am not one to end with questions. Many of these questions can be answered through actively supporting the restructuring of politics as a key to economic growth with justice. The international community, which participated with such solidarity and clarity at the Social Summit in Copenhagen and the Fourth World Conference on Women in Beijing, should see these types of arrangements as a means of moving beyond postulating goals and providing critiques, to offering a substantive, viable alternative for action.

The Women's Movement and PRI

The women's movement continues to support the PRI "revolution". Examples of this support include:

o facilitating their meetings across districts, offering women representatives fora to discuss issues e.g. the end of their term and the possibility of suspension of key organisations;

o transforming women's perceptions of the training they need away from traditional women-oriented training such as home economics, towards the provision of workshops where they can share, develop and refine their political views;

o ensuring that the women are not marginalised in the revenue and expenditure committee structures that will emerge to manage the development in these bodies;

o ensuring the devolution of project design and monitoring powers from central government to the elected bodies, so that the latter can develop their own policies, reflecting the views of their own representatives rather than those of central government, and be held accountable for them;

o strengthening the identity and feminist consciousness of women representatives, for example, by leadership training;

o building global coalitions through the activist, as distinct from the academic mode. This includes bringing women into political structures and supporting the backward and forward linkages of women's presence in politics, linking household and family priorities with macro-planning processes;

o pressing for South Asian regional economic cooperation amongst women to be based on regional support to empowering woman's role in local and national governance;

o campaigns and training programmes to prepare the women both as electors and elected; and

o urging multi-and bi-lateral agencies to revise their own patriarchal structures.

5

GENDER AND LOCAL GOVERNANCE A NEW DISCOURSE IN DEVELOPMENT

In India and Bangladesh, the recent Constitutional Amendments have brought a considerable number of women into the mainstream political arena, bringing to the fore a range of issues involving not only women's rights but their role in politics. It had enabled women to come to power, but not actually empowered them in the political sense of the term.

However, there was a considerable status enhancement among women and has made a difference in the perception among the men in the society with regard to their credibility in politics. The attitude of a large number of men towards women in politics has been changing from one of hostility and underestimation to reconciliation and trust.

The empirical study of the Panchayati Raj Institution and the Union Parishad has brought to the fore some emerging leaders among women at the grassroots level.

The reservation given to women seemed to be quite inadequate as far as their empowerment was concerned since the number of women who came to power exceeded even the 33 percent mark in most of the states in India. However, in Bangladesh the one-third mark in the Union Parishads was more of a move in the opposite direction and a disabling factor since as against men who contested from one ward, a woman had to cover three wards with all odds stacked against her to contest for one position.

As far as the inspiration factor behind joining politics was concerned, majority of women and men revealed that it was because of a sincere urge for public service and for developing the village that they took such a step despite the fact that family response towards their joining politics were sometimes negative. Politics as a profession was not worthy, because of the dominance of muscle and money power, and that there was too much threat of violence.

It was evident that lack of effective and timely planning, lack of political background, absence of suitable socio-economic and political environment, lack of appropriate organizational framework, lack of skill and training put women behind in proving their competencies compared to their male counterparts. It had been identified that women had limited scope to exercise political rights, lack of control over resources and had a limited choice in decision-making.

The hurdles faced by women in participation started at the nascent stage itself, especially in Bangladesh where most of the women were not even allowed to vote due to religious fatwas by the fundamental groups. The Indian scenario is not diametrically opposite, but to a great extent still witnesses a great deal of forced silence among the elected women representatives. The women Panchayat members were the worst hit and the most peripheral in this 'silent revolution.'

Most of the women emphasized the fact that their participation could be better if they had functional education and also training on the various intricacies involved in the political field.

STATEMENT OF THE PROBLEM

The process of globalization has led to discourses on development having different perspectives. One of the major upcoming development discourses puts gender and governance on the forefront of these. In this context, the governments of India and Bangladesh have amended their laws for fair representation of gender in the local government to ensure good governance. Not withstanding the fact that constitutional support and legislative measures are necessary for bringing about social change, but this however, cannot be achieved single-handedly. Constitutional efforts are needed to strengthen and consolidate them for meaningful empowerment. The question is whether an intervention like the constitutional amendment is able to ensure women's empowerment or whether the patriarchal structures, manifested in the household and the state, will continue to dominate.

In recent times, there has been a common realization in Bangladesh and India, that a strong and effective local government is one of the essential preconditions for ensuring good governance. It is generally agreed that an empowered local government is the key foundation on which the success of any democratic nation rests.

In this regard, one of the significant goals set out by the Fourth World Conference on Women, 1995, in Beijing was adequate representation of women in all decision-making bodies (Beijing Platform for Action, 1996). It was suggested that in any representative body there should be a 'logical balance' of men and women to voice the concerns of the society en masse. Good governance means being participatory, accountable, predictable and transparent which reasonably calls for a gender balance in political decision-making. It is believed that women's insights and values of governance can enhance and enrich the overall decision-making process. It is also generally observed that women at the local level are more sensitive to community issues.

Local government is part of overall governance. Local government institutions, being nearer to people, can involve them in various ways: (a) planning and implementation of projects (b) supervision of educational institutions, hospital and other government financed units (c) mobilization of support for new initiatives like campaign against dowry, child labour etc. (d) enforcement of laws regarding gender discrimination, violence against women, environment protection (e) mobilization of resources in the form of taxes, fees, tolls etc. Popular participation also assumes importance because of its potentials for holding the local government institution accountable to the community. On the other hand, local government institutions as the representative organization of the people can enforce accountability the central/

national government authorities. The more aware, vigilant and active the community becomes through their participation in local government bodies, the greater is the pressure on both local government institutions and the government authorities to become transparent and responsive.

The potentials of local government institutions can be realized more effectively where there is decentralization and devolution of powers. Accountability, transparency, participation, empowerment, equity and all other attributes of good governance can be in full play and become a part of the daily work of both the government and local government bodies when decentralization and devolution take place. Without decentralization and devolution, local government bodies remain paper organizations without any effective role. It will be no exaggeration to say that it is in a decentralized local government system that most of the attributes of good governance have a chance to survive and prosper. Strengthening of local government institutions can, therefore, be seen as a positive trend towards good governance.

All successive governments in Bangladesh, since its independence, felt the need to have viable local government for ensuring effective governance. As a result, we have seen 'decentralization' as an important policy agenda of all governments. Thus, reforming local government is not a new phenomenon in Bangladesh. The repetitive process of local government reform has been handed down to the sovereign state of Bangladesh from Pakistan as a postcolonial extension. However, the necessity to reform the existing structure of local government by various successive government in Bangladesh indicates their failure to create effective institutions for enhancing local democracy and delivering development programmes.

In Bangladesh there have been five major attempts to reform local government under five different governments. The objective of all, at least at the level of rhetoric, was to introduce participatory and accountable local governance through decentralisation of functions and powers to locally elected institutions. All these governments also recognised the relevance and important of the role of decentralised local institutions in planning and implementing need-based development projects for poverty alleviation and reduction of socio-economic inequality. However, the objectives were not realised and the governments failed to keep their commitment towards grassroots democracy and to devolve power to the people at lower levels to manage their own affairs. Consequently, the primary goal of poverty reduction, economic equity and gender balance remained unfulfilled (Khan, Z.R., 1999).

One of the important reasons why women have not received adequate benefits from years of planning and development was their inadequate representation, non-participation and non-involvement in the preparation and execution of plans for their economic development and social justice through decentralized institutions.

In Bangladesh, Article 9 of the Constitution promotes the special representation of women in local government. In recent years, a constant pressure on the Union Parishad from the academia, citizens and women's groups, a protected process, to provide adequate gender representation has lead to the Union Parishad Amendment Act 1997. This is, in itself, a remarkable initiative for providing adequate representation to women.

The Constitution of Bangladesh provides for equality of men and women. There is no legal barrier to women contesting or voting for any elective office, including that of the head of the State Article 9 of the Constitution promotes the special representation of women in local government (Constitution of the People's Republic of Bangladesh, 1972). Although the constitution grants equal rights to all citizens in all spheres of life, there have been very few women in local government. In 1976, provision was made for two nominated female members in addition to nine elected members and one chairperson in each Union Parishad, which increased to three nominated women members in 1983. In 1992, it was changed to indirect election where three women members in each local government body were supposed to be elected by the chairperson and other elected members. This process of filling women's seats in the local councils totally ignored the scope of women's active participation and role in these political organizations where policies are decided and crucial plans for local development are formulated. The nominated women could not play more than the role of a 'yes' person of the chairperson and members, who were predominantly men (Khan, Z.R., 1998).

In 1997, the Union Parishad Ordinance of 1983 was amended and through this Amendment, for the first time, provision was made for direct election for the female members to three reserved seats for women in the Union Parishad (The Local Government Union Parishad Amendment Act, 1997).

In 1997, again for the first time in the history of Bangladesh direct election for women representatives was provided in the local government at the lowest tier, the Union Parishad. Much enthusiasm has been observed among the women centering Union Parishad election. The number of voters was 50 million and the most striking feature of the election was the overwhelming participation of women voters. About 210,334 candidates including 45,000 female candidates contested in the Union Parishad election. A total of 13,000 women candidates were elected in the election to represent women's reserved seats (The Daily Janakantha, 15 December 1997). The whole process was a major breakthrough for the rural women in Bangladesh.

These are indeed, unique experiments in the world of democracy, wherein women at grassroots level of Bangladesh, irrespective of their educational, occupational and socio-economic background, have been found suitable enough to occupy political positions and participate in decision-making and economic development through local governance.

In Bangladesh, though the female chairpersons and members have gained enough confidence in their ability to discharge administrative duties, the discriminatory attitude of their male counterparts has been the main stumbling block. According to the Local Government Ordinance, elected women Union Parishad members will act as chairperson in at least three of 12 standing committees of the Union Parishad. But in reality it is found that in many of the Union Parishads, the Standing Committees have not yet been formed. Moreover, where they are formed, the women members have no responsibilities despite their inclusion in the committees (Shamim, I., 1999).

Women, however few, have been articulating and trying to sensitize local and national leaders and decision makers of the need for women's participation in the political process. Efforts are underway to take political scene more democratic, participatory, accountable and transparent so as to ensure a just, humane and equitable society. The urgency for political empowerment of women has therefore, increased manifold.

There is a need to enable women to be more effective members of local government bodies. Two aspects of effectiveness need to be considered, i. e. effectiveness in participating in overall Union Parishad operations and their involvement in the development issues.

The Indian Constitution has been committed to introduce socio-economic and political transformation. The initiatives of empowering women and the marginalized sections are the reflection of its democratic spirit that can be noticed from a number of amendments in these fields. Especially, the 73rd and 74th Constitutional Amendment Acts provide for an opportunity for women's entry into political spheres. These Amendment Acts provide for a 33 percent reservation of seats for women in the governance of local bodies (rural and urban) with aspiration of good governance and fair representation in the development process at grassroots level. The 73rd Constitutional Amendment Act is an important landmark in the history of Indian women's participation in the formation of democratic institutions at grassroots level. Not only do they have one-third membership, they also head, as chairpersons, one-third of the Panchayats. According to the estimates, three would be a total of 7.95 lakh women in leadership roles in three tires of the Panchayati Raj alone. In fact, in Karnataka, 43.88 percent of seats were won by the women in the 1994 and 1996 elections, much beyond the stipulated 33.3 percent in the Constitution. The new government system in India has shown that given an opportunity, women too can perform very well in public life.

The most significant aspect is that the gender representation in the decision-making has been taken into account. Although, the Acts have enabled women to participate in the PRI as members, Sarpanch, Block and Zilla Panchayat Adhyakshas throughout the country for over five years, an urgent need is felt to strengthen them.

The reservation in Panchayats have provided for the erosion of the traditional gender, caste, class roles and hierarchy but it is a long and difficult process. Women not only have to fight for their right to be more than proxy members but also to break the barriers of gender division of labor, illiteracy, low level of mobility, seclusion, lack of training and information, which still continue to exist without enough support from the power structure. Women's low self-esteem at the household level and their new role in local politics where they are now expected to function as leader creates a contradiction between women's role at home and in local government.

It has only been four years for Bangladesh and about a decade for India since the enactment of these constitutional changes. This however, is too short a period to modify the dominant patriarchal structure of society that has continued to exist for last many millennia via the historical processes and social formations. The process of empowerment in the local government institutions will enable women to re-examine their lives, recognize the source and structure of power and of their own subordination and initiate action to challenge the existing ideology as well as structures and institutions.

By contesting and getting elected to local government, women have shattered the myth of their own passivity-that women are not willing to enter politics. However, women's representation in the decision-making positions with monitoring power, is still negligible. The present rules of the game and decision-making procedure do not allow a greater participation of women and in the absence of women, there is no effort to recognize or change the game. The very absence of women at these levels thus leads to preservation and reinforcement of male-oriented and male benefiting types of decisions.

OBJECTIVES OF THE STUDY

The study is broadly an attempt to analyze the emerging scenario of women leadership at local politics by focusing on the elected women representatives of Union Parishad of Bangladesh compared to their counterparts in Panchayats of India. More specifically, the study will focus on the views, opinions, activities and training of the local government representatives in the following areas:

- Understand the grassroots level democracy, the decentralization of power and women's political participation
- Examine the role of gender in the functioning of local political institutions and focus on a comparative perspective on the experiences of India and Bangladesh
- Constraints and problems faced by women and men in the electoral process and as representatives in the local bodies
- The extent of devolution of power and active participation in the various committees
- The role of family networks, political parties and government and non-governmental organizations in their attainment of power
- Their participation in developmental works and programs
- Gender related obstacles encountered by women and men while undertaking development programs
- Strategies to overcome the barriers
- Needs, level of awareness and training as well as initiatives taken by the government and non-government organizations in those areas.

Theoretical Framework

In recent times, the process of 'globalization' of goods, market expansion, liberalization, commercialization of agriculture and market-oriented growth has been profoundly influencing the rural areas. The fact remains that whether in terms of 'food security', feminization of poverty', the rising environmental crisis, the import of worldwide economic and political change falls most heavily on women, especially rural women.

There can be no second opinion about the fact that national development cannot occur without broad based rural development and for rural development to happen there is an urgent need to empower the rural people, especially the rural women-politically, socially and economically. In this regard, it must be stated that the framework employed here shall work within the parameters of the 73rd Constitution Amendment Act, Schedules 5 and 11 of the Constitution of India and Article 9 of the Constitution of Bangladesh.

The new leadership that has emerged at various levels, especially at the level of local government seems to have posed a serious challenge to the traditional power structures. The women emerging from their traditional household roles and demonstrating their capacities of decision-making, administration and execution at the local level have been observed in different forms in the two countries under study. These examples are few and far between and yet they reflect a great degree of hope for a positive change.

The main problem that concerns us here is whether the representation of such a large number of women in the local government institutions has made any significant departure to affect the existing gender biased social structures and norms. These changes need to be assessed in terms of:

- Whether recognition of such constitutional structures, especially leadership of women for collaboration and joint efforts have been accepted by the traditional power structures
- Whether the new Amendment of the Union Parishad Act of Bangladesh and 73rd CAA in India have led to the overall empowerment of elected women and other marginalized sections of the society
- Whether the bodies of local self-governance have been liberated from acting as line agents of the State and empowered with functional autonomy
- Whether women have been able to bring in any new developmental alternatives as far as the local governance is concerned.

Relevance of the Study

The present study will be of some great significance as it is one of the few studies that attempt at linking gender issue with that of local governance. The study gains further importance due to the fact that it is a comparative study of two similar, neighboring countries and yet encrusted with significant differentials. As far as women at the grassroots are concerned, the study intends to give a new perspective on the prevalent notions of 'women are not interested in politics,' 'women do not have the qualities and capacities to run local governing bodies,' that the really marginalized women will not be able to benefit from the new set of arrangements since the upper caste/class women will usurp all the new forms of devolved power, etc.

The study will be extremely relevant in the growth of some comprehensive models and encourage further research within academia as well as the voluntary sector. Some of the significant features are noted below:

- To provide suggestions for the effective performance of both men and women as political leaders by understanding the constraints as well conducive factors in the process
- To bring out the needs and requirements of men and women leaders and suggest necessary measures
- To evaluate the necessity of training for them
- To analyze the need of reservation to involve a large number of women in decision making institutions at the local government level
- To focus on the change in attitudes and opinions of the people at large about women from one of hostility and underestimation to reconciliation and trust.

Methodology

The study focuses on the gender issues in the reconstituted local government system in Bangladesh and India and the extent of devolution of power to women and men in the latest amendments of the two countries.

The methodology for the study of local governance in Bangladesh and India differed to some extent because of some contrasting socio-cultural and political characteristics found in these two countries. These broad dissimilarities pertain to the domination of religion in Bangladesh and that of caste in India.

The study was limited to six districts of Bangladesh and two districts of India given the availability of time and resources. The primary sources of data were a combination of qualitative and quantitative methods such as interview using structured interview schedule, Focus Group Discussion, case studies and observation. Statistical information were processed, analyzed and presented in tables and graphs to present the major findings.

SELECTION OF THE STUDY AREA IN BANGLADESH

Six districts were purposively selected from six divisions of Bangladesh. A total of 202 Unions have been selected randomly from 34 Upazila of six districts. Since the districts have unequal number of Union Parishads, the number of sample Unions was unequal. A sample of 602 women and 399 men Union Parishad members were selected randomly from the list of Union Parishad members. These men and women members were selected from the sample Union Parishads.

Table : Study Areas and Sample Size by Sex in Bangladesh

Name of Division	Name of the District	Total Upazila	Number of Union Parishad	Female	Male	Total
Dhaka	Mymensingh	9	31	91	64	155
Sylhet	Moulvibazar	5	40	120	80	200
Rajshahi	Bogra	6	33	99	58	157
Barisal	Jhalakati	4	29	87	57	144
Khulna	Jessore	6	43	129	89	218
Chittagong	Cox's Bazar	4	26	76	51	127
Total		34	202	602	399	1001

Selection of the Study Area in India

Uttar Pradesh (UP) and Madhya Pradesh (MP) were selected for the Indian study, which are very large states that have a very large number of districts and population within their territory. The selection of the districts was based on the nature and level of development with reference to literacy, health, life expectancy, sex ratio, access to basic amenities, etc. Indore and Varanasi were the most developed districts within their respective states, while Etawah and Chhatarpur are among the most backward ones.

The target group, i.e., elected representatives was selected on the basis of sex and elected hierarchy in the Panchayati Raj structure. They were members and chairpersons of the Gram Panchayats, Block and Zila level Panchayats of Madhya Pradesh (Indore and Chhatarpur) and Uttar Pradesh (Varanasi and Etawah). The sample included 600 women and 400 men.

Table : Study Area and Sample Size in India

State	District	Blocks
Uttar Pradesh		
(501)	Varanasi (251)	Chairaigaon
	Haraua (125)	
	Etawah (250)	Chiraigaon (125)
	Saifai (125)	
Madhya Pradesh		
(504)	Indore (253)	Indore (126)
	Mhow (127)	
	Chatarpur (251)	Nowgong (126)
	Ishanagar (125)	

Organization of the Study

The study is divided into five chapters. The first chapter is the introduction with the statement of the problem and the methodology used in the study. Chapter two focuses on the local governance in South Asia and the institutional background of local government system in Bangladesh and India. Chapter third is on the socio-economic profile of local representatives, both men and women with special emphasis on the emerging women leaders in local self-government. Electoral democracy at grassroots level is the focus of the fourth chapter which includes women's political participation as candidates, motivation for joining politics and problems faced during elections and overall obstacles encountered by women representatives, as well as training needs and interventions for capacity building.

HISTORY OF THE LOCAL SELF-GOVERNMENT AND THE SILENT REVOLUTION

Local Government System in South Asia

The different countries in South Asia followed different paths towards political, social and economic development. India became a republic, a democratic and secular nation with a mixed economic setup that was overtly centralized, top-heavy and bureaucratic, besides taking recourse to import substitution and state sponsored industrialization. The state of Pakistan had experiments with the democratic form of governance at various intervals but remained largely and intermittently a military state where the State itself was the biggest producer of goods and services. Sri Lanka took the democratic road with great emphasis on social development. Bangladesh became a hostage to military rule for a while but settled on a democratic political system with increasingly greater emphasis on exports along with regional and global integration. The huge size at which the various activities were undertaken by these countries, viz., nation-building activities, development planning, economic stability, multi-level reforms and pressure for improving the quality of life led them largely to neglect their own local government systems at the micro-levels.

In India, Bangladesh and Sri Lanka, as well as in Pakistan the national political scenario as well as the national economic initiatives have generally tended to over-centralize resulting in the gross neglect of their own grassroots governance (Rahman, S., 2000.). A recent study of local government system in Bangladesh concluded that although the constitution provides for an autonomous local government system the provisions have not been implemented. The local government system has been subject to many changes and experiments, which has not only destabilized the system, but has caused the community to distance itself from the local government which it was supposed to serve (UNDDSMS, 1996).

Women and Local Governance in South Asia

Women leaders in South Asia had and have been occupying the highest positions in their in their respective governments, e.g., from Indira to Sheikh Hasina, Khaleda Zia and Benazir Bhutto to Sirimavo Bandaranaike and Chandrika Kumaratunga. And yet, the statistics tell a different story. The vast majorities of South Asian women are illiterate, in poor health, invisible in the system of national accounts, and suffer legal, political, economic and social discrimination in all walks of life. Women in South Asia also have the lowest rates of participation in their governance structures. Except for India where more than 33 percent members of local government are women (Mahbub ul-Haq Human Development Centre, 2000).

The 1999 Report on Human Development in South Asia advocated that if governance is to promote human development, it has to go beyond being pro-people or people-centered. It has to be owned by the people. Women account for half the population of South Asia, yet they remain mostly invisible in all governing institutions. Women hold the top positions in major political parties of the region, yet these powerful positions have not translated into positive outcomes for the majority of South Asian women. Most political parties do not even maintain data on their women membership and few women are granted party tickets for elections. In some countries, women are more visible in local governance structures than in any other governing institution. Most gains have been made in India, where one-third of the seats in Panchayats is reserved for women. However, gender bias pervades at all levels of governance in South Asia, which may be one of the reasons for the region's governance crisis (Mahbub ul Haq Human Development Centre, 2000).

Organization at the grassroots level allows people to contribute significantly to the governance of their communities. For women, successful grassroots experience has meant a chance to form coherent voice, to be heard and to make a difference in their communities. Across South Asia, the experience of women in local government has been varied, with some countries being more successful than others in attaining greater women's participation.

With the exception of India and Bangladesh, women's representation within local bodies in South Asia remains minimal. But even in Bangladesh, female representation barely rises above 20 percent. In 1992, the Government of India passed the 73rd and 74th Amendments to the Constitution of India. Termed the 'silent revolution', these Amendments paved the way for women's entry into local governance by reserving 33 percent of seats for them in the Panchayats at all the levels, including that of the chairperson's seat. In most states, reservation of seats has met with success, with female representation exceeding the 33 percent quota in states such as Karnataka, Kerala and Manipur.

Experience over the last decade has shown that women who have gained access to the Panchayats and Municipalities have performed well. Some of them have already established excellent records of service and even won distinguished awards for their performance. Being mostly illiterate, a large number of them have placed a high priority on acquiring literacy to be able to perform better at their jobs. Substantial numbers of teachers, lawyers and other functionaries at the grassroots level have been able to win elections and become members of the Panchayats.

In Bangladesh, women have been incorporated into local governance through reservation at the Union Parishad level. Bangladesh has experimented different forms of local government throughout its political history-sometimes at the village level, the Gram Sarker and sometimes at the sub-district level, the Upazila. But the Union Parishad, which consists of representatives from several villages, has remained the most effective local body at the local level. Currently there are about 4,276 Union Parishads in Bangladesh. Since 1997, a quota of three seats or one-fourth of the total has been reserved for women in the Union Parishads. This has brought up women's representation from a very few to over 20 percent. However, reforms suggested for one-third female participation at the sub-district and district levels remain unimplemented.

Local government is also an integral part of the Nepalese governance system. Since adopting a policy of decentralization, local governing bodies have over the years acquired increasingly greater authority in Nepal. The Local Self-Governance Act of 1999 is by far the most progressive Act in terms of devolving authority from central to the local governing bodies. Local governing institutions now have some taxation authority at the local level as well as limited judicial authority to tackle local level disputes.

However, female representation in local governing institutions has been very limited in Nepal. Currently, there is less than 10 percent of women in the District Development Committees (DDC) and Village Development Committees (VDC) combined. Not a single woman is the chairperson of a DDC or mayor of any municipality. Out of 3,913 VDCs, there are only 13 chairpersons who are women. On the positive side, one of every five seats in each ward of a VDC and municipality that is reserved for women candidates has ensured the participation of an additional 36,023 women at the ward-level governance of VDCs and municipalities.

Sri Lanka's Current System of Governance Consists of Three Tiers-the Municipal Councils, Urban

Councils, and the Pradeshiva Sabbas. While total membership of these councils exceeds three thousand, less than 3 percent are women. In the last bodies' elections, held in 1997, only one woman was elected mayor of a municipal Council in the province of Jaffna. Unfortunately, in 1998 she became the victim of political assassination. In the Urban Councils, while there are currently two female Vice-Chairpersons, women occupy none of the 36 posts for Chairperson. At present, three of the Chairpersons and two Vice-Chairpersons in the Pradeshiya Sabbas are women. Despite this, women represent only 1.72 percent of the total membership of the Pradeshiya Sabbas. Currently the government has also put forward a recommendation for fixing a quota of 25 percent for women in local government.

Until recently, female representation in local governance in Pakistan was negligible. The current government has scheduled fresh elections, starting December 2000, for local government at three levels-the Union Council, the Tehsil Council and the District Assembly. Fifty percent of seats at the union level have been reserved for women. At the Tehsil and district levels, women will be allocated 5 and 10 seats respectively, forming roughly about 15 percent of the total seats.

Since politics is traditionally a male domain and all financial, economic, commercial and political negotiations conducted outside the home are by males, South Asian women have very limited access to decision-making process, and they have a severe lack of access to and control over financial resources. This effectively reduces women's chance of contesting elections. Political equality is still elusive in most South Asian countries, though some progress has been made. As men have control over assets and have relatively better education, they have a dominant position in terms of political power remain surrogate actors in the political process. Tokenism is more evident and problematic at the local level than at higher levels of government. Women councilors may not necessarily be educated. Lack of awareness leads to situations where they may become dependent on male councilors or political parties, focusing more on issues of men's interest than on women's concerns. In some cases women are elected as councilors without actually participation in the functioning of local bodies. Most women lack any effective power or influence in local governance structure. Many of them do not have the necessary skills to present ideas effectively. Lack of awareness of the possibilities of political participation means inadequate contribution to public affairs on the one hand and women's empowerment at the other. Women councilors themselves recognize these problems.

Local bodies, if properly utilized can vehicle of women's active participation when it is effectively mainstreamed. Since these institutions function at the grassroots level, representatives, both men and women, are more aware of, and can be more responsive to the needs of women and children as well as to the problems of rural communities. Tapping into the latent capacity of women is essential to substantially enchanting the socio-economic development of South Asia. Decentralization is thus a prerequisite for effective mainstreaming of women's concern in development. However, unless existing mechanisms and attitudes that deny women equal chances in decision-making are not modified, simple devolution of power will not be enough to ensure greater female participation in decision-making (Mahbub ul Haq Human Development Centre, 2000).

Decentralisation and Functioning of Local Government in Bangladesh

The history of local government in Bangladesh goes way back to the British Colonial period. It can be traced back to the Bengal Local self Government Act of 1855, which established the three-tier system: District Board, Local Board and Union Committee.

During the British period, several acts were passed to promote local-level self-rule and people's participation in the administration was almost absent (Siddiqui, K., 1994). A study of local government system in Bangladesh concludes that although the constitution provides for an autonomous local government system these provisions have not been implemented resulting in a local government system that is not functioning properly. The local government system has been subject to many changes and experiments, which has not only destabilised the system but also caused the local government system to distance itself from the community it is supposed to serve (UNDDSMS, 1996).

Local Government Upazila Parishad Act was passed in Parliament in December 1998, providing for creation of an elected council at the Thana/Upazila level. In the new Upazila Parishad system, the chairman to be elected directly by the people, will head the Parishad and have the executive power. Chairmen of the Union Parishads and municipalities will be the members of the Upazila Parishad. One third of the total number of women members of the Union Parishads and municipalities concerned will be the members of the Upazila Parishad. The women members of the Union Parishads (UP) and the municipalities will elect them (The Local Government, Upazila Parishad Act, 1998).

According to the Local Government, Union Parishad Ordinance 1983, a Union Parishad shall consist of one chairman, nine elected members and three nominated women members. The Union Parishad Act, 1993 has brought about some changes in the composition of Union Parishad. The Union Parishad shall be divided into 9 wards and 9 members, one from each ward shall be elected by the voters of the concerned wards. Instead of nomination, the 3 women members will be indirectly elected by the Chairman and members of the concerned Union Parishad.

The right to vote in local bodies was dependent on the possession of property, tax payment and education. Women ordinarily being deprived of property and educational opportunities were automatically left out of this voting right, which in a way amounted to discrimination. Till 1956, women were not even able to cast vote in the election to rural local bodies, when for the first time election was based on the basis of universal suffrage.

However in 1997, on the basis of the recommendations of the Institutional Review of the WID Capability of the Government of

Bangladesh and the Local Government Reforms Commission, direct election for women representatives was provided in the Union Parishad. According to the new law, a Union is divided into wards. One member will be elected from every ward. Furthermore every Union comprising 9 wards has been divided into three parts for women members who will be elected through direct vote.

Women and Panchayati Raj: A Story of Token Representation in India

It would be least incorrect to state that none of the successive governments at the Centre or at the State levels went beyond paying a ceremonial lip-service of promising empowerment to the Indian women and took no serious measures to alter the existing power relations to bridge the gender-gap. It took almost half a century for the Indian Parliament to understand the rationale behind providing reservations for women at the Panchayati Raj level. In fact, there appears to be little difference between the attitude of the British colonial regime (whose one the deliberations with regard to the franchise of Indian women vide the Act of 1919 was that it was a matter to be settled by the legislative councils of India through legislation) and that of the makers of the COI. The Constitution of Independent India, similarly, after quarantining equality to all women in all spheres, left their political representation to their own willingness, opportunity and support even while providing for reservations for Scheduled Castes and Scheduled Tribes.

As far as the Panchayats are concerned the question of reservation for women sounded meaningless, once the enactment about PRIs was pushed into DPSP. Like the Act of 1919, the Constituent Assembly also left the issue of reservation for women to the various state legislatures.

The decade of the 1980s was one that saw a movement and a general consensus building up towards reservation of seats for women of not less than 33 percent. But before the much required corrective via the 73rd Constitutional Amendment Act (CAA) came, another bill in 1989 had been tabled before the Indian Parliament, known as the 64th Amendment Bill, seeking "as nearly as may be" up to 30 percent seats in favor of women in the membership of Panchayats at all the three levels, including in the provided for SC/ST and in the total seats. However, it did not provide for reservation among chairpersons. It is important to mention here that after the 64th Amendment Bill fell and before the 73rd CAA was passed, several States initiated some correctives in their Panchayat laws in order to bring reservation for women as if in sheer anticipation of the 73rd CAA. These States were Orissa, which provided 30 percent reservation for women in the membership of the Panchayat; Maharashtra, which introduced a 30 percent reservation for women in the membership of the Panchyats in 1991; and Kerala, which also late did before 1992. The most crucial difference between the 73rd CAA and the earlier 64th Amendment Bill was the fact that there was not provision for reservation for the seat of chairpersons in the 64th while the 73rd contained it.

PANCHAYATI RAJ: AN ACT OF POSITIVE DISCRIMINATION

In India, the government functions at three levels-the federal, the state or regional leveland grassroots level, called the Panchayati Raj. The Panchayati Raj system covering thevillage, tehsil and district has brought government to the doorsteps of the masses.

In 1992, the government of India enacted the 73rd and 74thAmendments to the Constitution of India toprovide for one-third representation of women in local government. By 1993 all states except Bihar hadratified these amendments. Previously, Panchayats were governed by State Panchayat Acts, which allowedthe nomination of only two or three women. As a consequence, in all the 223,000 Panchayats across India,only 13 percent members were women. However, with the onset of the silent revolution in the form of theseConstitutional Amendments, the numbers of women rose to 33 percent or one million. Presently, there are 655,629 women members in the Gram Panchayats, 37,523 in the Panchayat Samitis and 3,161 in the ZillaParishads. Under the Constitutional Amendments, women can be members as well as Chairpersons of theselocal government institutions. Elections under this system have already been held once, and some states arepreparing for a second round. The experience has been positive in states such as Gujarat and West Bengal but hosts ofissue still remain. Resistance from male power centers to devolution, discrimination on thebasis of class and casts and opposition from religious elements are just some.

Whatsoever might have been the logic behind zeroing in on not less than 33 percent figure, the number was inadequate to represent women. Unfortunately, a 33 percent only for all the states, on the one hand, and on the other, even this 33 percent was not vertically maintained to the level of various quorums of Panchayat meetings where the most crucial decisions regarding Panchayats were taken.

It can be concluded that despite some advances, both in terms of devolution and delegation to the local government system of South Asia, with a fair degree of certainty the local government systems are generally handicapped and ill-governed. Most of them lack technical as well as functional know-how, and in the absence of adequate financial resources to undertake the activities within their domain they still continue to be largely dependent on the Central and State government. As a matter of fact, dependence on grants from higher levels of government has increased overtime instead of declining. A prime example of such micro-management and intervention is the practice of deputized central administrators to the local government systems. There is also a strongly prevalent myth across the subcontinent that local governments are incapable.

EMERGING LEADERSHIP AMONG WOMEN IN LOCAL SELF-GOVERNMENT

The Constitutional Amendment Acts of both India and Bangladesh have brought in a large number of women into the realm of politics at the local level, which was unthinkable earlier. Before these Acts women did take part in the political process at the national, regional and local levels but their presence was negligible. This glaring lack of representation can be attributed as a spin off factor of the larger socio-cultural and politico-religious dimensions of the South Asian structural reality. This then meant that in a democratic setup where numbers tend to be crucial, women and their issues were always marginalized. The emerging trend of women's leadership in the local self-government shows that a large number of women were young, married, illiterate/ literate, and agriculturist by occupation and equally divided between very poor, poor and middle-income groups in India. Secondly, there were two elections in India as against Bangladesh where there was only one election. In India, about 83.4 percent women were first timers in local politics. On the other hand, 16.6 percent women had contested and won posts in Panchayats at different levels even for the second time, especially when the seats were not reserved.

Socio-Economic Profile

Women leaders' socio-economic profile provides the background the representatives have come from. When we take a gender perspective in political leadership, the socio-economic profile becomes even more important standard to analyze the impact of women's political leadership, whether their background is a hurdle/barrier or a major constraint for quality functioning.

Age

In Bangladesh, majority of the women members were in 25-34 years age group, in contrast to 55-64 years 65 years & above majority of men members who were in 35-44 years age group. However, 16 percent among men members were in the age group of 55-64 years, while there was only one percent among women who belonged to the same age group. Moreover, it is interesting to note that men continued to be involved in local politics even when they were above 65 years of age. On the other hand, there was no elderly woman member of that age. Only 4 women members were below 25 years of age. It might be explained by the fact that men members were in politics for longer time, but women began their political career at the local level in 1997 after the amendment of the Ordinance.

In India, there were hardly difference in percentage of men and women of the different age groups. Nearly 10 percent of women members were below 25 years of age. They were not only new to politics, but were also new to the functional maintenance of society. However, overwhelming majority of 84 percent of women were of the age group of 25-50 years who were expected to bring change in village development. The same was true for men (82 percent). Women once taken as the maintainers of status quo were now expected to be the 'change agents.'

Marital Status

Marital status signified a change in perception and attached honor and responsibility of the representatives for community work, whether married or not made a tremendous difference in a traditional society. While a married woman was considered to be responsible, the single woman was taken on a tentative basis. As long as she was unmarried, she was considered to be irresponsible, while the stigma on a widow was appalling in our society. The level of participation in such hostile circumstances does affect quality representation.

Marital status played an important role for participation in politics at the Union Parishad level in Bangladesh. An overwhelming majority of both men and women were married, with higher percentage for men (97 percent) compared to that for women (91percent) as married people were more accepted as political leaders in rural Bangladesh due to maturity and stable family life.

Only one man was a widower, while 43 females were widows was significant because they were usually the heads of their households and hardly received support from other men members of their in-law households. Only 2 percent of both men and women members were unmarried, as they were less acceptable due to their age as well as their lack of experience.

The same trend was found in India where nearly 90 percent women were married which was nothing, but a mere reflection of kind of women socially accepted as representatives. As such, there were only a few single men and women at local level politics.

Moreover, in both India and Bangladesh we find the practice of child marriage quite prevalent. Nearly 54 percent of the women in India said that they were married before they were 18 years of age, which is quite alarming although the government is continuously trying to make it obvious that child marriage is illegal.

Cristian Hindu Hindu

Religion

Religion had been a major source of enforcing the gender-gap in our society. In Bangladesh the number of Muslim women representatives was almost 83 percent, while in India, 96.3 percent women representatives were from the Hindu religion.

Level of Education

It was assumed that women could not fare well in politics since they are neither literate nor exposed. In Bangladesh, majority of the members both women and men were educated up to the secondary level. In India, 30 percent women were illiterate compared to only 7 percent men.

Women were found to be at the receiving end of the patriarchal set up since only 5 percent were found to be graduates in India. However, majority of women as well as men had primary and secondary education. However, interestingly in both the countries, some of the women were graduates and masters degree holders despite class, caste and religious fundamentalist forces in these countries.

Occupational Status and Income

In Bangladesh 82 percent women were housewives and had the strict sense of purda culture, which made their quality representation impossible owing to lack of exposure and movement. Unlike their Indian counterparts, they had only the domestic chores to deal with while the Indian women representatives were more involved with outside work as well as for their livelihood as they were mostly from below poverty line families. Men were mostly farmers and businessmen.

In the rural area, the economic set-up is characterized by land holdings that are 'inherited' through male line. Women are excluded from owning any land/property. Access to land control over material and economic resources, especially land, the single most important means of production in rural Bangladesh and India, women were ingeniously removed. They are merely working on it but not owing it. However they do earn, especially for their family's livelihood.

In India, housewives were only 7 percent. Majority men as well as women were involved in agriculture-related work and agricultural laborers, while very few were involved in business, non-agricultural work, different professions and service.

Monthly income of women representatives was an important indicator of economic solvency as well as economic empowerment. In Bangladesh, there were sharp differences between the level of income of women and men members. Majority of the women members (84 percent) had income below taka 4,000 per month, while the men members (89 percent) were in higher income brackets of taka 4001 and above. Moreover, 32 percent of women members earned as low as taka 500 per month. Women were mostly dependent on their husband's incomes and her income was perceived as a supplement to the household income. As such, women members were dependent on family decision for contesting in the election and getting financial support.

In India, women as well as men were mostly in the lower income category, hardly earning 2000 rupees a month, while only a few had a viable income. However, case studies from all over India revealed that Panchayat work had not suffered because of their poor economic status.

In Bangladesh as well as in India, majority women members were above the age of 25 years and married. It seemed that maturity of the members was a very significant criterion not only during election campaigns but also as an important factor to have an impact on the decision making process. Maturity in age and honor attached to marriage were yardsticks to be acceptable to the members of the community. Level of education was very depressing for both men and women, but for women it was even worst. For example, about 30 percent women were illiterate in India.

However, in Bangladesh, they could at least sign their names owing to NGO programs related to adult literacy. Occupational status of women in India and Bangladesh were different. In Bangladesh, majority of women representatives were housewives, unlike in India where they were more involved in agriculture work and laborers outside their home. In both the countries, women earned far less than men. Given the deprived socio-economic status, women had to face more hurdles than men during elections and as members of the local self-government.

DEMOCRATIZATION AND GENDER ISSUES

Political participation is one of the major ways to ensure women's empowerment, to increase decision-making power and greater ability and to influence matters that affect their lives in the community and the larger society. In the broader sense, participation in politics goes far beyond electoral politics, such as voting and election to public office. Women's empowerment begins with their consciousness-perceptions about herself and her rights, her capabilities and her potentials, awareness of her gender and socio-cultural, economic and political forces that affect her. Women's political empowerment and equal representation in all decision-making institutions are critical inputs in their struggle for freedom from patriarchal subjugation. Local government bodies have a vital role in the developmental processes. Therefore, importance of local level government to women and men is twofold. First, decisions made at the local levels have implications for the distribution of resources and opportunities between women and men. Second, the lower tiers of government are also arenas in which individuals gain experience and knowledge and a political base for seeking office at higher levels. Within local bodies, women are generally, expected to represent women's interests. That is, women's development is seen as women's business rather than the responsibility of both men and women members. Allied to this is the perception that women serving at the local level should focus on women and children's issues rather than the full range of issues at the grassroots level.

Nomination to Indirect Election of Women Members in Bangladesh

In 1976, provision was made for two nominated women members in addition to nine elected members and one chairperson in each Union Parishad, which was increased to three nominated women members in 1983. The nomination system in local government was changed in 1992 to indirect election where three women members in each local government body will be elected by the chairperson and other elected members.

There was an extremely low level of women's presence in the most important local council, the Union Parishad. No woman was elected in the local government elections of 1956 and 1969. One woman was first elected as chairperson in 1973. Although in 1992, the number increased to thirteen women, Union Parishad chairpersons being elected and subsequently twenty in 1997, still in the case of local government bodies, women were grossly under represented. However, the process of filling women's seats in the local councils totally ignored the scope of women's active participation and role in these political organizations where policies are decided and crucial plans for local level development are formulated. The nominated women could not play more than the role of a 'yes' person of the chairperson and members, who were predominantly men. In addition, such nomination also takes away the credibility and acceptability of the women to the women's constituencies whose causes they represented. Once again, in the provision of reserved seats for women to be filled through nomination reflects the male biases in policy making with the net result that the elected bodies become extremely male dominated (Khan, Z. R., 1998).

The 'selected' or nominated women members usually came from a rural elite group. In the nominating process-status, kinship and especially the relationship with the chairman were considered. The constituents, especially the rural women, had no way of 'electing' their own representatives. As the 'selected' representatives do not come through the election process, they usually do not know or care about their role and functions as people's representatives. Even most of the women voters do not know who their representatives are in the local government and what responsibilities and duties the representatives have towards constituents.

Therefore, the nominated female representatives are far less accountable to than those elected. In fact, they are more accountable to the men who have 'selected' them, if they wish to retain their posts, than to the electorate or the people who should really matter (UNDP, 1994). Hence in 1997, direct election for women representatives was provided in the local government at the lowest tier, the Union Parishad.

Reservation for Women in India

In India, reservation for women in political bodies became necessary, considering the social conditions in which women of the country lived even after the constitutional guarantee of their rights to equality and political participation it became necessary for the state to remind the political institutions at different levels, particularly the Panchayat level (district, block, village) to give adequate representation to women. The 73rd Amendment envisaged a significant structural change by decentralizing power and redressing the gender imbalance in the institutions of self-governance. Once the bastion of upper caste/class male power structure is now forever changed. What reservation has basically done is to give the other half of the state, i.e. women a say in the political system in a country, albeit at the grassroots. If we see it in another way, once these women taste power at the local level and understand its intricacies, they could very well enter national politics, with or without reservation, provided the political parties give party tickets to the women participants. After all, in a plural society like India, the political system has to ensure a modicum of equality between all the groups and communities if history's longest oppression is to be seriously tackled.

The 73rd CAA has certain intricacies. The Act suggests that the constituency at each election keeps rotating, the constituency reserved for women will be chosen by lottery, with those that have just been reserved excluded. Consequently it would damage both women and the parliamentary system. For women, since the fixed reserved constituency would mean ghettoisation, they would forever keep campaigning only against other women.For parliament, it would be destabilizing since with a minimum of two-third of the sitting members are due to change at every election (The Hindu, May 20, 2000). Another argument is that if a particular constituency is declared reserved for women for more than one term it would end up in the hands of those with vested interests. The rotation system gives more women the opportunity to participate (The Deccan Herald, October 22, 2000). But the purpose of reservation is not only giving an opportunity to women in politics but also for the betterment of the society and to quicken the process of development; the whole purpose behind decentralization of power. This could happen only when those participating are for a longer term in the office and are experienced in the art of politics.

The discussion on reservation after almost a decade needs to appraise the impact on the society at large and in particular its effect on the village power structure. While the positive side shows women's alacrity in participating, in managing funds, on developmental works and last but not the least in cutting across the class-caste-gender barriers. The other side has a grim picture, where once the male bastion of power/status is challenged, changed and given a new meaning, 'full-fledged democracy', led to averse male response leading to violence, public ridicule, defamation, no-confidence motion, etc. The aversion was not only because women have entered their space but also because women's work procedure is different compared to the men counterparts. Moreover, women laid emphasis on development works to be planned and executed-a phenomenon not appreciated by many who had been in the past siphoning off the development funds by showing most of the works on paper (The Deccan Herald, January 1, 1997). It was assessed that women in politics would affect development in a profound manner. A global assessment of women in politics arrived at three conclusions. "Firstly women choose issues of importance to themselves using a variety of meanings in different cultural contexts.

Secondly, no issues are tied solely to one political context and a condition and thirdly the political problems, facing women cluster into four topics: personal safety, security and autonomy, reproductive rights and maternal and child health problems, equalizing access to public, communal and market resources for problem solving and empowerment, and remaking the political and legal rules of the game" (Sharma, 1998). Women are closer to the environment and demand facilities that affect their immediate surroundings like drinking water facilities, healthcare, education, etc.

Making of the Sarpanch-Pati in India

The emerging women's leadership and the making of the Sarpanch-Pati was a pattern emerging among the young, new, development-seeking men and women with constraints that hampered their work, but it was the women who were bigger losers at the present state owing to the guile of their men folk. The flow chart given below explains the whole process of how men have become Sarpanch-Pati.

So that their own wife/ mother/ daughter may occupy the post and they may command via proxy rule and once the reserved seat becomes vacant they may retrieve the seat or get elected to it by virtue of their rk durin wo g the proxy rule.

73RD CAA ENABLES THEM IN OBTAINING SECURED

How?

Women are concerned about the development in their area and are committed to public service.

What motivates and encourages them?

But why such young and married women are encouraged/ allowed to leave homes and join politics when they themselves note that 'perception of politics' and 'neglect of family front' is a constraint

But why should they encourage?

A large number of young women are joining politics and getting elected.

EMERGING WOMEN'S LEADERSHIP

Sarpanch-Pati

Even after all these mechanisations by male counterparts of the elected women members, a considerable number of them (13.5 per cent) came back for a second time.

Women's Political Participation

What participation means is the functioning of the whole array of public institutions and forces which are involved in molding the lives of the people by way of decisions and policies that impinge on their relations with one another (Kaushik, 1992). Participation of women in the local bodies would include:

- Women as voters

- Women as members of political parties
- Women as candidates
- Women as elected members of local government bodies taking part in decision-making, planning, implementation and evaluation
- Women as members of women's organizations, their association with voluntary organizations
- Women in developmental works and dealing of priority issues in the village level.

Gender empowerment is determined by the degree to which women and men participate actively in economic, professional and political activity and take part in decision-making. Women's political participation was hindered by a system of social relations in the male-dominated society, reflecting the orthodox male-centric mentality like religious fundamentalism. Only men were consistently educated and trained for leadership, while very few rural women had the opportunity to pursue their education because of tradition. Women themselves had been strongly influenced by male-dominated village communities and had little faith in their own capacities to take on leadership roles.

In India, among the women who became Sarpanches, elected Panchayat members, intermediaries in Panchayati Samitis and chairpersons at Zilla Parishads, nearly 83 per cent of these women

Public service were first timers in politics and 74 per cent of the women stood independently. About 23 per cent stood as party candidates. These women were predominantly married, illiterate/literate and from very poor families. This trend focuses on whether these rural women, always in veil, inarticulate and ignorant of the rules of the political game would be able to make even a dint in their self-identity.

While in Bangladesh, most of the women members attained school level education and were married. Though these women had attained some school level education, they were not employed thus leading to dysfunctional educational syndrome. This was one of the major reasons for the lack of effective participation among these women in Union Parishads in Bangladesh. But we still find some sporadic cases among these women who have made a mark in the Parishad cutting across the gender-class-traditional bias of a primarily Islamic society.

Motivation for Joining Politics and Election Process

The level of participation could be understood from the reasons to get interested in politics in the first place and what were the issues promised in the election manifesto and their success and failures in implementing them.

Both men and women who became representatives of the Panchayat, i.e. 40 percent men and 38 percent women were interested in village development, while 27 percent men and 28 percent and women respectively were interested in public services. The assumption that only women take up social development issues and men opting for infrastructure development was grossly mistaken.

Improvement Inwomen/social Welfare

The way a man aspired for a link road closest to the city was also a woman's aspiration. The difference was that women's priority lies in the development of the immediate surroundings due to the fact that they were the ones who suffered the most without the civic amenities, water supply, fodder and fuel sources and access to credit. It was clear from the election promises the men and women candidates had made before the elections.

In Bangladesh, women who contested elections were usually motivated by NGOs or came from families having political background where male family members were active in local level politics. Very few entered politics as replacement after their husband's death.

There were hardly any differences in priority areas and election promises between men and women candidates. Education and improvement in civic facilities were commitments of an overwhelming majority of men and women candidates in both Bangladesh and India. In India, nearly 34 percent women as well as men contesting elections had priority areas such as women development and social welfare. The myth that women only feel about women's needs and problems no more holds true.

Issues Hindering Election Process

In Bangladesh, lack of economic resources was a major obstacle because most of the candidates were not very well off. It was more true in the case of the women candidates. Women candidates hardly had viable income or landed property of their own and were usually dependent on their husbands' earnings. As such, they also encountered social constraints and lack of family support. However, social security, especially during campaigns seemed to be a major problem, irrespective of gender and it was mostly threats from opposition. In the case of a woman candidate, opposition even tried to convince the candidate to withdraw her nomination paper. Lack or lower level of education of candidates also played a negative role during campaigns and receiving votes. Women candidates often suffered from lack of self-confidence. However, an overwhelming majority of the candidates did not face any problems during the election, 82 percent among women and 84 percent among men candidates.

Problems Faced During Elections

In Bangladesh, professionals stated that campaign for votes at night were difficult and risky for the women candidates, especially because women could not move easily as men did. Moreover, women candidates had to face some social and religious constraints during their campaigns. They also faced financial problems due to lack of political support. It was very difficult for women candidates to campaign throughout the constituencies under three wards. Violence was more pronounced due to the fundamentalist forces by not even allowing the women to vote.

The major fact that cannot be ruled out while discussing of women's participation in the Panchayats in India is the "violence" in the Panchayats that rather increased with the 73rd CAA. Violence against women, which in the villages was usually confined to their houses and of course inter-community violence had now spread its diabolic tentacles in the socio-political arena. During elections and decision-making also in everyday matters, violence against women was ever present. Beating up these women or their husbands, sexual harassment in public and molestation were imploring the society's equality front. Women due to the very patriarchal structure were as it was submissive and could not speak freely. Violence was the only aspect impeding women's ultimate overt participation in the Panchayats. Apart from overt violence, the fear of violence was something that had severely impaired women from actively participating in the Panchayat activities.

Fulfilling Election Promises

As to the extent of fulfilling election promises, both men and women in India initiated debates on the issue or persuaded these with higher authorities. But, unfortunately a vast majority did not response, which may be owing to the fact that they could not accept the work on their terms and complete it or maybe they did not understand the questions.

In Bangladesh, majority of the members had no problems in fulfilling the commitments they gave during election campaigns as they had not many priority areas except expansion of education and infrastructure development which were also priority areas of the annual development plan of the local government. However, both men and women could not fulfill some promises due to their own economic impoverishment, social and family problems, lack of education and security and last but not the least threats from political groups.

Though a large proportion of women and men in India mentioned that lack of funds had tied their hands, lack of knowledge, coordination, planning strategy and confrontation of party politics lead to hindrances. The main reason behind decentralizing the power structure was that corruption would not/could not reach the grassroots. Here comes the effective role of women, who were considered to be less corrupt in management.

There were some common obstacles that had hindered women's political participation in Bangladesh and India. Some were socio-economic, while others were mainly political.

Attendance and Participation in Meetings

Attendance of meetings is not only an important indicator for active participation but also a forum to discuss development activities and decision-making. Moreover, active participation of members and the level of acceptance at meetings were important indicators of their involvement in development activities at local level.

In Bangladesh, an overwhelming majority of 96 percent among men members and 88 per cent among women regularly attended the meetings. But the majority of the women members who attended the meetings could not play effective roles in the decision-making process except giving support to their male counterparts.

In India, nearly 68 percent women attended the meetings regularly, against 72 percent men. At least 32 percent women were either irregular or never attended the meetings. This was also true of 28 percent men. 88% 12% Regular

Unfortunately in Bangladesh, there were about 12 percent women and 3 percent men members who were irregular at meetings. Majority of them explained that they did not get notices of the meetings in time (39 percent women and 43 percent men). A few members reported that although they did not attend the meetings, their signature in the resolution book and attendance registers were collected after holding the meeting. As for other reasons, there was a difference between men and women members. For example, 18 percent women members complained that they were not given any responsibility, and that was why they lacked the interest in attending meetings regularly. Sickness was another factor for irregularity, which was as high as 21 percent among men and only 8 percent among women. Family problems were another valid reason for 10 per cent women such as household work, lack of cooperation of in-laws and husbands, child rearing responsibilities, etc. A few women members about 4 per cent did not trust the chairmen.

In Bangladesh, an overwhelming majority of 83 percent women were active participants against 92 percent men who attended the meetings. Partial participation and non-participation were very low among both men and women. In Bangladesh, there were several reasons for the acceptance at meetings. Women members reported that their opinions were accepted because their

With regard to partial and non-acceptance of the opinions of women at the meetings, majority of women reported that because they had minority representation in the Union Parishad, their voices were not heard. It was also pointed out by a large number of women (56 percent) that their identity as 'women' worked as barrier for their opinions to be accepted at meetings. Among other reasons given by women was the chairman's ignorance of women's opinions and reluctance of men members to allow women colleagues to speak. On the other hand, men's opinions were fully accepted more than partial acceptance. Their opinions were only rejected when they did not have a good relationship with the chairmen.

Khadiza Khanom: Conflict with Chairman

Khadiza Khanom, elected from the reserved seat of Chakmerpull Union of Cox's Bazar, came froma renowned family. She was a strong willed widow. She gets moral support from her educated sonHowever, Khadiza gathered measurable experiences as a woman Union Parishad member. At themeetings the chairman misbehaved with women when they talked about their rights. The chairmanmisappropriated government allotments with the help of his musclemen. No one had courage toprotest against the chairman's illegal activities for fear of being harassed by his musclemenHowever, Khadiza published all the chairman's illegal activities in the newspaper.

The chairmanbecame angry and published false news in the newspaper about Khadiza to smear her image. TheDeputy Commissioner of Cox's Bazar helped to minimize the dispute between the two andcompelled the chairman to apologize to Khadiza. The chairman, however, felt insulted but therewas no change in his behavior towards Khadiza. Khadiza felt the necessity of the interference of thehigher authority to solve the problem.

Problems Encountered at the Local Level

Active participation not only included their attendance at meetings, level of participation in the meetings, how acceptable were their opinions, but also the hindrances while undertaking development works at the local level. At the same time, their election promises were important indicators of whether they were able to fulfill them and if not what were the obstacles.

As far as women and their new relationship with politics is concerned, there were two kinds of women representatives in the Panchayats: those who had and are facing problems, and those who have had a smooth entry.

Smt. Dhan Devi, a Panchayat member of Bahadurpur Luhiya Gram Panchayat, Basrehar Block of EtawahDistrict said, "In our Nyaya Panchayat the Pradhan and other officials work according to their personalwhims and fancies. Though we attend the meeting but deliberately keep quiet. In my locality not even a brick lane has been made and the common passage that existed earlier has been closed down indefinitely.We women have been made Panchayat members only to behave as passive 'yes' people sans respect and importance whatsoever."

Women representatives faced problems when she did not have any political or organizational affiliations, did not have any family members in politics and fought independently without any party support for which she had to contest elections. On the other hand, women who were associated with political parties, claimed to have a family member in politics, accepted party ticket for election and was elected without contesting and did not even made any promises had hardly any problems. Moreover, 79 percent women did not face any election violence due to the fact that they had political backing and about 49 percent women were encouraged by the male members of their families. While 40 percent opined that just being a woman, male dependency, dual responsibilities and purdah were some of the social problems that women had to live up with. The above analysis clearly indicates that women who were active in party politics had support from political groups and gained more recognition in the Panchayat meetings. On the contrary, women who were independent of party affiliation had to struggle on their own to establish their rights and get things done because their voices were hardly considered in the local level meetings.

In Bangladesh women had some schooling, still there were orthodox fundamentalist patriarchal men in the Union Parishad. A case in retrospect was of Saleha Khatun, an elected Union Parishad Member of Sukhpuria Union of Chougcha Thana under Jessore district. She faced various problems while performing her duties. Saleha knew that according to Union Parishad Ordinance, each female Union Parishad member should preside over at least one project. She also learnt that they had the right to participate in one-third of development programs. However, the chairman did not respect the Ordinance and left women out of development activities. Moreover, he threatened women if they raised their voices. There were no arrangements for holding monthly meetings. As a result, women failed to participate in the decision-making process and undertake development activities.

Thus we find that the Bangladeshi counterparts faced a stronger opposition in participation itself, while in India women representatives did participate but their voices got submerged in the men's groups where the actual decisions were taken, as it was a forbidden space for women.

In Bangladesh, professionals opined that communication was the main problem that they faced. Women were unable to communicate with all the people of the three wards. Sometimes their men colleagues ignored them. Social and religious barriers, non-cooperation from husbands and small honorarium were among other problems. Chairman, politicians and others mentioned that communication with voters, family affairs, illiteracy, physical incapability, insecurity, disturbance by miscreants, etc. were faced by women members. Housewives observed that financial crisis was the main problem that women members faced as honorarium given to them were not enough. Moreover, their husbands did not cooperate with them.

Aparna Rani: Saga of Misfortune

Aparna Rani was a woman Union Parishad member of Moulvibazar. Her husband, who was aPrimary School Teacher, encouraged Aparna to compete in the Union Parishad election. She waselected from the reserved seat. During the early stages of her time in the Union Parishad, Aparna did not face any problem but the situation changed later. She was more vocal than other womenmembers and often argued with the chairman, which took a serious turn. The chairman did notapprove of her active participation in the meetings and tried to teach her a lesson. A friendly male colleague used to help Aparna in performing different

Union Parishad activities. The chairmanspread rumours using Aparna's friendly relationship with her male colleague. This shatteredAparna's married life. She was almost ostracised in the society. Finally she had to leave the UnionParishad.

The problems of men as Union Parishad members were different from their women counterparts. Problems were encountered by 47 percent men Union Parishad members, which was 60 per cent in the case of women members. Majority of the women who faced problems mentioned that chairmen did not allocate development works for them and men members opposed females' involvement in development activities. Women members also mentioned problems of non-cooperation from local people, for example people did not give land for road construction work to women members. Other problems included corruption of higher authority and men colleagues, less allocation to female, less value given to women, lack of security, etc.

About 53 percent men did not face any problems at all in performing Union Parishad activities. Men who faced problems reported that they did not get cooperation from local people while land acquisition was necessary for road construction, as well as chairman's negative attitudes towards allocating work and money to members. Other problems faced by men members included political interference, irregular meetings held by the chairman, delay of receiving project money and so on. WomenProblem with chairman regarding allocation of development work & fundsProblems faced from men members who opposed womenmembers, to get work and laugh at them Villagers do not cooperate Corruption at the higher levelLack of fund/less allocation for development work Lack of education, confidence, security, honorarium andfinancial problem Women members were not informed about their rights &dutiesNo problem

The reasons faced by both men and women members while undertaking any development work in the Panchayat of India were numerous. But for women, household workload, the attitude toward the caste and gender were the most dominating factors. Nearly 49 percent women representatives were ignorant of the power and duties specified to them, while 31 percent of the women representatives were not able to participate properly owing to the heavy workload at the house. Other obstacles faced by women were lack of information and mobility. While these were also handicaps of men representatives, they do not have the household to deal with. Apart from the impediments faced by them, some of the women and men felt that the decisions were usually taken and influenced by the rich and influential people.

- The women did not allow me to attend meetings
- I am not given an opportunity to speak at the meetings
- Women did not have any recognition in Saifai Gram Panchayat
- We did not have any rights except for the fact that we were members of the Panchayat.
- We did not get assistance from the Block

Cooperation Received at Local Level

Although women and men faced various types of problems both at the household level and in the community, still they could carry out their activities with the support and cooperation they received from other groups and people. Moreover, election promises can only be materialized when there was cooperation from the community from where the members have been elected. Level of cooperation received by members also helps in understanding the success of carrying out the work successfully.

In Bangladesh, Union Parishad members received cooperation from colleagues, family members, relatives, members of the community, Union Parishad chairmen and NGOs to carry out their development activities. Local government representatives elected from the grassroots level received cooperation mostly from the community people, 36 percent women members and 44 percent men members. Regarding other sources of cooperation, there was different scenario by gender. Women members received the highest cooperation from their women colleagues (38 percent), compared to 14 percent from their men members. On the other hand, only 4 per cent men members reported to have such cooperation from their women colleagues. Regarding cooperation from the men colleagues, 14 percent women and 44 percent men reported in favor. On the other hand, only negligible 4 percent women members got support from their husbands. The same trend was true of men members, where men got more cooperation from men colleagues (44 percent) than from their wives who were hardly involved or consulted by their husbands. Support from the NGOs was also very low in the case of both among women and men members.

There were not many proxies in the Panchayats, but on the other hand nearly 33 percent of women were helped by their husbands in the Panchayat work. Initially, most of these women were helped by their husbands and men colleagues, but once they understood the intricacies on the work front, they took charge. The community members cooperated with 29 percent of the women members and 38 percent of the men members. This would lead to better coordination and also speedy development through the group effort.

Capacity Building through Training Interventions

The need of training and awareness could bring women representatives in a better position not only in the participation level but also at the decision-making levels. The assistance given by the NGOs through the various training programs and general awareness programs is worth noting. The need for training of women does not mean that women were incapable of undertaking development at local level perceived by men politicians, but for qualitative input in development works taken up by the government, which did not reach those who actually needed it. Training has been identified as an important tool to carry out development activities. Training is essential, especially for women because their participation in local government and in the public sphere is a new phenomenon

In Bangladesh, 71 percent women members received training from government and NGOs, compared to only 45 percent men members.

Training received by women members from government organizations were mainly on health, sanitation and family planning. Women Union Parishad members also received training on fisheries, poultry, dairy farm and horticulture activities, child rights and early marriage.

In India, the scenario of training was minimal. However, the Panchayat representatives had identified some major areas in which they need training. Most of them emphasized planning procedures, as developmental issues could be dealt successfully only when the planning agendum was taken up with full conviction. The next priority was education, as owing to lack of training, people do suffer in taking quick and emphatic decisions.

The governments of India and Bangladesh provided a major opportunity to include provisions to ensure greater participation by women in local government and greater responsiveness of local government authorities to women's interests and needs. In India, reservation for women in the Panchayat level had basically given women a say in the grassroots political system. On the other hand, the emerging women's leadership, there evolved the Sarpanch-Pati where women may occupy the post but the men may commend via proxy rule.

Women's political participation in the local bodies included mainly women as voters, as candidates, as elected members taking part in decision-making, planning and implementation.

In India, the problems faced by women during the election and while implementing development works in the Panchayats were mostly caste/class factors, while in Bangladesh, it was the religious fundamentalist and the purdah restriction.

The women representatives were designated as change agents for rural development, but unfortunately they did not have enough knowledge or training on development and organizational issues to provide a support system for rural women.

CONCLUSION AND RECOMMENDATIONS

The essence of good governance lies, on one hand, the inclusion of local level planning in the national government and on the other hand, the success of a local government depends on peoples' participation. It is the grassroots level people who could contribute significantly to the governance of their communities. However, unequal participation of women and men in the government planning works as a barrier to ensure good governance in both Bangladesh and India. After three decades of research focused on gender equality, it is clear that there is a crucial need for a gender-specific development paradigm into all areas of policy making and planning so that women's needs can be met and their participation ensured. Decentralization has been identified as one of the important prerequisite to ensure gender balance into development process.

The present study was an attempt to review the participation of women at grassroots level democracy in Bangladesh and India. The study examined the role of government of Bangladesh and India to ensure gender balance at local level policy planning. In Bangladesh women's participation at local level politics has been recently ensured through the constitutional reform, while in India it had been for sometimes. It has been found in both the countries that although a large number of women were elected as local representatives, obstacles related to women's gender identity refrained them to play their roles effectively. It was evident that lack of effective and timely planning, lack of political background, absence of proper socio-economic and political environment, lack of appropriate organizational framework, lack of skill and training placed women behind to prove their competencies compared to their men counterparts. It had been identified that women have limited scope to exercise political rights, lack of control over resources and limited choice in decision-making. However, women had been trying to overcome the barriers through their active participation in the local level policy-making.

Attempts had also been taken to sensitize communities as well as local and national leaders and policy makers to the need for gender balance in the political process. Efforts are going on to make politics democratic, participatory, accountable and transparent so as to ensure a just, humane and equitable society. The urgency for political empowerment of women has therefore increased manifold. There is a need to enable women members to be more effective members of local government bodies. Two aspects of effectiveness need to be considered: effectiveness in participating in overall operations and effectiveness in stimulating attention to women's development issues.

That being the case, the foremost task is to reach out to women to make them politically aware and conscious. This task requires to be taken up on a mass and intensified scale. Coordination and cooperation of both government and NGOs are necessary to achieve this goal. Political parties have a significant role to play as well.

At the same time it must be acknowledged that the effort becomes even more difficult when precautions have to be taken to make governance more streamlined, empowering and development oriented while at the same time ensuring that the plurality of the multilayered cultural complexes enmeshed and intertwined with centuries of constructive accretion are not disturbed in any simplistic and radical manner.

Recommendations

Suggestions and recommendations are under three heads, viz., the role of government, role of political parties and role of NGOs and civil societies.

Role of Government

Election rules and regulations to be restructured: Both in India and Bangladesh, election rules should be restructured in the light of facilitating women's participation in the electoral processes, i.e. right to choose their representatives, freedom to express their views and opinions, freely allowed to cast their precious vote, strict ban on use of violence in elections, limits on expenditure and its strict implementation.

Representation of women members at the local level committees: Both in India and Bangladesh, at the local level, planning and decision-making committees should comprise at least 50 percent women. Social programs should be introduced to encourage women's effective participation in such activities.

Fair representation of minorities: The Bangladesh government should also let the minorities like Hindus and Christians be represented in the decision-making process, which could be facilitated by the help of reservation or through fair entry basis.

Information and training to women members of local bodies: The government along with the NGOs imparting training should provide information and training to women members of local bodies to increase their knowledge of local government, responsibilities and functions. This could be through information manuals, mobile training program and through audio-visual mediums. Women should be given various opportunities for leadership training and education in order to encourage them to take up political and leadership position in all fields. Supportive services should be provided to allow women to participate in local bodies.

Exchange of information and experience: Through the Local Government machinery, program or project should be developed that would allow for meetings for the exchange of information and experience on the ways in which women members can pursue issues of women's equality and development as members of local government.

The effectiveness of all Union Parishad and Panchayat members must be increased in promoting women's development. Training materials and courses for members of local government bodies should be revised to include components on women's equality and development. This should include components on changing attitudes to women's participation in decision-making bodies as well as components on assessing programs and projects to ensure that women benefit.

Literacy in legal rights and politics: In all formal and non-formal schools, proper training and exposure to the legal and political rights of women should be given to bring about attitudinal changes among both men and women.

Improvement of motivational programs: To create greater awareness among women about their low status in society and the need to improve it, motivational programs for expanding opportunities for education, health care and employment should be launched.

Participation of women in all activities: To ensure participation of women in development and social activities equal importance should be given to their opinions. To ensure an active participation of women in all activities of Union Parishad and Panchayat, government should monitor that women representatives are given their due respect to undertake and participate equal partners with men in development works at the local level.

Implementation of all kinds of activities: To ensure suitable training on proper implementation of all kinds of development activities and for the proper advancement of grassroots level poor community.

Role of Political Parties

Need for democratization from within: If women are to come even without reservation, as was not approved by some sections of the women's groups and the academia, the foremost responsibility should be that of the political parties who should recognize the capability and success of women and give party tickets to those who are interested to stand for the said post.

Party manifestoes and constitutions should include gender equity as one of their goals and have a plan of action for its achievement.

The present system of reserved seats is a necessary evil that may continue until greater representation of women is achieved. However, political parties in Bangladesh should work together to amend the system of nomination to direct election of women to the reserved seats for the Parliament as well.

Conscientisation to Women's Issues: To raise the political consciousness of the people and to sensitize them about women's issues, political parties should organize workshops, dialogues, discussions and mass meetings. Political parties should also sensitize party leaders and party workers about women's issues by organizing discussion sessions.

Maintain Linkages with Voters: Political parties should encourage their women candidates to maintain a continuous linkage with the voters, with special emphasis on women voters, so that they are not misled by the male members of their families.

Fair Elections at All Levels: Political parties should work towards free and fair elections so that women candidates can contest. Awareness programs for the voters should be undertaken so that they can cast their vote in favor of eligible candidates.

Stand against Fctionalism: Political parties should take a positive stand against factionalism, fundamentalism and misinterpretation of religious beliefs, which stands in the way of

women's political participation. In order to develop political awareness and consciousness, women should be involved in social, economic and political activities.

Implementation of Legal reforms and UN Conventions: Political parties should ensure the implementation of legal reforms and UN Conventions relating to women.

To Change the Policy of Political Parties: Women belonging to all political parties have to take organized steps to change the discriminatory policy and approach political parties in the matter of financial support to women candidates in elections. Political parties should provide financial allocations for the campaign expenditure of women candidates.

Role of NGOs and Civil Society

NGO Agenda: Political empowerment of women should be incorporated in the NGO agenda. They should consciously make an effort to emphasize the issues of gender equity and women's empowerment in its right perspective. Both men and women leaders at the grassroots and national levels must be sensitized to women's issues, and form pressure and advocacy groups for the realization of gender equity. Women should be made aware of their potential political power and their contribution to the political process as voters.

Networking: To facilitate the inclusion of women's issues in the political and public agenda, networking between the women's organizations and women politicians, in particular, is necessary. Curriculum and media should be adequately utilized so as to change patriarchal social values and encourage women towards leadership roles and activities.

Organize Pressure Groups: To support women candidates and mobilize funds for increasing women's participation in politics, NGOs should organize support groups and raise the political consensus of women through seminars, workshops, orientation training, mass media, etc. To lobby for increasing women's participation in politics, pressure groups should be formed within and outside the Parliament.

Participation in Political Parties: To increase the number of women in the rank and file at all levels of political parties, grassroots women's organizations should mobilize women at all levels. They should also highlight the potentials of women and their competence as candidates.

Knowledge about the functions of Panchayats and Union Parishads: Most of the women members had lower levels of education. Their training may be conducted by the relevant training institutes or by the respective district authority with the financial support of the government or assistance from the donor agencies/ development partners. A training or instructional handbook on women's power, rights, functions and management of the Union Parishad should be provided to them after being elected as women members of the Union Parishad.

To participate in the local bodies meeting: In order to ensure proper participation in the local bodies, the government may undertake the membership of women members in the different committees, specially the committees dealing with family planning and women's development. A mechanism should be developed to ensure regular attendance of the women members at the meetings.

Selection procedures of party's candidates: Rural women do not have a clear appreciation and adequate awareness of the issues faced by the women because of the respective environment. Women members, whatever may be their selection procedure, are recognized as leaders at the grassroots level by the government and by the local community. They should, therefore, be given adequate training and exposure to the issues, which stand in the way of the integration of women with the socio-economic life of society.

6

REPORT OF THE STEERING COMMITTEE

BACKGROUND

In the context of the preparations for the Tenth Five Year Plan (2002-07), Planning Commission constituted a Steering Committee on 'Empowerment of Women and Development of Children' under the Chairpersonship of Dr. K. Venkatasubramanian, Member, Planning Commission, with the following Terms of Reference.

i) to review the existing approach, strategies/and priorities; the ongoing policies and programmes of empowering women and development of children in the Ninth Five Year Plan; and suggest, if necessary, alternative strategies, priorities, policies and programmes to accelerate the empowering process;

ii) to assess the effectiveness of the implementation of 'Women's Component Plan' and suggest specific measures and mechanisms to ensure that the funds/benefits flow to women from other development sectors;

iii) to assess the impact of the on-going economic reforms and progressive globalization / liberalization of economy on the conditions of women and children and suggest effective strategies to cope up with the situation;

iv) to review the effectiveness of the existing women & child-specific and women and child-related legislations and their enforcement and suggest corrective measures;

v) to review the effectiveness of the existing Institutional Arrangements for implementation of policies and programmes relating to women and children, both at Central and State levels and suggest improvements, if necessary;

vi) to assess the role of NGOs and the status of devolution of Powers and resources to Panchayati Raj Institutions and Local Self Government Bodies, as per the 73rd and 74th Constitutional Amendments and suggest specific measures for their involvement in the planning policies; and

vii) to suggest an approach and necessary strategies, priorities, policies and programmes along with physical and financial targets, in pursuing the commitment of Empowering Women and Development of Children during the Tenth Five Year Plan (2002-07).

Simultaneously, Planning Commission had also set up two Working Groups at the ministerial level-one on the 'Empowerment of Women', and the other on the 'Development of Children' under the Chairpersonship of Shri B.K. Chaturvedi, Secretary, Department of Women and Child Development.

Besides the above two Working Groups, Planning Commission also set up, for the first time, a Working Group on the Welfare and Development of Adolescents under the chairpersonship of Dr N.C. Saxena, Secretary, Planning Commission, to look into the developmental needs of the Group on priority basis, as they have been identified as the most neglected lot during all these fifty years. Details of the Composition and the Terms of Reference of the Working Group is at Annexure-IV. While the nodal responsibility of taking the follow-up action lies with the Department of Youth Affairs and Sports, recommendations having a direct bearing on the well-being of adolescent girls will be taken note of by the Steering Committee on Empowerment of Women and Development of Children.

The Steering Committee, in its First meeting held on the 31.1.2001, took stock of the status of women and children in the country, besides deliberating upon-(i) the fast-changing situations and persisting as well as emerging problems/issues that should

receive priority attention during the Tenth Plan; and (ii) the line of approach required to be adopted in the Tenth Plan to ensure empowerment of women and the development of children. The Steering Committee, in its Second meeting held on 9.5.2001, discussed in detail, the Reports of both the Working Groups with a special reference to-the gaps/problems identified and the priorities/approach suggested for the Tenth Plan and accepted them. With regard to the Report of the Working Group on Adolescents, the Committee decided to hand over the same to the Steering Committee on Sports and Youth Affairs which in turn is expected to pass on to the nodal Department of Youth Affairs and Sports for necessary action. However, the recommendations relating to the Adolescents Girls would be taken into consideration by this Steering Committee also.

Based on the detailed deliberations that took place in the Meetings of the steering Committee and also taking into consideration the suggestions and recommendations of the Working Groups, the Steering Committee on the Empowerment of Women and Development of Children finalized its Report. The same is presented here below in two parts-Part A on the Empowerment of Women and Part B on Development of Children:

EMPOWERMENT OF WOMEN

According to the 2001 Census, women as an independent target group account for 495.74 million in actual numbers and represent 48.3 % of the total population of the country. Depending upon the developmental needs of the individual age-group, the entire female population projected for 2001 can be categorized for the planning purposes into the following five distinct sub-groups:

i) Girl children in the age-group of 0-14 years who account for 169.03 million (34.6%) deserve special attention because of the gender bias and discrimination they suffer from at such a tender age;

ii) Adolescent girls in the age group 15-19 years who account for 51.39 million (10.5%) are very sensitive from the view-point of planning because of the preparatory stage for their future productive and reproductive roles in the family and society;

iii) Women in the reproductive age group of 15-44 years numbering 230.35 million (47.1%) need special care and attention because of their reproductive needs;

iv) Women in the economically active age group of 15-59 years, who account for 285.22 million (58.4%) have different demands like those of education/training, employment, income generation and participation in the developmental process, decision making etc.; and

v) The elderly women in the age group of 60+ numbering 34.36 million (7.0%) who have limited needs mainly relating to health, emotional and financial support.

The principles of gender equity and equality and protection of women's rights have been the prime concerns in Indian thinking right from the days of Independence. Accordingly, the country's concern in safeguarding the rights and privileges of women found its best expression in the Constitution of India. While Article 14 confers equal rights and opportunities on men and women in the political, economic and social spheres; Article 15 prohibits discrimination against any citizen on the grounds of sex, religion, race, caste etc; and Article 15(3) provides for equality of opportunities in the matter of public appointments for all citizens. Yet another Article 39 mentions that the State shall direct its policy towards providing to men and women equally the right to means of livelihood and equal pay for equal work. Article 42 directs the State to make provisions for ensuring just and humane conditions of work and maternity itself. Article 51(A)(e) imposes a fundamental duty on every citizen to renounce the practices derogatory to the dignity of women. To make this de jure equality into a de facto one, special legislations have been enacted from time to time in support of women

The realization of the significance of investing in the nation's women has grown over the plan periods. Women as a separate category for planning interventions came to focus upon increasingly over the plan periods as it became clear that the development of women has a direct bearing upon the country's total development. Women who represent 90% in the Informal Sector have been the backbone of the rural economy, but unfortunately their contribution to the economy and to

development process remains invisible. They are, in fact, getting adversely affected in the wake of the changing developmental paradigms, especially those of economic liberalization and globalisation, besides their own sufferings of social backwardness. Therefore, they form a priority group requiring special attention of the Government.

DEVELOPMENT OF WOMEN THROUGH FIVE YEAR PLANS (1951-2002)

First to Eighth Five Year Plans (1951-97)

Development of women has been receiving attention of the Government right from the very First Five Year Plan (1951-56). But, they have treated development of women as a subject of 'welfare' and clubbed it with the welfare of other disadvantaged groups requiring attention of the Government. The First Five Year Plan (1951-56) sought to 'promote the welfare of women' by helping them to play their legitimate role in the family and the community and stressed that 'the major burden of organizing activities for the benefit of vast female population has to be borne by the private agencies'. The Central Social Welfare Board (CSWB) was set up in 1953 to act as one Apex Body at national level and to promote action organizations at various levels, especially at the grassroots; to take up welfare related activities for women. The Second to the Fifth Plans, including the Plan holidays also continued to reflect the same welfare approach, except according priority on education for both men and women besides launching of measures to improve maternal and child health services, supplementary feeding for children and expectant and nursing mothers.

The shift in the approach from 'welfare' to 'development' of women could take place only in the Sixth Five Year Plan (1980-85), which made the Planners and Policy-makers recognize women not only as partners but also as stake-holders in the development of the country. The report of the Committee on the Status of Women in India which was published during the same period also highlighted the imperatives for Women to be considered as an independent target group requiring special focus in planning and development. The Sixth Plan adopted a multi-disciplinary approach with a special thrust on the three core sectors of health, education and employment. Accordingly, priority was given to programmes for women in agriculture and its allied activities of dairying, poultry, small animal husbandry, and handlooms, handicrafts, small-scale industries etc.

In the Seventh Plan (1985-90), developmental programmes continued with the major objectives of raising their economic and social status and bring them into the mainstream of national development. A significant step in this direction was to identify/promote the 'beneficiary oriented programmes' for women in different developmental sectors which extend direct benefits to women. The stress on generation of both skilled and unskilled employment through proper education and vocational training continued.

The Eighth Five Year Plan (1992-97) with its major focus on `Human Development' played a very important role in the development of women. It promised to ensure that benefits of development from different sectors do not bypass women, implement special programmes to complement the general development programmes and to monitor the flow of benefits to women in the three core sectors of education, health and employment. Women must be enabled to function as equal partners and participants in the developmental process. This approach of the Eighth Plan marks a further shift from `development' to `empowerment' of women.

Some of the Policy Programme Initiatives undertaken for empowering women during the Eighth Plan period include the following: (i) setting up of a National Commission for Women in 1992 to safeguard the interests of women; (ii) setting up of Rashtriya Mahila Kosh in 1993 for women to meet the credit needs of poor and assetless women; (iii) adoption of the National Nutrition Policy in 1993 to fulfil the Constitutional commitment to ensure adequate nutritional standards to its people; (iv) launching of the scheme of Mahila Samriddhi Yojana in 1993 which seeks to empower women by institutionalising their savings so that they can have greater control over household resources (later merged with Integrated Women's Empowerment Programme); (v) setting up of National Creche Fund in 1994 so as to meet the growing demand for crèche services which is a support service for working

mothers; (vi) launching of Indira Mahila Yojana in 1995-96 (renamed as Integrated Women's Empowerment Programme in 1999); and vii) formulation of a National Policy for Empowerment of Women (a draft-1996).

THE NINTH FIVE YEAR PLAN (1997-2002)

The Ninth Five Year Plan made a major commitment of `Empowering women as the Agents of Socio-Economic Change and Development', through the following strategies--(i) to create an enabling environment for women to exercise their rights, both within and outside home, as equal partners along with men, through early adoption of `National Policy for Empowerment of Women'; (ii) to legislate reservation of not less than 1/3 seats for women in the Lok Sabha and in the State Legislative Assemblies and thus ensure adequate representation of women in decision making; (iii) to adopt an integrated approach towards empowering women through effective convergence of existing services, resources, infrastructure and manpower in both women-specific and women-related sectors; (iv) to adopt a special strategy of `Women's Component Plan' to ensure that not less than 30 per cent of funds/benefits flow to women from other developmental sectors; (v) to organize women into Self-Help Groups and thus mark the beginning of a major process of empowering women; (vi) to accord high priority to reproductive child health services and thus ensure easy access to maternal and child health services; vii) to universalize the on-going supplementary feeding programme-Special Nutrition Programme (SNP) and Mid-Day Meals (MDM); (viii) to ensure easy and equal access to education for women and girls through the commitments of the Special Action Plan of 1998; (ix) to initiate steps to eliminate gender bias in all educational programmes; (x) to institute plans for free education for girls up to college level, including professional courses; (xi) to equip women with necessary skills in the modern upcoming trades which could keep them gainfully engaged besides making them economically independent and self-reliant; and xii) to increase access to credit through setting up of a 'Development Bank for Women Entrepreneurs' in small and tiny sectors. The following paragraphs give a detailed account of the efforts put in by both the women-specific and women-related sectors to translate the Ninth Plan commitments into action during the Ninth Plan period.

Women and Child Development

Keeping the commitments of the Ninth Plan in view, the nodal Department of Women and Child Development which is responsible for empowering women initiated action in finalising the Policy. The Group of Ministers (GOM) which examined the draft Policy made certain changes to make it more effective and recommended the same for approval of the Cabinet. Finally, it got approved in March, 2001. The other major step in this direction was to seek 33-1/2 per cent reservation of seats for women, both in the Lok Sabha and in the State Legislative Assemblies. To this effect, a Bill on the subject was introduced in the Lok Sabha in September, 1996, but the same is yet to be passed.

Besides setting up of a Standing Lok Sabha Parliamentary Committee on Empowerment of Women in March 1997 to review the progress of empowering women from time to time, a Task Force on Women and Children was also constituted in August, 2000 to review all the related measures and to draft a Programme for Celebrating 2001 as the 'Year of Women's Empowerment'. The Task Force which met on 12 September, 2000 has finalised a Programme for Celebrating the Women's Empowerment Year. Further, to have a detailed review of all the legislations relating to women, the Task Force set up two Sub-Groups-Sub-Group I and Sub-Group II. The two Sub-Groups, while submitting their reports, have recommended certain amendments. The Task Force, after having a detailed discussion on the amendments proposed, accepted the reports of the Sub-Groups in its meeting held on 6.9.2001.

With regard to earmarking of funds/benefits under Women's Component Plan, the Planning Commission, as reported, requested all the Central Ministries/Departments and the State Governments to draw up Women's Component Plans. The Minister for Human Resource Development had also requested all the Central Ministers for their personal intervention in the matter of earmarking of funds/benefits under Women's Component Plan in the plans/ programmes of their respective Ministries/Departments. The nodal

Department of Women and Child Development also made a request to all the Ministries/Departments to-(i) set up Advisory Committees to help the Ministries/Departments in the preparation of Women's Component Plan; (ii) set up a 'Women's Cell' to monitor the implementation of Women's Component Plan; and (iii) include a chapter on Women's Component Plan in their Annual Reports. As per the information available, 12 Central Ministries/ Departments, viz.-Health and Family Welfare, Education, Labour, Agriculture, Urban Affairs and Employment, Rural Development, Social Justice and Empowerment, Textiles, Industries, Non-Conventional Energy Sources, Science and Technology and Information & Broadcasting, have confirmed their efforts of extending benefits for women under Women's Component Plan. While the State Governments of Karnataka, Kerala, Gujarat and Himachal Pradesh have made a bold initiative of earmarking funds for Women's Component Plan, Rajasthan is also trying to follow the path very soon.

Although, it is difficult to quantify the efforts of various Ministries/Departments in terms of allocations, yet the flow of benefits to women from the core sectors of health and family welfare, education, labour and employment, rural development, urban development, agriculture, science and technology etc. can be easily enlisted, as reflected in the chapters of this document. Efforts have already been on for preparing a Gender Development Index to assess the impact of various policies and programmes in improving/raising the status of women at regular intervals. A set of 18 Developmental Indicators selected for the purpose are being field-tested to find out the feasibility of data being available at the district level on a regular basis. Results are still awaited from the respective State Governments. The Committee on Empowerment of Women, referred to above, also inter-alia, reviews the implementation of the progress of the Women's Component Plan from time to time, as part of the strategy for empowering women.

Besides formulating policies and programmes, enacts/amends legislation concerning women; and reviews, guides and coordinate the efforts of both governmental and nongovernmental organizations, the nodal Department also implements a few innovative programmes. They include--(i) empowering strategies;

(ii) employment and income generation; (iii) welfare and support services; (iv) awareness generation and gender sensitization; and (v) other enabling measures. These programmes, in fact, play the role of supplementary/complementary to the other general development efforts for women. Progress of some of the important on-going programmes is given below:

Empowering Strategies

Indira Mahila Yojana (IMY), launched in 1995-96 was recast and retitled as `Integrated Women's Empowerment Programme (IWEP)' in 2001 to empower women through the following: (i) generate awareness amongst women by disseminating information and knowledge; (ii) help women achieve economic strength through micro-level income-generating activities; and (iii) establish convergence of various services such as literacy, health, non-formal education, rural development, water supply, training for capacity building, entrepreneurship, etc. Merged with the programme of Mahila Samriddhi Yojana, IWEP will be an effective instrument for empowering women, both socially and economically, besides organising them into Self-Help Groups (SHGs) to form a strong institutional base. More than 42,000 Women SHGs were formed by the end of 2000.

The Rural Women's Development and Empowerment Project (RWDEP), now being called as Swa-Shakti Project sanctioned in 1998 as a Centrally-Sponsored Project, is yet another governmental intervention which was already put to test in Tamil Nadu and found to be successful in empowering women through awareness generation and income generation. The same is being replicated in the States of Bihar, Haryana, Gujarat, Karnataka, Madhya Pradesh and Uttar Pradesh with the assistance from IDA and IFAD. The Women's Development Corporations and the NGOs in these States are actively associated in implementation of the programme. As the Project is still in its infancy, it is too early to assess its impact.

Employment and Income Generation

The Support of Training and Employment Programme (STEP) provides a comprehensive package of up-gradation of skills through training, extension inputs, market linkages etc. in the

traditional sectors of Agriculture, Dairying, Handicrafts, Handlooms and Animal Husbandry, Sericulture, Fisheries etc. Since inception of STEP in 1987, till date, about 4,91,795 women have been covered under 96 projects launched in the States of Andhra Pradesh, Bihar, Gujarat, Haryana, Himachal Pradesh, Karnataka, Kerala, Madhya Pradesh, Maharashtra, Manipur, Nagaland, Orissa, Tamil Nadu, Tripura, Uttar Pradesh and West Bengal. Setting up of Employment and Income Generation Training cum Production Centre for Women (NORAD) extends training for poor and needy women in the age-group of 18-45 years in the up-coming non-traditional trades. Since 1982-83 when the programme was started, 1477 projects benefiting 2.28 lakh women have been approved. The Socio-Economic Programme (SEP) provides `work and wage' to needy women such as destitutes, widows, deserted, disabled etc. By the end of the Ninth Plan 50 new units are likely to be set up under SEP. The Condensed Courses of Education and Vocational Training (CCEVT) provides new vistas of employment through continuing education and vocational training for school drop-outs. A total number of 3753 courses is likely to be started by the end of the Ninth Plan.

Welfare and Support Services

Support services to working women are being extended through the programme of Hostels for Working Women (HWW) which aims to promote greater mobility for women in the employment market through providing safe and cheap accommodation to working women of lower income strata. Since inception of the Scheme in 1973 till February 2001, 861 hostels have been sanctioned to provide accommodation to 60,865 working women. A nation-wide study conducted in 1998 by the Tata Institute of Social Sciences, Mumbai suggested expansion of the scheme to meet the ever-increasing demand for such hostels. The Master Plan of Operations (MPO) prepared by the Department in 1992 also indicated the need to provide hostel accommodation for about 1.35 lakh working women throughout the country. Not even half of this target could be achieved, so far. The other two major support services include-i) ICDS through its nation-wide networking of 6 lakh anganwadi centres and ii) creches/day-care centres for working and ailing mothers. Details of these two programmes are given under the section `Development of Children' of this Report.

The welfare programme of Short Stay Homes (SSH) for Women and Girls has been under implementation since 1969 to protect and rehabilitate those women and girls who are in social and moral danger due to breakage of families, mental strain/stress, social ostracism, exploitation etc. During the year 1999-2000, the financial pattern and norms under the scheme were revised as mid-term corrections during the Ninth Plan. At present, there exist a total number of 339 SSHs benefitting about 10,170 women/girls. The scheme of SSHs was evaluated in 1998 by Programme Evaluation Organisation (PEO) of the Planning Commission. Based on their recommendations, the scheme has been transferred to Central Social Welfare Board (CSWB) to develop linkages/get merged with another alike scheme called Family Counselling Centres launched to help those families which are on the verge of break-down.

Awareness and Gender Sensitization

The Ninth Plan attaches great importance to those efforts which trigger changes in societal attitudes towards women and the girl child. An integrated media campaign projecting a positive image of both women and the girl child through electronic, print and mass media forms the most important component of the government's communication strategy. Also, a set of 10 Legal Literacy Manuals were brought out in 1992 with the aim of educating women about the laws concerning their basic rights. These Manuals being simple and illustrated, even semiliterates and neo-literates can easily comprehend the messages. The manuals have been distributed to all the State Governments and NGOs for wider dissemination and the same are also being translated into all other Indian languages.

Other Enabling Measures

Rashtriya Mahila Kosh (RMK) is a national-level mechanism to meet the micro-credit needs of poor and asset-less women in the Informal Sector. Since inception of RMK in 1993 till February 2001, a total credit worth Rs.100.27 crore was sanctioned to benefit more than 4 lakh women through the medium of 827 NGOs

spread all over the country. Disbursements already made are worth Rs. 74.92 crore. RMK has been maintaining a very creditable recovery rate of 90 to 95 per cent. It also ventured to develop an institutional base at the grass-root levels hrough Self-Help Groups for expanding its credit services. In this process, it also started developing linkages with the existing Women's Groups of IMY and DWCRA. For expansion of these activities, RMK needs financial support from the Government.

The National Commission for Women, set up in 1992, has a mandate to safeguard the rights and interests of women. The Commission continued to pursue its mandated activities viz- safeguarding women's rights through legal awareness programmes; looking into the individual complaints/pre-litigations, sexual harassment of women at work place; organising `Parivarik Mahila Lok Adalats' with the help of local NGOs and Legal Aid Boards; and review of the existing legislations and preparation of new Bills relating to Prevention of Inter-Country trafficking in the SAARC Region, framing of Rules under Dowry Prohibition Act of 1961 etc. The Commission accords highest priority in securing speedy justice to women. A statement showing the physical and financial targets and the achievements made during the Ninth Plan is at

MONITORING THE BENEFICIARY-ORIENTED SCHEMES (BOS)

At the instance of the Prime Minster's Office, the nodal Department of Women and Child Development monitors the progress of implementation of the 27 Beneficiary-Oriented Schemes for Women through the mechanism of Inter-Ministerial Review Meetings. Based on the findings of the review, the nodal Department plays an interventionist role with the help of PMO in removing the obstacles/impediments and thus improve the implementation of the 27 BOS. Status Reports prepared by the nodal Department form the base for the necessary follow-up action by the individual Ministries/Departments. A review of the 27 BOS reveals that-i) a total outlay of Rs. 20688.70 crore representing 2.4 per cent of the total public sector outlay is available in the Ninth Plan for empowering women; ii) of this, while Rs. 12878.28

crore (62.2 %) flow from 6 women-related Ministries/Departments, the rest of Rs. 7810.42 crore (37.8%) flow from one single Department of Women and Child Development. This justifies the fact that the women's component plan needs to be concretized right from the very beginning of formulation / launching of the Plan so that the benefits from other developmental sectors do not by-pass women.

Review of Legislation (women-specific & women-related)

As per the mandate, the National Commission for Women reviewed all the 39 legislations which have bearing upon women. The two Sub-Groups of the Task Force on Women and Children examined a total of 22 women-related legislations and completed the task of giving recommendations with regard to the following- (i) Employees' State Insurance Act, 1948; (ii) Factory Act, 1948; (iii) Minimum Wage Act, 1948; (iv) The Bonded Labour System (Abolition) Act, 1976; (v) Legal Practitioners (Women) Act, 1923; (vi) Maternity Benefit Act, 1961; (vii) The Child Labour (Prohibition & Regulation) Act, 1986; (viii) The Equal Remuneration Act, 1976; (ix) The Beedi and Cigar Workes (Conditions of Employment) Act, 1966; (x) The Cinematograph Act, 1952 and related Laws; (xi) The Contract Labour (Regulation and Abolition) Act, 1970; (xii) The Inter-State Migrant Workmen (Regulation of Employment and Condition of Service) Act, 1979; (xiii) The Payment of Wages Act, 1936; (xiv) The Plantation Labour Act, 1951; (xv) The Workmen's Compensation Act, 1923; (xvi) The Commission of Sati (Prevention) Act, 1987; (xvii) Indecent Representation of Women (Prohibition) Act, 1986; (xviii) Family Courts Act, 1984; (xix) Indian Penal Code, 1860; (xx) Criminal Procedure Code, 1973; (xxi) The Immoral Traffic (Prevention) Act, 1956; and (xxii) Dowry Prohibition Act, 1961;

Health And Family Welfare

Improvement in health status of women is sought to be achieved through improving the access to and utilization of health, family welfare and nutrition services with a special focus on under-served and under-privileged segments of population. Technical improvement and increased access to health care have resulted in fall in mortality rates, but the disease burden continues

to be high. Substantial variations exist between States and districts in availability, quality and utilization of health care services and women's access to such services, as well as the health status. Bihar, Uttar Pradesh, Madhya Pradesh, Rajasthan and Orissa, are areas where reduction in the IMR has been slow and pre-natal and neonatal mortality rates have not declined.

Anaemia is the most widespread yet most neglected micronutrient deficiency/disorder in India. Poor dietary intake of iron and folic acid are the major factors responsible for anaemia. Pregnant women and pre-school children are the worst affected. Prevalence of anaemia among pregnant women ranges between 50%-90%. Training programmes to improve screening of pregnant women for anaemia and initiating appropriate therapy have been initiated as a part of Reproductive and Child Health (RCH) programme. However, the programme is yet to be operationalised. In the past serious shortage and poor quality of iron and folic acid tablets had crippled the programme. The RCH aims at eliminating these.

The issue of maternal and child health are given high priority through the RCH programme which is proposed to be universalized by the end of Ninth Five Year Plan. Improvement in the indicators like life expectancy, maternal mortality, gaps between male and female infant and child mortality, female literacy and participation in grassroots level democracy are noticeable positive changes. The Ninth Plan sought to address the issue of high population growth rate by bringing about a shift in focus from reducing infant mortality to reduce high desired fertility and by encouraging contraception to reduce unwanted pregnancies. Integrated reproductive and child health care were to be provided and Area specific strategies for microimplementation of the RCH programme were to be adopted. RCH focuses on the obstetric care aimed to achieve substantial reduction in maternal mortality and morbidity through-early registration of pregnancy, screening of all pregnant women at least thrice in pregnancy for detection of risk factors; appropriate referral and care for at risk person and safe delivery.

The strategy aimed to achieve substantial reduction in maternal morbidity through the Contractual appointment of additional

Auxiliary Nurse Midwifes and Public Health Nurse/Staff Nurse to improve institutional deliveries. Safe delivery component of the RCH Programme was to be strengthened through provision of Kits and the training of Dais. Initiatives to Promote Safe home deliveries in poorly performing states were also envisaged such as screening of all pregnant women to detect and refer high-risk group, Training of Traditional Birth Attendants (TBA) regarding danger signals and timely referral, and the promotion of use of disposable delivery kits to reduce infection. Referral units were identified and strengthened but did not become fully operational due to lack of skilled manpower, adequate infrastructure, equipment and medicines. STI/RTI prevention, detection and management in women are priority areas as parts of essential RCH care at all levels of health care. Fall in routine immunization is a matter of concern. Poor coverage is mainly due to vacancies of staff, poor access, distribution and storage of vaccines, lack of supervision and monitoring, and ongoing campaign mode programmes disrupting routine activities. Role of Panchayati Raj Institutions was envisaged to improve the health services.

Efforts to educate the girl, her parents and the community to delay the marriages of their daughters were to receive focused attention during the Ninth Plan. Effective management of nutritional and health problem in adolescent girls was also proposed. Health care needs of adolescents were addressed under the RCH Programme in coordination with Integrated Child Development Services (ICDS) Scheme in blocks where ICDS Centres exist. The impact of this however has been negligible.

The National Population Policy adopted in 2000 seeks to address the issues related to population in the country and ensure universal access to quality contraceptive services towards attaining two-child norm. It calls for full coverage of registration of births, deaths and marriage and pregnancy and universal access to information/counseling services for fertility regulation. Reduction in Infant Mortality Rate and immunization of children are priority areas identified. It seeks to promote delayed marriage for girls and reduction in Maternal Mortality Rate, and enhance the number of institutional deliveries. It emphasizes the containment of Sexually-Transmitted Diseases (STD).

Food and Nutrition Security

States where the incidence of poverty is maximum, are also the States where the Public Distribution System (PDS) is least developed. Studies have shown that only 15 per cent of the needs of rural poor households are in fact met by the PDS and they are compelled to go to the open market for their needs. This has led to severe nutritional deficiency among the majority of the people, especially among women and girls. Apart from the PDS, the ICDS and the Mid-Day Meal Programmes are the two other schemes of the Central Government that address the issue of food security and seek to reduce household malnutrition.

The National Nutrition Policy adopted in 1993 advocates a comprehensive intersectoral strategy for alleviating the multi-faceted problems of malnutrition and achieving an optimal state of nutrition for all. Closer collaboration between the ICDS and the health functionaries at all levels is being attempted. The current norms provide for distribution to the various anganwadi centers, but only 30 million out of the country's 162 million children are covered and there are no guidelines or strategies suggested to ensure outreach to the most needy.

Education & Training

The thrust areas for educational development in the Ninth Plan include Universalization of elementary education, achievement of full adult literacy, raising the quality of education at all levels, improving learner achievement, upliftment of the educational status of disadvantaged groups including SC/ST/ girls and disabled children, among other issues. Female Literacy rates increased at a faster rate than male literacy rates for the decade reaching a level of 75.85 for males and 54.16 for females. The gap in male and female literacy rates stands at 21.69 per cent for population above 5 years of age. There are still a large number of districts especially in

BIMARU states with female literacy rates below 10%.

The National Literacy Mission Authority played a critical role in the Total Literacy Campaign (TLC) phase to mobilize NGOs, experts and volunteers in large numbers and recorded significant participation of women-over 60 %. For the first time the number of female literates outnumber the illiterates. There are currently 450 Total Literacy Campaigns (TLC) and 250 Post Literacy Campaign (PLC). Continuing Education (CE) projects are being implemented in 68 districts but are yet to gain momentum, with little energy and few creative ideas to sustain people's interest in reading and learning.

The alternative models like Mahila Samakhya, non-formal education, adult education, early childhood education etc. contributed in various ways. Some programmes like District Primary Education Program, Operation Blackboard, Lok Jumbish, Shiksha Karmi, National Open School etc. have considerably improved female literacy. A focus on qualitative aspects has brought about substantive change in the education of girls.

The Mahila Samakhya (MS) is the only women focused programme of the Department of Education, reaching out to more than a lakh women in 10 states through its state societies. Through its strategy of building grassroots women's organizations the MS programme has created a forum and environment for women's education at the community level and has also been influential in raising issues related to the education of girls in a number of areas. Although MS has highlighted the need for a gender focused and holistic approach to women and girls education, it continues to be viewed as marginal in the department's efforts of education despite its successes and long years of existence.

The Sarva Siksha Abhiyan has committed to provide useful and quality elementary education to all children in the 6-14 age group by 2010 and bridge the gender and social category gaps at primary level by 2010. Plans for free education for girls up to college level, including professional courses have not been instituted universally in the Ninth Plan period although some State Governments have made education free for girls at all levels.

Economy, Work and Employment

The increasing growth rate of the economy at 6 per cent per annum1 of the period was accompanied by policy initiatives towards expansion of social security to workers through selffinancing systems; addressing the conditions of workers and elimination of evils of child labour and bonded labour and strengthening of accreditation facilities for vocational training institutes including services sectors and better coordination of vocational training imparted by various departments were attempted.

The Ninth Five Year Plan strategy envisages a growth of 4.5 percent per annum in agriculture sector, and a target of doubling food production and making India hunger-free in 10 years. The concept of food security has been broadened to include accessibility and availability of basic nutritional requirements. The priority to access to food grains for the poor has been emphasized in the plan document, the reality seems rather bleak in that context especially for women.

Women in Agriculture

New initiatives taken for achieving the Ninth Plan objectives include introduction of crop insurance scheme "Rashtriya Krishi Bima Yojana (RKBY)", establishment of Watershed Development Fund (WDF), launching of Technology Mission on Cotton (TMC), launching of Kisan Credit Cards. These have little significance for women as invisible family workers or as labourers.

Focused programmes for women in agriculture have been introduced, and have been quite successful in addressing technology, food security, access to information and resources such as land leases etc., yet these experiences and issues of equity are not adequately reflected in the mainstream policy on agriculture. Programmes for women include:

(i) 'Women in Agriculture' scheme to extend support services such as technology, extension etc.

(ii) Empowerment of Women Farmers which provides micro capital assistance and revolving funds exclusively for women to purchase inputs, land base, undertakes land development activities, risk coverage collective farming and hiring of equipments etc.

(iii) Agricultural Cooperatives, which provide a special protection to women in the form of assured work by organizing cooperative societies for women in agricultural based sectors.

Besides these, specific areas have been identified in 6 other schemes that could provide for spaces for incorporation of women's needs and target them as a beneficiary constituency. Despite these measures and the progressive perspective that they reflect for women's concerns in the agriculture sector, creating access to resources for acquisition of assets and production inputs and access to technologies and inputs, the larger perspective of the agriculture sector seems to remain gender blind.

Poverty Alleviation

The Ninth Five Year Plan envisaged a creation of entitlements (through self-employment and wage-employment schemes, food security and social security) and building up of capabilities through basic minimum services like education, health and housing. The Integrated Rural Development Programme (IRDP) continued as a major self-employment scheme till April 1,1999 and 53.50 million families have been covered at an expenditure of Rs.13,700 crore since the inception. Rural poor families have however remained constant in number at 55 million in the last 20 years despite high growth and high investment in IRDP and wage-giving programmes as investment per family remained at sub-critical levels. Investment at the beginning of Ninth Plan of Rs.16,753 was not much higher in real terms and could not finance viable projects to offer adequate incomes on a sustained basis. The restructured IRDP, Swarnajayanti Gram Swa-Rozgar Yojana (SGSY), aims at self-employment of the rural poor. The Development of Women and Child in Rural Areas (DWCRA) scheme which was a women focused intervention was also merged as part of these initiatives.

IMPACT OF POLICIES, PLANS AND PROGRAMMES

The impact of various developmental policies, plans and programmes put into action during the last few decades have brought forth a perceptible improvement in the socio-economic status of women in the country. The following paragraphs give an account of achievements in the selected areas of demography, vital statistics, health, education, employment, decision-making, political participation, etc.

(i) The Population figures exclude the area under illegal occupation of Pakistan & China

(ii) The 1981 Census was not held in Assam. The figures for 1981 include the inter-polated population of Assam.

(iii) The 1991 Census was not held in J&K. The figures for 1991 include the population of J&K as projected by the Standing Committee of Experts on Population Projections, (October, 1989).

Source: Census of India, 2001, "Provisional Population Totals" & Census of India, 1991.

There has been a slight increase between 1991 and 2001 in the size of the total female population of the country. While the actual increase recorded refers to a very marginal increase of 0.2 per cent, it was 88.6 million in terms of absolute numbers, as against the 77.1 million during 1981 to 1991. The growth rate of female population for 1991-2001 decade was 21.79 per cent, which was 0.86 percentage points higher than that of males and 0.45 percentage points more than the total population.

The Sex Ratio which illustrates the survival scene of women registered a very marginal improvement from 927 in 1991 to 933 in 2001, as shown above. Although the Sex Ratio increased in respect of all ages, it declined in the most crucial age group of 0 to 6 years from 945 in 1991 to 927 in 2001. The very same declining trend got reflected in most of the states, (Annexure-VIII) even in the States like Punjab and Haryana which are economically more progressive states. This clearly points to the fact that economic growth may not necessarily bring about improvement in the status of women. This could be attributed mainly to the discrimination that the girl child faces and the consequential problems of poor health and nutritional status. Adding to these are the problems of female foeticide and female infanticide practised and now increasing in the country.

The Expectation of Life at Birth in respect of females has been rising very steadily, from 40.6 years in 1961 to 65.3 in 2001, by-passing even the male life expectancy and recording an all-time high of an increase of 5.6 years from 59.7 years in 1989-93, as detailed in Table 3. 4.5 Similarly, Mean Age at Marriage for females has also increased from 15.5 years in 1961 to 19.5 years in 1997, as per the details given in Table 4. The Child Marriage Restraint

Act of 1976 which raised the age of marriage for girls from 15 to 18 years has, no doubt, helped prevent the child/ early marriages and the consequent early pregnancies and birth of premature babies. But at the same time, education and greater employment amongst women/ girls has also played a role in raising their age at marriage.

Health and Nutrition

While the Birth Rate has declined by 15.6 percentage points from 41.7 in 1961 to 26.1 per thousand in 2001, the Death Rate has gone down by 14.1 percentage points from 22.8 in 1961 to 8.7 per thousand in 2001 as shown in Tables 5 and 6. The Death Rate of women declined from 15.6 in 1970 to 8.8 in 1998.

Although the Maternal Mortality Rate has declined from 468 in 1980 to 407 in 1998, the same continues to be very high and therefore, is a matter of great concern. This high rate of maternal mortality is attributable to the major causes of bleeding in pregnancy and puerperium, abortion, anaemia and toxemia, as per the details given below. 4.8 As can be seen from above, the highest number of maternal deaths in 1998 was due to haemorrhage which is preventable through better reproductive health care. Abortion was legalised as early as 1972 as a health measure through the Medical Termination of Pregnancy (MTP) Act, 1971. Despite this special sanction, illegal abortions still continue to be performed by unauthorised persons like local quacks and untrained persons under unhygienic and unsafe conditions because of the non-availability of MTP services within the easy reach of most of the rural population. In 1998, abortions accounted for 8.9 per cent of the maternal deaths. Women's morbidity continues to be relatively high due to causes such as Reproductive Tract Infections (RTIs) and Sexually Transmitted Diseases (STDs) related ailments, as well as their higher vulnerability to succumb to malaria and tuberculosis and diseases due to their lower access to health care facilities.

Literacy and Education

Increase in the female literacy rate from 12.95 per cent in 1961 to 54.16 per cent in 2001, reflecting the sound gains in women's education, grew at twice the rate than that for males during the same period. For the first time, the number of absolute female illiterates has come down from 200,068,077 in 1991 to 189,554,886 in 2001. The gap between female and male illiterates and dropouts has started narrowing down. Some states, however, continue to have very large inter-State variations in education. However, there are still 299 districts with lower female literacy levels than the national average. Amongst the States, while Kerala recorded the highest literacy rate of 87.86 per cent for females, Bihar recorded the lowest at 33.57 per cent.

The Gross Enrolment Ratio (GER) of girls at the primary level has also increased from 41.4 in 1960-61 to 85.2 in 1999-2000 representing more than two-fold increase. In just one year between 1998-99 and 1999-2000, GER at the primary level has gone up by 2.3 percentage points, while at the middle level, it could go up only 0.6 percentage points. Detailed information is given at Table 25 of Part B on `Development of Children' of this Report.

The number of women in higher education which includes colleges, universities, Professional colleges of Engineering, Medicine and Technology, increased from 13.60 lakh (33.2%) in 1990-91 to 30.81 lakh (39.9%) in 1999-2000. Except in Courses of Bachelor of Education and Bachelor of Teachers' Training, women in Graduate Courses, Post Graduate Courses and Doctoral Courses have all shown an increase in relative terms.

The drop-out rates which have a direct bearing on the school retention rates, have also shown a definite declining trend both in the case of boys and girls at all levels of school education from 1960-61 to 1999-2000. Although the drop-out rates for girls at primary and middle levels reduced from 70.9 and 85.0 in 1960-61 to 42.3 and 58.0 in 1999-2000, respectively, the rates are still higher than those for boys. Data on the subject is given in Table 26 of Part B on `Development of Children'.

The female work participation rate registered an increasing trend, the increase being from 14.2 per cent in 1971 to 22.3 per cent in 1991 as can be seen from the above Table. But, at the same time, it is much lower than the male work participation rate in both urban and rural areas. There are wide regional variations ranging from as high as 34 per cent to as low as 4 per cent amongst the major states. The data for the 2001 census is not yet available.

However, work participation rate for females is expected to record a rise in 2001. But the NSSO, 55th Round data paints a contradictory picture for 1999-2000, recording a decline in the female participation rate to 20.3. Moreover, total work participation rate also shows a decline. This is highly unlikely.

Table: Women in the Organised Sector (1971-99)

(Figures in lakhs)

Year (1)	Women (2)	Men (3)	Total (4)
1971	19.30 (11.0)	155.6 (89.0)	174.90 (100.0)
1981	27.93 (12.2)	200.52 (87.8)	228.45 (100.0)
1991	37.81 (14.1)	229.52 (85.9)	267.33 (100.0)
1997	43.88 (15.9)	48.29 (17.2)	231.77 (84.1)
1999	232.84 (82.8)	275.65 (100.0)	281.13 (100.0)

Note: Figures in parentheses are percentages.

Source: Director General of Employment and Training, Ministry of Labour, Govt. of India, New Delhi.

Women's share in the organized sector workforce has shown an increasing trend; increasing from 19.30 lakh (11%) in 1971 to 48.29 lakh (17.2%) in 1999. In two years between 1997 and 1999, the rise in percentage points of women in the organised sector has been 1.3. But their share still stands very low when compared to men.

Table: Women in the Public Sector (1971-99)

(Figures in lakhs)

Year (1)	Women (2)	Men (3)	Total (4)
1971	8.6 (8.0)	98.7 (92.0)	107.30 (100.0)
1981	14.99 (9.7)	139.85 (90.3)	154.84 (100.0)
1991	23.47 (12.3)	167.1 (87.7)	190.57 (100.0)
1999	28.11 (14.5)	166.04 (85.5)	194.15 (100.0)

Note: Figures in parentheses are percentages.

Source: Director-General of Employment & Training, Ministry of Labour, Govt. of India, New Delhi.

Women's employment in the public sector has also recorded an increase from 8.6 lakhs (8%) in 1971 to 28.11 lakh (14.5%) in 1999.

While representation of women in the Administration (Government) increased marginally from 11.0 per cent in 1981 to 13.9 per cent in 1996, representation at the decision-making levels through the Premier services in the country viz. Indian Administrative Service (IAS) and Indian Police Service (IPS) accounted for only 5.4 per cent in 1987, as shown in Tables 14 and 15. Although, the same has risen marginally to 7.6 per cent in 2000, yet it stood at a very low ebb, requiring both affirmative action and special interventions to help raise the number of women at various decision-making levels.

Table: Women in Panchayati Raj Institutions (1995-2001)

(Figures in lakhs)

Year (1)	Women (2)	Men (3)	Total (4)
1981	11.9 (11.0)	97.1 (89.0)	109.0 (100.0)
1996	15.0 (13.9)	92.7 (86.1)	107.7 (100.0)

Note: Figures in parentheses are percentages.

Source: Director-General of Employment & Training, Ministry of Labour, Govt. of India, New Delhi.

Table: Women in the Government Sector (1981-96)

(Figures in lakhs)

Year (1)	Women (2)	Men (3)	Total (4)
1995#	3.18 (33.5)	6.30 (66.5)	9.48 (100.0)
2001@	7.25 (26.7)	19.96 (73.3)	27.21 (100.0)

Note: Figures in parentheses are percentages.

Data refers to 9 states-Gujarat, Haryana, Karnataka, Kerala, Madhya Pradesh, Punjab, Rajasthan, Tripura and West Bengal.

@ For whole of India.

Source: Department of Rural Development, GOI, New Delhi.

As the data above speaks, the landmark achievement of both 73rd and 74th Constitutional Amendments in 1993 brought forth a definite impact on the participation of women in the grassroot democracy through the Panchayati Raj Institutions (PRIs) and Local Bodies. In fact, these amendments are expected to achieve effective participation of women in the grass-root democratic institutions and its processes, both as individuals and as representatives of interest groups.

Out of 475 Zilla Parishads in the country, 158 are chaired by women. At the Block Level out of 51,000 members of Block Samitis 17,000 are women.2 In addition nearly one third of the Mayors of the Municipalities are women. In the elections of PRIs held between 1993 and 1997, women have achieved participation even beyond the mandatory requirement of 1/3rd of total seats in States like Karnataka (43.45%), Kerala (36.4%) and West Bengal (35.4%). However, the all India figures for women show a decline from 33.5% in 1995 to 26.7% in 2001.

Table: Representation of Women in Parliament (1952-2001)

Year (1)	**Females** (2)	**Males** (3)	**Total** (4)
1952	37	676	713
1980	52	47	723
1989	721	775	768
1991	63	707	770
1998	59	761	820
1999	67	70	723
2001	750	790	820

Source: 1. Election Commission of India 2. National Informatics Centre, Parliament of India

4.19 In the State Legislative Assemblies, although the number of women has increased from 102 (2.5%) in 1977 to 162 (3.9%) in 1997, the same stands at a very low ebb. Similarly, the number of women in the Parliament has also increased from 37 (5.2%) in 1952 to 70 (8.5%) in 2001, as shown in Table 17, but the same continues to be very low.

Table: Representation of Women in the Central Council of Ministers (1985 &1999)

Year	Women	Men	Total
(1)	(2)	(3)	(4)
1985	4 (10.0)	36 (90.0)	40 (100.0)
1999	8 (11.1)	64 (88.8)	72 (100.0)

Note: Figures in parentheses are percentages.

Source: National Informatics Centre, Parliament of India,

The number of women in the Central Council of Ministers has increased from 4 in 1985 to 8 in 1999 recording a marginal increase of 1.1 per cent.

These trends point to the urgency of addressing these issues in a systematic and expeditious way so that women's concerns gain political prominence and a fairly representative number of women are in position not only at grass-roots level, but also at the state and national levels.

PERSISTING PROBLEMS REQUIRING PRIORITY ATTENTION

The Mid-Term Appraisal (MTA) of the Ninth Five Year Plan (2000) while appraising the progress of the implementation of policies and programmes of the Ninth Five Year Plan (2000) has also surfaced certain Critical Issues and Persisting Problems that were standing as the major obstacles for the advancement/ empowerment of women, including the Girl Child. The same are discussed below:

Declining Sex Ratio

Despite the marginal improvement shown in the over-all sex ratio from 927 in 1991 to 933 in 2001, the sharp decline in the juvenile sex ratio from 945 in 1991 to 927 in 2001 bear the evidence of the incidence of gender discrimination besides reflecting the survival scene of both women and the Girl Child in India.

The adverse sex-ratio and its decline since 1901 can be attributed mainly to higher mortality among females, as compared to males, in all age groups right from childhood through child-bearing ages. Limited access to health care services contributing to high maternal mortality and relative deprivation of the female child from nutrition, health and medical care have also been identified as some of the other contributory factors. Interventions to this effect have already been in action.

Related to the problem of gender bias and the persistent discrimination against the girl child are the harmful practices of female foeticide and female infanticide leading to the unwanted abortions and the present high rates of IMR / MMR. The sample studies sponsored by the Department of Women and Child Development in 1993 confirm that-while the female foeticide is widespread in a most rampant form in the urban areas, female infanticide continues to be prevalent as a localized/community-based phenomenon in the States of Tamil Nadu, Madhya Pradesh, Bihar, Rajasthan, Punjab and Haryana. As per the 2001 Census, only in 73 districts of the country, the sex-ratio is in favour of females. The long-term measure of sensitizing the society to change their mind-set which is negatively disposed towards the girl child-as unwanted, neglected and discriminated both within and outside her home, is also very important.

Inaccessibility to Health and Nutrition

Although, the Infant Mortality Rate (IMR), Child Mortality Rate (CMR) and Maternal Mortality Rate (MMR) have been showing a very steady declining trend during the last decade, yet they still stand very high when compared to many other developing countries. In respect of individual States, 10 major States viz. Andhra Pradesh, Assam, Gujarat, Haryana, Karnataka, Kerala, Madhya Pradesh, Maharashtra, Orissa and Punjab have also shown an increasing trend. This demands careful investigation of the factors responsible for such a situation and effective action to intensify those measures of new-born care and institutional delivery systems. MMR which also stands at a very high rate of 407 maternal deaths per 1,00,000 live births (1998) needs special attention on priority basis through a wide-spread coverage of RCH services.

Mental health continues to be a neglected area, despite it being recognized as a major health concern in the context of the discriminatory practices against women. The present health care delivery system remains ill equipped to tackle these problems specially in rural areas.

The burden of AIDS is experienced disproportionately by women and girls as in their traditional gender roles they are responsible for caring for the sick. This enhances their risk and susceptibility to the disease. The issue on women's control over their bodies also needs to be addressed in that context.

Women's reproductive health continues to be the focus of policy and programmes in the limited context of maternity at the cost of reproductive choices and other health aspects. Given the swelling numbers of women in the older age group as well as the large adolescent age group it is necessary to move to a broader range of services and problems to be served by the health care system.

Women's Access to Health Care Services for treatment continues to be neglected due to their low mobility and the fact that their health needs remain low priorities in the household. The decision to access health care for them seems to be determined by the perception of health, permission or decision for seeking health care, the availability of alternatives and costs involved and the ability to access place. Several studies have indicated inadequacy in the delivery of even primary health services by the Government adversely affecting women's health status. Faith and emphasis in traditional and alternative health systems is also reduced due to which women's access to health care is further adversely affected.

The National Population Policy has set a target free approach, but the State Population Policies do not seem to reflect a similar perspective. Linking up incentives/disincentives with social security measures and socio-economic development plans further reduce women's freedom and choices in these domains. Indiscreet introduction of contraceptives in the name of cost effectiveness, at the cost of women's health reflects an approach of negating the value of women for achievement of family planning goals.

Inaccessibility to Education & Training

Almost half the female population is still illiterate, as the female literacy rate as per 2001 census still stands at 1,89,554,886.

The euphoria of women's high participation in literacy camps of the initial phases of the TLC campaign and significant gains of the TLC may be lost unless the follow-up and CE phase are not undertaken with renewed energy and focus.

Women's education is not given the priority it deserves despite the commitments of the Government in the National Policy on Education and the International Convention of Education For All (EFA), which incorporate the provision of educational opportunities and removal of gender discrimination. The Mahila Samakhya continues to be the only programme that focuses exclusively on women's education. Its strength lies in the approach to address women's education in a responsive framework while creating opportunities for women's empowerment. It is important that the programme is strengthened and its learnings are incorporated in the framework of other initiatives to enhance educational opportunities for women.

Programmes for women and girls' education still remain few. While various innovative education programmes are focusing on the needs of girls to enhance their access to education, there is little effort to engender systems. Incentives are also required to overcome the constraints that women experience in sustaining literacy. Also, the proportion of resources allocated to adult education has decreased to only a 2.5% share of the education budget, compared to 65.7% for elementary education in the Ninth Plan Period. The gap between male (75.85%) and female literacy (54.16%) remains high and regional disparities in female literacy remain stark.

Efforts towards the integration of gender concerns in the framework of key education programmes including the Sarva Siksha Abhiyan, the District Primary Education Programme, Distance education, Operation Blackboard etc. while focusing on girls' participation are far from adequate to correct the gender imbalances; efforts towards integration of gender in curriculum and training of teachers remains inadequate. Even though enrolment among boys continues to be higher than girls, the gap is narrowing. As a result, in 1998-99, 74 per cent of girls and 83 per cent of boys between 6-14 years were attending school. There is much, however, that needs be done to improve the school infrastructure, access and retention of children in schools. For example, even though 94 per cent of India's rural population has a primary school within a walking distance of one kilometer, there are at least 1,00,000 habitations without this kind of physical access. Girl children remain particularly disadvantaged as a result. At the same time, efforts are required to improve the quality of education and improve learning achievements am··ng children.

Invisible Women's Work

Women workers continue to be the most 'invisible', despite their high levels of contribution to the national economy, especially to the informal/unorganized sector. Being predominant in the marginal workers' category, women's contribution in the informal sector is neither recognized nor finds a place in the official records. Impressive performance at macro economic level has not much improved the economic position of women specially women from rural areas. The lack of continuity of women in the employment market with a high rate of withdrawal and late entry in the labour market results in their confinement in lower levels despite their better qualifications in many areas. Post globalization women are also likely to be rendered jobless in traditional sectors in larger numbers. The prevailing social constraints of gender largely relegates women to the inside sphere. Adding to this are the dual responsibilities of women tagged with heavy work responsibilities in agriculture, animal husbandry and other 3 Annual Report, 2000, Department of Secondary Education & Higher Education, M/ HRD, Govt of India. traditional sectors which create a syndrome of gender stereotypes, marginalisation, alienation and deprivation of women in the informal sector.

The rate of increase in women's employment in the organized sector has slowed down, so future opportunities for absorption of women workers will be fewer. The higher numbers of women in the category of wage labour and reducing numbers in the self employed category mark a further marginalisation of women as workers. There has also been an increase in casualisation of the rural women work force.

Programmes for women in agriculture that have been introduced remain marginal and despite creating access to information and resources their influence is negligible in the macro policy. Role of women remains unrecognized to the sector and its productivity. Labour and social legislation for safety net benefits for women workers like maternity benefit, child care support, safeguards from sexual harassment, etc. continue to exclude women in the informal sector.

Degradation of Natural Resources

Women have traditionally played an important role in managing and protecting natural resources and their access to natural resources like land, forest and water, especially for tribal and other disadvantaged groups of women are significant factors. With increasing commercialization and corporatisation of management of these resources, however, women are being marginalized from their traditional roles and access, which very clearly has an adverse impact on the sustainability of these resources themselves, apart from increasing women's vulnerability in the struggle for survival. The increasing pressure for access to these resources also has an adverse impact on women in the family, with the incidence of violence increasing.

Initiatives for the development of natural resources must not be at the cost of livelihoods and means of survival of large number of indigenous populations and communities dependant on these resources. Women are major contributors in these economies and bear the brunt of these developments. They are also increasingly the victims of violence in instances of a conflict of interest between the state and the users. Current policy trends of joint management of resources have implied the intrusion of government departments in the traditional management systems. Women's roles are reduced to nominal in the management of these resources in these new systems. The processes of planning have thus currently become the means of women's alienation from their resources. Women's roles and community needs for fuel, fodder, water and other natural resources need to be strengthened with equity as the guiding principle.

Land Rights for Women

Very strong gender inequalities exist in various inheritance laws, especially in land reform laws passed by various states. In a number of North Western States, including Haryana, Punjab, Jammu & Kashmir, Himachal Pradesh, Delhi and Uttar Pradesh, the land inheritance devolves on male lineal descendants and consequently, widows and daughters inherit only in the absence of male heirs. In Uttar Pradesh section 171 of the Zamindari Abolition Act bars any female child from inheritance of agricultural land. In some States women cannot even buy agricultural land because of the absence of land records to prove their rights as Agriculturists

Ineffective Food Distribution

Despite the strides in agricultural production and food surplus and State intervention through Special Public Distribution System (SPDS) and various poverty alleviation programs, consumption levels are abysmally low due to poor distribution policies and low purchasing power of the poor. This has led to severe nutritional deficiency among the majority of the people, especially among women and girls. States where the incidence of poverty is maximum are also the states where the PDS system is least developed. Studies have shown that only 15 per cent of the needs of rural poor households are in fact met by the PDS, and they are compelled to go to the open market for their needs. This has lead to severe nutritional deficiency among the majority of the people, especially among women and girls. Apart from the PDS scheme the ICDS and the mid day meal programmes are the 2 other schemes of the Central Government that address the issue of food security and seek to reduce household malnutrition. PDS schemes are limited in their impact due to operational mal-efficiencies. Large numbers of women continue to suffer from mal-nutrition as the distribution systems are not in sync with the regional requirements, and poverty ridden areas continue to be ill-served by the PDS system.

Gender and Poverty

Several micro-studies have indicated that adverse consequences of SAP are disproportionately borne by women. Increased mechanization leading to displacement of female unskilled workers, increased movement of male workers into traditionally women dominated areas, increase in female headed households due to migration of males are some of the trends established, indicating a growing incidence of the feminization of poverty. Even within households which may otherwise fall above the Below Poverty Line (BPL) the situation of the women is known to be at levels below poverty. Female headed households are among the most impoverished. The incidence of landlessness and consequent impoverishment is highest among women headed households and is reported to be rising. The incidence of poverty is also known to be maximum in the states of Bihar, Orissa and Uttar Pradesh, which contribute more than a third of the country's poor and are known to be areas of male out-migration. These are also the states where the Public Distribution System (PDS) system is the weakest.

Despite the reported decrease in poverty, intra household disparities persist in the experience of poverty based on gender. Employment rates for women in the formal sector have reduced, and opportunities for self-employment have also diminished. Women continue to be the greater victims of layoffs and displacement, as men take over tasks traditionally considered women's tasks. Decreasing earning opportunities and the lowering Work Participation Rates and incomes having recorded no significant changes in relative and absolute terms in relation to the inflation rates, the reality for women is rather bleak. Studies reveal that only 15-17 per cent participants in the Poverty Alleviation programmes for wage employment through the Jawahar Rozgar Yojana (JRY) Programme have been women, due to the lack of provision of services and support for child care, and no flexible hours.

The burden of poverty upon women has been increasing, as they are being more vulnerable to the extremes of poverty and its consequences as they push them to abject poverty. For poor households, women's capacity to work, her health, knowledge and skill endowments are often the only resources to fall back upon for survival. In other words, poorer the family, more the dependency upon women's earnings. Women are thus critical to the processes of moving their families out of poverty. Therefore, they require special attention as extreme poverty by definition implies low absorptive capacity for development programmes.

Media and Women

Current media trends indicate a strengthening of stereotypes, and reinforcement of traditional roles; the portrayal of women continues to be as objectification rather than rational human beings. Portrayal of violence and using women in negative sense create a mindset that only perpetuates discrimination and the exploitation of women through violence of various kinds.

Legislative Loopholes

Violence against women in the home is the most sinister and is the least likely to be reported or acknowledged. A review of the legislative framework and the law enforcement agencies of the country reveals an inherent gender bias. The law itself reflects assumptions of patriarchy, and girls continue to be denied the right to property in the inheritance of agricultural property, as also highlighted in the MTA report. In this direction, some progress was already made by the National Commission for Women and later by the Task Force on Women to review a majority of laws related to women as already mentioned. This process should be completed during the 10th Plan.

Inadequate Mechanisms

The infrastructure needs of women are related to their various roles. Women's access to economic infrastructure such as capital and credit has increased over the last decade with the focus on micro-finance through the alternate institutions and to a lesser degree through mainstream financial institutions and commercial banks. Their economic viability however remains at risk with few channels of support for marketing and technological support. Apart from the burden of arduous domestic chores, women's time is spent to a great extent on these tasks, denying them other opportunities and time for rest, reducing their role to low levels of efficiency. Recognition of women's specific needs in the provision of social and economic sectors is still hardly recognized. Despite the recent initiatives to extend credit and micro finance to them, the follow-up requisites of support for raw material sourcing, marketing, etc are still to be addressed. Support to reduce the burden of drudgery of domestic chores and to create alternative opportunities for addressing their fuel and energy requirements, as well as child care remain low developmental priorities. There is an increasing number of women workers attached with various agencies and needing suitable accommodation for single / married women. Location and construction of hostels to cater to their needs would reduce the risks and apprehensions of working women. The problem of shelter for homeless women below the poverty levels needs urgent attention especially for the 37 per cent female heads of household and women in specially vulnerable circumstances.

Lack of Dissemination of Information

The development of technologies that are women-friendly are few and far between and the investment in these activities remains marginal to the realm of Science and Technology. Women's access also remains constrained by low mobility and access to information and education attainment apart from the inherent gender based impediments. Efforts should also be made to assess the impact of new technologies on women, and to counteract the negative impacts through technological innovations or enhancement of women's skills.

Women's Component Plan

Reports received hitherto from the various departments by the Planning Commission in response to its directions have indicated that the Women's Component Plan (WCP) Planning process is viewed as an extension of the Beneficiary oriented programmes of the PMO. Departments have in most cases included figures of women specific schemes as the WCP inputs, while some departments have declared that their schemes are gender neutral. This reveals that the concept of Women's Component Plan needs to be clarified and strengthened and streamlined for greater efficacy.

Limited Representation in the Decision-making

Adding to the serious problems listed above, lack of education and training, information and awareness generation and low rates of literacy aggravate the situation of deprivation of women, thereby excluding them not merely from political, social and economic processes, but also from decision-making. As per 55th Round of NSSO, 1999-2000, women's work participation is as low as 20.3% as their contribution in the informal sector is neither recognized nor finds a place in the official records. Further, while their representation in the organized sector is only 17.2 % (1999), they are 14.5% (1999) in the public sector; 13.9% (1996) in the Government; and 7.6% (2000) in administrative decision-making. No doubt, they represent 26.7% (2007) in Panchayats against the 33-1/3 per cent reservation for women. When more and more women are positioned at various levels of decision-making, it is bound to have a definite impact on public policy in favour of women and thus, women's issues will get transformed into societal issues.

Besides the participation of women in local self-governance in the past decade, an equally significant factor is the extent to which the systems and institutions are geared to respond to the needs and issues that women are prioritizing in the governance agenda. While women have gained access to the Panchayats and Local bodies, the resistance from men to their leadership continues in various forms. Women in these positions have the disadvantage of a shifting constituency which implies that reflection may only be possible on a general seat or after a rotation of a few years.

Representation of women in the Legislatures and Parliament is still very low, ranging between 4-8%. The number of women Members of Parliament has increased from 37 in 1952 to 70 in 2001. Parties in the country also field very few women candidates in the general seats. Very few women are office bearers or occupy key portfolios in the major political formations of the country. There is also resistance across party lines to the proposal to provide for reservation for women in the Parliament and state legislatures. Despite the gains in the political arena therefore there are still many frontiers that challenge women on the way to political empowerment.

Violence against Women

The increasing violence against women is yet another manifestation of their low and unequal status and continues to be a big threat to their development. Violence against women and the girl-child, both domestic and at work-place, has been showing an alarming trend especially during the recent past.

Incidence of atrocities against women ranges from female infanticide, foeticide, molestation, sexual assault, sexual-harassment at the workplace to rape, caste-based violence, trafficking, forced marriage, domestic violence, dowry related murders, enforced sterilization and custodial violence. Physical, mental and psychological violence against adolescent girls is a growing phenomenon.

The National Crime Record Bureau (NCRB), New Delhi in 1999 recorded an increase in the total number of cases of crimes related to women like kidnapping, abduction, dowry death, torture and molestation from 1,15,723 in 1996 to 1,35,771 in 1999. Out of the total cases related to women and registered under IPC in 1996, rape accounted for 14,846 (12.8%), dowry deaths 5,513 (4.81%) and cases of torture 35,246 (30.5%). In 1999, the corresponding figures rose to 15,468 (11.4%), 6,699 (4.9%) and 43,823 (32.3%), respectively. Most rape victims are in the age group of 10-16 year and a significant number are under 10 years of age. The media plays a role in perpetuating the gender-stereo types, undermining the contribution of women to society.

As per NCRB 1999 data, there was an increase of 8.4 per cent in the total number of crimes committed against women between 1997 and 1999. While the total number of cases registered under IPC stood at 1.36 lakh, torture claims the highest share of 32.3 per cent; followed by molestation (23.8%); kidnapping and abduction (11.8%); rape (11.4%); sexual harassment (6.5%); and dowry death (4.9%). Amongst the States, while Madhya Pradesh reports the highest incidence of 12.6% of the total crimes, Uttar Pradesh (12.5%) and Maharashtra (10.0%) followed suit. Delhi which shares 1.3% of the country's total population, accounts for 1.8% of the total crime, and reports the fourth highest crime rate in the country with 17.9 (number of crimes per one lakh population), while the all India crime rate stands at 13.8.

APPROACH TO THE TENTH PLAN (2002-07)

It is the empowerment strategy that has emerged as the most challenging task during the Nineties. It is, therefore, necessary to ensure that women are empowered socially, economically and politically. If women are to be empowered socially, it is necessary to make everyone of them literate, reach them information and generate awareness, equip them with legal literacy and thus conscientise them to realize their own potential. If women are to be economically empowered, it is necessary to equip them with vocational skills; provide employment and income-generation, extend free channels of micro-credit, provide management/ entrepreneurial skills, social security and thus allow greater visibility. If women are to be politically empowered, the immediate need is to resort to different forms of affirmative discrimination so that women in proportionate numbers reach critical places to ensure that their voices are heard.

The Ninth Plan's commitment to empower women through the adoption of a National Policy has come true when the Government adopted a National Policy on Empowerment of Women in April 2001. The country has now got a mandate to translate the Policy into Action. Therefore, nothing could provide a better approach in the Tenth Plan other than the National Policy itself.

The objectives of the National Policy for Empowerment of Women include: (i) creating an environment through positive economic and social policies for full development of women to enable them to realize their full potential; (ii) the de-jure and de-facto enjoyment of all human rights and fundamental freedom by women on equal basis with men in all spheres-political, economic, social, cultural and civil; (iii) equal access to participation and decision making of women in social, political and economic life of the nation; (iv) equal access to women to health care, quality education at all levels, career and vocational guidance, employment, equal remuneration, occupational health land safety, social security and public office etc.; (v) strengthening legal systems aimed at elimination of all forms of discrimination against women; (vi) changing societal attitudes and community practices by active participation and involvement of both men and women, (vii) mainstreaming a gender perspective in the development process; (viii) elimination of discrimination and all forms of violence against women and the girl child; and (ix) building and strengthening partnerships with civil society, particularly women's organizations.

For achievement of the above objectives, the National Policy lays down certain policy prescriptions. They include-i) towards mainstreaming gender perspectives in the development process, policies, programmes and systems will be established to ensure mainstreaming of women's perspectives in all developmental process. Wherever, there are gaps in policies and programmes, women-specific interventions would be undertaken to bridge them; ii) all measures will be taken to guarantee women equal access to and full participation in decision-making bodies at every level, including the legislative, executive, judicial, corporate, statutory bodies, as also the advisory Commissions, Committees, Boards, Trusts etc. Affirmative action such as reservations/quotas, including in higher legislative bodies, will be considered whenever necessary on a time-bound basis. Women-friendly personnel policies will also be drawn up to encourage women to participate effectively in the developmental process; and iii) legal-judicial system will be made more responsive and gender sensitive to women's needs, especially in the cases of domestic violence and personal assault. To this end, new laws will be enacted and existing laws reviewed to ensure that justice is quick and the punishment meted out to the culprits is to commensurate with the severity of the office. Also, gender discrimination in personal laws relating to marriage, divorce, maintenance and guardianship and in laws relating to ownership of property and inheritance shall be eliminated with full participation of all stakeholders including community and religious leaders. A copy of the National Policy for Empowerment of Women is appended at Annexure-XI.

Economic Empowerment of Women

The suggested policy measures for economic empowerment of women in the Tenth Plan will be:

a) Macro economic policies and poverty eradication programmes will specifically address the needs and problems of women who comprise the majority of the population below the poverty line and are very often in situations of extreme poverty.

b) New micro-credit institutions shall be established and existing institutions strengthened to enhance women's access to credit for consumption and production.

c) Women's contribution in the informal sectors (including home based workers) will be recognized by way of reinterpretation and redefinition of conventional concepts of work wherever necessary and this will include Census records, preparation of satellite and national accounts etc.

d) Strategies will be designed to empower women to meet the negative social and economic impacts, which may flow from the process of globalization and at the same time enhance their capacity so that they can utilize the opportunities opened by this process.

e) In view of the critical role of women in the agriculture and allied sectors, as producers, concentrated efforts will be made to ensure that benefits of training, extension and various programmes will reach them in proportion to their numbers. The programmes for training women in soil conservation, social forestry, dairy development and other occupations allied to agriculture like horticulture, livestock including small animal husbandry, poultry, fisheries etc. will be expanded to benefit women workers in the agriculture sector.

f) The important role played by women in electronics, information technology and food processing and agro industry and textiles has been crucial to the development of these sectors. They would be given comprehensive support in terms of labour legislation, social security and other support services to participate in various industrial sectors.

Social Empowerment of Women

For social empowerment of women, Policy prescribes the following measures as the approach in the Tenth Plan.

a) Equal access to education for women and girls will be ensured and special measures will be taken to eliminate discrimination, universalize education, eradicate illiteracy, create a gender-sensitive educational system, increase enrolment and retention rates of girls and improve the quality of education to facilitate life-long learning as well as development of occupation/vocation/technical skills by women. Reducing the gender gap in secondary and higher education would be a focus area. Sectoral time targets in existing policies will be achieved, with a special focus on girls and women, particularly those belonging to weaker sections including the Scheduled Castes/Scheduled Tribes/Other Backward Classes/Minorities. Gender sensitive curricula would be developed at all levels of educational system in order to address sex stereotyping as one of the causes of gender discrimination.

b) A holistic approach to women's health which includes both nutrition and health services will be adopted and special attention will be given to the needs of women at all stages of the life cycle. Measures will be adopted that take into account the reproductive rights of women to enable them to exercise informed choices, their vulnerability to sexual and health problems together with endemic, infectious and communicable diseases such as malaria, TB, and water borne diseases as well as hypertension and cardio-pulmonary diseases. The social, developmental and health consequences of HIV/AIDS and other sexually transmitted diseases will be tackled from a gender perspective.

c) Men and women will have access to safe, effective and affordable methods of family planning of their choice. The child marriages shall be eliminated by 2010 by measures like compulsory registration of marriage, spread of education and programmes like BSY.

d) Focused attention would be paid to meeting the nutritional needs of women at all stages of the life cycle, particularly of the adolescent girls and pregnant and lactating mothers.

e) All forms of discrimination against the girl child and violation of her rights shall be eliminated by undertaking strong measures both preventive and punitive within and outside the family. These would relate specifically to strict enforcement of laws against prenatal sex selection and the practices of female foeticide, female infanticide, child marriage, child abuse and child prostitution etc. There will be special emphasis on the needs of the girl child and earmarking of substantial investments in the areas relating to food and nutrition, health and education, and in vocational education.

f) Special attention will be given to the needs of women in the provision of safe drinking water, sewage disposal, toilet facilities and sanitation within accessible reach of households, especially in rural areas and urban slums.

g) Special attention will be given for providing adequate and safe housing and accommodation for women including single women, heads of households, working women, students, apprentices and trainees. Women's perspectives will be included in housing policies, planning of housing colonies and provision of shelter both in rural and urban areas.

h) Measures will be undertaken to provide women in difficult circumstances such as destitute, disabled and old women, women heading households, women affected by natural calamities, those displaced from employment, migrants, deserted women and women who are victims of marital violence and prostitutes etc.

Approach to the Tenth Plan should be governed by the policy prescriptions of the National Policy for Empowerment of Women. While the Policy has given a vision for the future, the Plan can facilitate realization of this vision by converging the approach and strategy of all the related sectors, fixing priorities, setting measurable goals and also allocating resources for the achievement of those goals within a time frame of a five year perspective. The Plan can also prescribe an implementation strategy and a monitoring mechanism for the realization of those goals.

The guidelines for the operational strategy, as prescribed in the National Policy, says,

"All the Central and State Ministries will draw up time bound Action Plans for translating the Policy into a set of concrete actions, through a participatory process of consultation with Centre/State

Departments of Women and Child Development and National / State Commissions for Women. The Plans will specifically including the following:

- Measurable goals to be achieved by 2010.
- Identification and commitment of resources.
- Responsibilities for implementation of action points.
- Structures and mechanisms to ensure efficient monitoring, review and gender impact assessment of action points and policies.
- Introduction of a gender perspective in the budgeting process".

Tenth Plan should be able to offer the opportunity for adopting this operational strategy in implementing the National Policy for Empowerment of Women. Preparation of an Action Plan giving the road map for the next five years is a must. It can fix certain measurable goals which can be achieved by he end of the Plan. It can allocate resources and also prescribe an institutional mechanism for the achievement of these goals. It can initiate the process of the development of Gender Development Indices (GDI) and Gender Auditing and Evaluation. It can strengthen the Women's Component Plan and further carry it forward by introducing a gender perspective in the entire budgetary process which will include both the plan and the non-plan as also the flow of institutional finance for the development of women.

RECOMMENDATIONS FOR THE EMPOWERMENT OF WOMEN

Keeping the suggested Approach in view, the Steering Committee made the following recommendations to initiate action during the Tenth Plan period (2002-07):

General

Challenge in the New Millennium

The global setting of the Tenth Five Year Plan is completely different from the earlier Plans. It is characterized by new challenges of 'market driven forces' on the one side, and expectations of the people-women and men-fast getting sensitized to their rights and entitlements, on the other. This new scenario calls for an approach based on recognition of 'people's entitlements' and the responsibilities of the State to facilitate and provide the conditions for achieving these entitlements.

Approach to Development

Limitations of earlier approaches to development that relied on 'trickle down effects' are well known. 'Access' to benefits of development was conditioned by the prevailing social environment of discrimination, which limited the outreach of the programmes. The everincreasing population, the burden of 'diseases of poverty', limited supply of services, and even more pathetic absence of 'effective' demand, further smothered the advantages of relatively 'meagre' investments in the social sectors. The challenge, more than ever before, is to design strategic investments whose outcome will sustainably enhance social gains in terms of good health, education and capabilities and usher in social justice and equity in distribution, in effect holistically bringing about empowerment of women in the entirety of its connotation.

Social Development and Economic Progress

The inevitable link between social and economic development has emerged as an important factor to be reckoned. The Annual Economic Survey 2000-2001 emphasizes the economic gains of investment on social sectors, particularly on women: "From the efficiency point of view, what is important is the social rate of return of investment in women, and in many cases, this can be greater than the corresponding rate for men".

Decline in Development Expenditure

The Economic Survey highlights that the total central plan outlay on social sector (education, health, family welfare, women and child development and social justice and empowerment) and rural development as percentage of total plan expenditure has declined from 27.13% in 1997-98 to 26.43% in 2000-01. Likewise, the percentage share of GDP on these sectors at current market prices has also declined from 1.21% to 1.08% during the same period. Further, actual plan expenditure has shown a consistent downward trend as compared to the budget and revised estimates.

This trend at a time when investment in development is very critical is a serious cause for worry.

It is therefore urgent to sharpen the approach in the Tenth Plan to focus on strategies to optimize the very scarce public resources to increase gains for larger numbers of people and remove inequities. Government resources have to be supplemented from the corporate sectors as well as the community to reach the aspired goals of social development.

Correction of Regional Imbalances

Regional disparities continue to prevail in the country, despite special efforts in the national planning process to bring up backward regions with special economic incentives. The process of liberalization has exacerbated existing imbalances and deepened the schisms since investments under the liberalized regime tend to flow in the direction of regions and States, which have a head start in infrastructure development.

The flagging economic situation of the less developed States has also slowed down the process of their social development further jeopardizing human resource development in those regions. Intra-state differences are equally marked creating pockets of prosperity amidst poverty and deprivation. It is urgent to evolve a new set of sustainable strategies to eliminate the regional imbalances in social and economic development.

Gender Equity

The planning process for the development of women has evolved through 'welfare' to 'development' to 'empowerment' to 'participation'. Despite the dynamism of the approach, the constitutional and legal provisions for affirmative action, the institutional build up and attendant step up in investments, gender discrimination continues to be a daunting challenge.

Significant gains have, however, been made in the life expectancy of women, literacy and representation in the local self-governing institutions. An active and grassroots level leadership is emerging from among women. If properly harnessed this can be a very effective and catalytic agent for transforming the social conditions of women in the country.

National Policy on Empowerment of Women

The National Policy for Empowerment of Women which was announced by the Government in April 2001 has outlined the approach to the whole gamut of issues for the empowerment of women and laid down a number of policy prescriptions for the national, state and local governments. Therefore, the Tenth Plan should essentially be in the nature of an Action Plan for the implementation of the National Policy, as given below:

Social Empowerment

Demographic Imbalances

Although the Census 2001 has registered a marginal improvement in the overall sex ratio in the country, the juvenile sex ratio (age group 0-6) has sharply declined from 945 per 1000 male in 1991 to 927 in 2001. It has declined in all the States and Union Territories except Kerala, Tripura, Mizoram and Sikkim. The decline has been very sharp even in the prosperous States of Punjab, Haryana, Maharastra and Gujarat. A massive awareness campaign involving the community, religious leaders and opinion-makers at all levels is necessary to counter this trend along with effective policies and programmes in favour of the Girl Child.

Gender Asymmetry in Population

A strange gender asymmetry in population pyramid is taking place, with 'males outnumbering females' and 'females outnumbering males' at the lower and upper end of the pyramid respectively, while the middle is swelling with numbers. This would create new demands for intervention at each level-protection and care of the girl child, social security for the aged, and training, capacity building and employment of more and more women in the working age group.

Rights of the Girl Child

Measures undertaken in the Ninth Plan do not seem to be having the desired impact on the condition of the girl child who is facing all round discrimination within the family and outside. The Pre Natal Diagnostic (Regulation and Prevention of Misuse) Act 1994 has completely failed to prevent female foeticide. Balika

Samriddhi Yojana (BSY) also could not enhance the value of girl child in society. Implementation of BSY has been tardy as is reflected in huge unspent balances with the State Governments and a complete mismatch between the birth of girl child and disbursement of incentives under the scheme. A completely new strategy based on a holistic approach of awareness, incentives, education, nutrition and enforcement need to be worked out to protect the rights of the girl child.

Women's Health and Nutrition

The complex socio-cultural determinants of women's health have cumulative effects over a lifetime. Discriminatory childcare, under-nutrition and micronutrient deficiency in early adolescence is compounded by early child bearing and consequential serious pregnancy-related complexities. This is reflected in very high MMR (407 per 100,000 live births), IMR (70 per 1000 live births) and underweight babies (47%). Therefore, interventions for women's health and nutrition are extremely crucial not only for the health and the well being of the women but of the nation as a whole. National Socio-Economic Goals of NPP 2000 aims, inter alia, to bring down MMR to 100 and IMR to 30 by 2010. These goals should be broken into certain achievable targets upto the year 2007 and measured by national level surveys.

Women should have access to comprehensive, affordable and quality 'health care' which should go beyond the 'reproductive health' to take into account their vulnerability to various endemic, infectious and communicable diseases. The social and health consequences of HIV/AIDS and sexually transmitted diseases also need to be tackled from a gender perspective.

Education and Training

Although the gender disparity in the level of literacy both in urban and rural areas continues, the urge for women's literacy has taken the shape of a movement through out the length and breadth of the country. For the first time, the number of absolute female illiterates has come down, rate of growth of female literacy has out-paced that of male and the gap between female and male illiterates and dropouts is narrowing down.

The Mission of Sarva Siksha Abhiyan should also be broken into measurable goals to be achieved by the end of Tenth Plan in 2007. Tenth Plan should also further focus on reducing the gender gap in secondary and higher education and on the special category groups including SC/STs, OBCs and Minorities.

The vocationalisation of secondary education and vocational training for women is another priority area, which would require greater attention during the Tenth Plan. The existing network of regional vocational training centres should be extended to all the States and the women IITs with residential facilities be opened in all districts and sub-districts. More and more women should be trained on the emerging areas of technical education such as bio-technology, bio-engineering, food processing, electronics and computer systems and applications, fabric designing, communications, media etc. which have high employment potential.

Women and Environment

Departmentalisation of forest management and commercialisation of forest extraction directly impinge on the interests of tribal and other women living in the vicinity of forest areas who depend on non-timber minor forest produce for their livelihood. The complementarities of relationship between the women and the forest can be strengthened and institutionalised through the proper implementation of the mechanism of Joint Forest Management. There are instructions that 50 per cent of the members of the JFM should be women and that the 50 per cent of women members should be present for holding the General Body meeting. There are reports that these instructions are not being followed in many States.

There is also a need for change in the silvi cultural practices in the forests so that trees and plants which generate a lot of fodder, fruits, nuts, twigs and branches are planted in place of timber and other conventional species. This will enable the local community driven by the women's groups to take greater role and interest in the management and conservation of the forests.

Women are the most interested group for consumption of domestic fuel and therefore their involvement for the spread of non-conventional energy sources like bio-gas, non-smoke chullahs etc. are of critical importance for success of this programme. Air pollution arising out of conventional cooking system affects the health and the respiratory system of the women. The existing programme of smokeless chullahs and other non-conventional energy resources should be taken up on a massive scale for the benefit of women.

Drinking Water and Sanitation

This is an area of critical concern for the public health. Although 85 per cent of the villages have been covered under safe drinking water supply, the actual coverage of the hamlets and households have been much less particularly in the hilly, tribal, drought prone and desert areas where women have to travel a long distance for fetching the drinking water. The priority concern for the Tenth Plan should be to ensure that every woman could access safe drinking water in the neighbourhood.

More than 70 per cent of the population in India are not covered by toilet and sanitation facilities. The women, particularly living in the urban slums, are the worst sufferers since their privacy is disturbed severely. The low cost sanitation scheme for the liberation of the scavengers had unfortunately a very tardy performance. Even the meagre allocation of the Plan resources are not being fully utilised by the State Governments and the demeaning practice of manual scavenging of night soil by the female scavengers is still continuing in many urban areas. The Tenth Plan should have a fresh look into the entire issue of urban sanitation in the country which badly affects the interests of the women.

Housing and Shelter

Although the women are the house-keepers their perspectives are not generally considered in the planning of houses and housing colonies and provision of shelters in both urban and rural areas. The gender bias in planning of human settlements should be removed by necessary amendments in the building bye-laws and the rules and regulations of the town planning. Special attention should be given for providing adequate and safe housing and accommodation for women including single women, heads of households, working women, students, apprentices and trainees.

Women and Media

A carefully planned mass media strategy is of critical importance for women's empowerment. Men and women in decision making position-in family, community, workplaces and society at large-can be gender sensitized through media intervention. The issues of women's rights, health and education, access to resources, men's sharing of domestic responsibility, girl child's right to be born, survive, develop and many other related issues can be packaged in interesting, viewer friendly programmes for assimilation and absorption in social psyche.

The Tenth Plan must consciously address to the need for a well-planned media strategy not only for bringing a massive awareness and education on the gender issues but also preventing a derogatory and biased portrayal of women in the media. Such a Plan would not only cut across issues but also across agencies, Ministries and Departments. The Plan should also provide adequate resources for implementation of such a comprehensive and holistic media strategy for social change.

ECONOMIC EMPOWERMENT OF WOMEN

Employment and Work

Census 1991 had registered that only 22.3% of adult female population of India are workers, which may be a gross under statement since much of the work that women do, other than in the domestic and care sector, is not recorded in the work participation format of the Census. This format was revised for the Census 2001, which is expected to give a more realistic assessment of women's work. A pilot Time Use Survey conducted by the Central Statistical Organisation came out with the startling revelation that 51% of the work of women which qualify for inclusion in GDP are not recognized and remain unpaid.

Census 1991 further recorded that 95.8% of the women workers in India are employed in the unorganized sector where there are no legislative safeguards even to claim either minimum or equal wages, leave aside the other benefits that the women in the organised sector enjoy. The Report of the National Commission of Self Employed Women Workers (1988) gave a comprehensive account of the problem of women workers in the informal sector and recommended an intervention strategy which is largely valid even today.

Access to Resources

Traditionally women have been discriminated in her access to the productive resources. She has been denied coparcenary rights over the ancestral property. She has been denied ownership of land, cattle, trees, harvest and shelter. She has been discriminated in accessing credit and marketing facilities for her economic activities. Major interventions at the macro economic and social policy levels are required to eliminate these age-old discriminations against women. While on the one hand there is there is the need to recognize women's economic activities in the domestic sector which largely go unpaid, on the other hand all the shackles should be removed for women's access to the productive resources so that she can be self-reliant and enjoy all the benefits of development. During the Tenth Plan various intervention strategy shall be required to improve the access of women to productive resources.

Women in Agriculture

The overwhelming majority of female workforce in the country are employed in the agricultural sector. Therefore concerted efforts should be made to ensure that the benefits of training, extension and various programmes reach women in proportion to their numbers. Programmes for training women in soil conservation, social forestry, and other occupations allied to agriculture, horticulture, livestock including small husbandry, poultry, fishery, etc. should be expanded to benefit women workers in this sector.

Women in Industry

The important role played by women in electronics, technology, food processing, agro industry and textiles has been crucial to the development of these sectors. They should be given comprehensive support in terms of labour legislation, social security and other support services to participate in various industrial sectors.

Women at present cannot work in night-shift factories even if they wish to. Suitable measures should be taken to enable women to work in night-shift in factories. This should be combined with support services for security, transportation etc.

Equal Wages for Women

Although the twin legislations of the Minimum Wages Act and Equal Remuneration Act have granted equal means of livelihood and equal pay for equal work to the women, these rights are violated with impunity particularly in the informal sector. Administrative infrastructure of the Labour Department is not conducive to the enforcement of the provisions of the Act through the functionaries of the Department. Therefore, a new approach for involving women's groups and other civil society organizations for facilitating the enforcement of the laws is called for.

Women and Poverty

Women comprise nearly 70 per cent of the population below the Poverty Line. Many women like destitute, disabled and female-headed households face extreme situations of poverty. Although 40 per cent benefits of Swaran Jayanti Gramin Rozgar Yojana (SJGRY) and 30 per cent under Swaran Jayanti Shahari Rozgar Yojana (SJSRY) have been earmarked for women, various studies have shown that the actual benefits have not flown to them in the same proportion. It has been experienced that these programmes have a greater chance of success in a group approach rather than individual beneficiary approach and therefore the women's self help groups should be fully mobilised at the block level and the programmes should be converged with the Block Level Action Plan of Integrated Women's Empowerment Programmes (IWEP).

Women and Micro-Credit

In order to enhance women's access to credit for consumption and production the micro credit institutions in the country should be further strengthened and the actual flow of fund should be substantially enhanced so that self-employed groups of women have access to adequate credit for the income generating activities.

Women and Globalization

With the removal of all quantitative restrictions on import of various products the selfemployed women's groups, mainly in the informal sector, have started facing competition of low price imported consumer goods which are invading the market. This has the imminent danger of throwing out a large number of women from their self employment. At the same time the process of globalization has opened up opportunities for exporting the products to new markets all over the globe. Unfortunately the country has not fully geared itself to face the challenges of the globalization. It is necessary to identify the areas where skill and quality upgradation is required to make the informal women's groups more competitive. The training, infrastructure and credit requirement of all such activities should be fully arranged by the Government. The scope of the existing Women's Employment Programme (WEP) and Support for Training and Employment for Women (STEP) should be restructured and the allocation of resources under these two programmes substantially stepped up to meet the new requirement.

Science and Technology

A number of women-specific technologies have been developed by the various research institutes to reduce the drudgery of women in their domestic and farm works. There is a need for dissemination of these technologies through the collaborative efforts of the research institutes, manufacturers and the women's groups. Research should be more focused for development of new technologies which would have greater chances of acceptability by the women.

Although more and more women students are taking up higher education in the fields of science and technology there is still a large gender gap in this area. Liberal scholarships and other incentives should be given to the girl students to pursue higher studies on scientific research and technology.

Women's Support Services

Department of Women and Child Development is implementing a number of schemes to provide social support services to the women. A number of State Governments have also initiated innovative schemes on support services which are duplicating the efforts of the Central Government. While on the one hand there is a need for merger and convergence of similar schemes and restructuring of many schemes according to the changing situations there is also pressing requirement of professionalisation of some of the services like Family Counselling Centres, Crèches, and Short Stay Homes etc.

Similarly there are new areas of support services which require the attention of Government. The long awaited scheme on Women in Difficult Circumstances which is expected to be launched during 2001-02, should be expanded to cover various types of women in distress like widows in religious places, prostitutes, migrant women, women affected by natural calamities, disabled women, women ex-prisoners, mentally retarded and disordered women, women in conflict situations etc.

Women and Social Security

Similarly there is a dire need for introducing social security system for women in the unorganised sector which employ maximum number of women but do not provide them any protection or safety network.

The Personal Accident and Social Security Insurance Scheme of the LIC and GIC which provide compensation for disability and death should be extended to the women in the informal sector. The women in the BPL families should be covered by insurance benefit when the male earning members sustain disability or die and the families are pauperised further.

Women and Legislation

Although the Constitution of India has granted equality to women and further empowered the State to make positive discrimination in favour of women for neutralizing the cumulative socio-economic, educational and political disadvantages faced by them, there are still some areas where rights of women are not fully secured by laws and there are laws which are either discriminatory against women or provide a week enforcement and punishment mechanism which do not deter the recurrence of crimes of against women. The entire gamut of laws on women or related to women need a comprehensive and thorough review. Some exercise has been done in the past by the National Commission on Women and some major legislative initiative has been taken in hand. This process should be continued and completed during the Tenth Plan

National Machinery for Women's Advancement

Considerable institutional development has already come about for facilitating women's advancement. Useful work has also been done by various institutions like the National Commission for Women, Central Social Welfare Board, National Institute of Public Cooperation and Child Development, Rashtriya Mahila Kosh, Parliamentary Committee for Empowerment of Women, State Women Development Corporations etc. While these institutions should be further strengthened and streamlined according to their felt needs, various grassroots level institutions and initiatives should be involved with the process of empowerment of women.

Panchayats and Municipalities

Panchayati Raj institutions and the Municipalities, created under the 73rd and 74th Constitutional Amendments, have both the Constitutional mandate and potential as grassroots institutions to bring about a sea change of development in the social sector. They should be empowered with resource support for the purpose of enhancing the status of women in societal as well as developmental terms. A nation wide capacity building exercise should be taken up for all elected women members of PRI and Municipalities. They should be given responsibility of planning, implementation and monitoring, particularly in the areas of health services, primary education, child development programmes, drinking water, irrigation, management of all natural resources land, forest and water, social security for women in BPL families, aged, disabled, deserted women de facto female headed households etc.

Women's Self-Help Groups

Self-help groups of women have been found to be very effective grassroots institutions in facilitating access for women to means of development, be it information, financial and material resources or services. The 'self-help group' mode should be encouraged, so that the groups become dynamic change agents in bringing about empowerment and socio-economic development of women.

Organizations of the Civil Society

Efforts of the governmental institutions have to be supplemented by the Organizations of the Civil Society (NGOs). Already a large number of such institutions have emerged in different parts of the country and they have to their credit significant contribution and experience at the grassroots level in projecting and addressing women's issues. The services of these institutions should be encouraged, supported and availed of, so that advancement of women becomes a truly national and people's movement.

Corporate World

The Corporate world, especially of late, has evinced significant interest in social development issues including women's development, transcending their limited business mandates. As employers, corporate bodies have strategic interface with the working people. Their services should be utilized for further gender sensitization of the corporate world as a whole as well as the working people. Their infrastructure and resources should also be drawn upon in implementation of women's development programmes.

UN and other Agencies

The United Nations and its various specialized agencies, as a matter of pro-active and coordinated in-house policies have taken very keen interest in women's development in their own respective areas of competence. They have been providing resource support for various gender-oriented programmes. More importantly, they have been facilitating sharing of international experience in addressing women's issues and catalyzing national action. Full support should be given to the efforts of these agencies at the national, regional and grassroots level. World Bank, Asian Development Bank and other multilateral as well as bilateral agencies are increasingly providing resource support for social development including gender development programmes. Their assistance should also be availed of to maximize investments in human resource development amongst women.

IMPLEMENTATION STRATEGY

Women's Component Plan

Ninth Five Year Plan adopted Women's Component Plan as one of its major strategies and directed both the Central and State Governments to ensure that "not less than 30 per cent of the funds /benefits are earmarked in all the women's related sectors". It also directed that a special vigil be kept on the flow of the earmarked funds/benefits through an effective mechanism to ensure that the proposed strategy brings forth a holistic approach towards empowering women.

Although 12 Ministries/Departments and 4 State Governments have confirmed their efforts to extend the benefits to Women's Component Plan, it has not been possible to exactly quantify the allocations, although substantial benefits from the core sectors of health and family welfare, education, labour and employment, rural development, urban development, agriculture, science and technology are stated to be flowing to the women.

The concept of the Women's Component Plan must not be abandoned or weakened merely because it was not operationalised effectively. Rather it should be further strengthened with comprehensive guidelines and instructions and an effective system for monitoring the progress should be developed both in the Planning Commission and in the Department of Women and Child Development.

Tenth Five Plan should also enlist the schemes and programmes of the various Ministries/Departments which will be covered under WCP. The estimates of allocation and expenditure of these schemes should be shown as a separate account head in the Demands for Grants on the pattern of Tribal sub-plan and Special Component Plan for Scheduled Castes. No re-appropriation from WCP to the general schemes should be permitted without the prior approval of Women and Child Development Department. Various schedules and formats for reporting progress should also be devised to include separate columns on men and women so that the benefits flowing to women can be monitored more closely.

Gender Budgeting

Gender budgeting is not a separate budget for women; rather it is a dissection of the government budget to establish its gender-differential impacts and to translate gender commitments into budgetary commitments. The main objective of a gender-sensitive budget is to improve the analysis of incidence of budgets, attain more effective targeting of public expenditure and offset any undesirable gender-specific consequences of previous budgetary measures.

The Department of Women and Child Development has taken the initiative of starting a gender budgeting exercise from the current year. For the first time a separate section on Gender Inequality has been included in the chapter on Social Sector in the Annual Economic Survey of the Government. An analysis of the Budget 2001 from the gender perspective has been carried out and this should be continued as a regular feature every year.

Convergence of Services

Various Ministries/Departments and their agencies engaged in women's development have often tended to function in a compartmentalised manner, leading to duplication of services, escalation of costs and fragmentation of efforts at various levels. Strategies and mechanisms for bringing about coordination and convergence of services and sequencing multi sectoral functions for social development have to be given priority in programme design and implementation. Identification of best practices, critiques on failures and the analysis thereof of the causes leading to those failures and adoption of measures for mid-course corrections would need to be a continuous process. Various bottlenecks that have been exposed in the implementation of several well-intentioned projects and programmes have to be identified for specific scrutiny to strategize the elimination of those bottlenecks.

The Integrated Child Development Services (ICDS) is almost universalized. The units under this programme (Anganwadis) have become the ubiquitous grassroots level institutions. This infrastructure should be used for converged delivery of a variety of social services-immunization, health, nutrition, preschool education. life-long education of adolescent girls, adult literacy, population education, AIDS awareness etc., apart from general Awareness Creation.

Restructuring of Programmes

With the introduction of Swarna Jayanti Gramodaya Yojana, Sarva Siksha Abhiyan, and success of National Literacy Mission and National Open School etc some of the existing schemes like Socio Economic Programme, Condensed Courses for Women's Education and Vocational Training etc have completely lost their relevance and should be converged with the new institutions and programmes. The women specific programmes of the Department should be completely restructured. There should be two main programmes, (a) Programmes for Social Empowerment, and (b) Programmes for Economic Empowerment, which should offer a wide range of choices according to the specific situations in particular States, regions and sub-regions.

Resources and Priorities

The share of women specific programmes constitute a fraction of the total fund allotted to the DWCD. During the financial year 2000-01 out of the total expenditure of Rs 1335.93 crores in the Department, expenditure on women specific programmes was only Rs 115.71 crores. This constituted a meager 8.57%.

It is also a matter of concern that the Central Plan investment on women-specific programmes has been shrinking over the years. The total outlay of Ninth Plan on women specific programmes of the DWCD was Rs.1238.76 crores, but the actual budget allocation during these five years was only Rs 851.49 crores (68.73%). The revised budget allocation for the first four years was Rs. 568.73 crores (45.91%), out of which only Rs 472.35 crores (38.13%) could be actually spent. It is unfortunate that nearly one-fourth of the sanctioned budget allocation of the Department on women specific schemes could not be utilized during the Ninth Plan and had either to be surrendered or diverted to some other schemes due to limited capacity of absorption of funds under existing strategy. Both these trends must be reversed during the Tenth Plan.

Delivery Mechanism

The existing mechanism of implementation of most of the schemes of the Department of Women and Child Development, either directly by the Department or through the Central Social Welfare Advisory Board, severely constraints the capacity of the system to reach the target women. This model had its relevance when no institutional machinery existed at the State level for the delivery of services to the women. Today every State Government has its Department of Social Welfare, besides Women and Child Welfare Department and Women Development Corporation. Panchayat Raj institutions with one-third women members and a large number of women self-help groups have come up at the grassroots all over the country. These new institutions can take up the responsibility of the implementation of most of the schemes on women. The Tenth Plan must recognise this changed scenario and accordingly restructure the entire institutional mechanism for the delivery of the programmes of women.

Research, Evaluation and Monitoring

Any developmental plan to be realistic is to be based on information on ground truths in terms of cultural traditions, practices, problems and their magnitude as well as developmental experience itself. Reports and feedbacks on all these factors have to be obtained through field level research conducted on credible and scientific basis. For the purpose, scientific researches would be undertaken on women's issues and concerns through various governmental and nongovernmental institutions having competence and credibility. The system of concurrent evaluation of the major schemes through independent organisations should be built into the programme itself. Important State and national level research organisations and other academic institutions and societies should be involved for the regular evaluation of the major programmes of the Department.

Monitoring systems and mechanisms need to be developed both at the community and Panchayat level at one end and State and National levels at the other end to ensure allocations, expenditure and implementation of programmes and projects as per the Component Plans. Evaluation and midcourse correction of the gender-budgeting and monitoring system should be done systematically and the experience gained there from should be applied to evolve and establish fine-tuned institutionalized procedures. The critical mass of technically qualified persons should be positioned in the Planning Commission, Ministries/ Departments and States to undertake this task on a half-yearly basis.

The system of concurrent evaluation of the major schemes through independent organisations should be built into the programme itself. Important State and national-level research organisations and other academic institutions and societies should be involved for the regular evaluation of the major programmes of the Department.

Gender Development Index

Gender segregated data on the various indices of human development at the State, district and sub-district level are not available for preparation of region specific projects for empowerment of women. D/WCD had taken an initiative for preparation of 18 minimum indicators on gender development at the district level There should be further discussions on these Indices for establishing certain uniform and comparable indicators at the national and international levels. The statistical system of the country should be strengthened for generating such data at district and sub district levels at a regular intervals.

DEVELOPMENT OF CHILDREN

Children form the first priority on the National Agenda not because they are the most vulnerable but because the foundations for life-long learning and human development are laid in the most crucial years of early childhood. This is the time when, even a small positive change yields long-term social benefits and even a temporary deprivation inflicts life-long damage. Thus, the opportunities of early childhood development determines the present and the future human resource development of a nation.

As per the 2001 Census, children in the age-group 0-14 years account for 347.54 million (33.84%) of the total population in the country. Of these, 169.03 million (48.64%) are female children. Of the total child population, 20.71 million population (5.96%) are infants who are below 1 year; 41.75 million (12.01%) are toddlers in the age-group 1-2 years; 77.32 million (22.25%) are pre-schoolers in the age-group 2-6 years; and another 207.76 million (59.78%) are in the age-group 6-14 years. While the children as a whole require special attention of the Government, the first 3 age-groups viz., Infants, Toddlers and Pre-schoolers require individual attention because of their vulnerability and age-specific needs.

Realising the vulnerability of the tender age of children, the Constitution of India laid down certain special safeguards to ensure their survival, protection and development. While Article 14 guarantees that the State shall not deny to any person equality before the law or the equal protection of laws within the territory of India, Article 15(3) empowers the state to make any special provisions in favour of children; Article 21 states that no person shall be deprived of his life or personal liberty except according to the procedure established by law; Article 23 prohibits traffic in human beings and beggary and other forms of forced labour and any contravention of this provision shall be an offence punishable in accordance with law; Article 24 prohibits employment of children below the age of 14 years in any factory or mine or other hazardous occupations; Article 39 states that the rights of the children and the young to be protected against exploitation and to opportunities for healthy development, consonant with freedom and dignity; Article 42 ensures right to humane conditions of work and maternity relief; Article 45 provides right for children to compulsory education upto the age of 14 years; Article 47 states that the State shall endeavour to raise the level of nutrition and standard of living and to improve the public health.

Also, some very relevant and crucial constitutional provisions relating to children are included under Directive Principles of State Policy, which are in the form of guidance to the State and cannot be claimed legally. The state should strive to convert these principles into fundamental rights at the earliest so that all the rights of children can be legally asserted and their withdrawal under any circumstances not permitted. The proposed 83rd Constitutional Amendment seeking to make elementary education a fundamental right, is a step in this direction.

All the initiatives and programmes for the development of children have been backed by strong legislative support. Primary amongst them are: The Guardian and Wards Act, 1890; The Child Marriage Restraint Act (Amended in 1979), 1929; The Factories Act (Amended in 1949, 1950 and 1954), 1948; Hindu Adoption and Maintenance Act, 1956; Probation of Offenders Act, 1958; The Orphanage & Other Charitable Homes (Supervision and Control) Act, 1960; Immoral Traffic Prevention Act, 1986; The Child Labour (Prohibition and Regulations) Act, 1986; The Infant Milk Substitutes, Feeding Bottles and Infant Foods (Regulation of Production, Supply & Distribution) Act, 1992; The Pre-natal Diagnostic Technique (Regulation, Prevention and Misuse) Act, 1994; The Persons with Disabilities (Equal Opportunities, Protection of Rights & Full Participation) Act, 1996; Juvenile Justice Act, 2000.

Also, there are instances where the judiciary has derived strength and support in giving their judgements to safeguard the interests of Children by upholding various Constitutional provisions, referred to above. For instance, following an order of the High Court in December 2000, Rule 37 of the Delhi School Education Act, 1973 allowing for corporal punishment for children has been struck down. The Court staunchly upheld the child's right to life and referred to the provision provided to this effect in the Constitution, the National Policy on Education and the Convention on the Rights of the Child (CRC). The Court defined the rights of the child in its widest sense of the term "encompassing all that which gives meaning to life and made it wholesome and worth living, still more than mere survival of animal existence".

DEVELOPMENT OF CHILDREN THROUGH FIVE YEAR PLANS (1951-2002)

First to Eighth Five Year Plans (1951-1997)

Child development has been a priority subject in the country's developmental planning right from the First Five Year Plan (1951-56). In the initial years, the responsibility of child care services had primarily rested with voluntary organizations under the charge of a national apex body, viz., the Central Social Welfare Board which was set up in 1953 to promote voluntary action in the field of women and child development. Subsequent reviews and assessments concluded that holistic development of the child requires integration with other developmental sectors and their services. Accordingly, during the Second to the Fourth Plan (1956-78), Child Welfare Services were linked to different sectors of the Plan such as Health, Family Welfare, Nutrition, Education, Rural and Urban Development. These Plans, besides according high priority to education for children, also introduced measures to improve maternal and child health services, supplementary feeding for children and expectant and nursing mothers. 9.2 The Fifth Plan (1974-78) has proved to be the landmark in the field of child development through the adoption of a National Policy for Children (1974), and launching of the Integrated Child Development Services (ICDS) with a shift from welfare to development in the approach towards development of children. The programme of ICDS, launched in 33 experimental blocks in 1975, aims to reach a package of 6 basic services, viz., health check-up, immunization, referral services, supplementary feeding, non-formal pre-school education and health and nutrition education for children below 6 years and expectant and nursing mothers living in the most backward areas through a single window delivery agency called 'Anganwadi Centre'.

The Sixth Five Year Plan (1980-85), i.e., the early Eighties witnessed an effective consolidation and expansion of programmes started in the earlier Plans. The National Policy of Health adopted in 1983 set certain specific targets like bringing down the high rates of Infant and Child Mortality and take up universalisation of immunization etc. by the year 2002 A.D. The National Policy on Education of 1986 emphasised universal enrolment and retention of children in the schools especially the girl children. Non-formal education programmes were also promoted intensively. Vocationalisation of education was given priority. Pre-school education centres were supported in the educationally backward states by extending grants to voluntary organizations.

The Seventh Five Year Plan (1985-90) continued the major strategy of promoting early childhood survival and development through programmes in different sectors, important among these being ICDS, universal immunization, maternal and child care services, nutrition, preschool education, protected drinking water, environmental sanitation and hygiene, and family planning. Under the maternal and child health services of the Ministry of Health and Family Welfare, the universal immunization programme to protect children from six major diseases which affect early childhood mortality and morbidity, viz. diphtheria, whooping cough, tetanus, polio, measles and childhood tuberculosis was strengthened for the development of children as a whole. ICDS continued to be the single nation-wide programme for early childhood survival and development during Seventh Plan. The Juvenile Justice Act (JJA) was enacted in 1986, to deal effectively with the problem of neglected or juvenile delinquents and provide for a standardized framework for dealing with such children. The Government of India enacted the Child Labour Prohibition and Regulation Act, 1986 and in 1987, the National policy on Child Labour was formulated. Projects were sanctioned to voluntary organizations for the welfare of working children to provide non-formal education, supplementary nutrition, health care and skill training. For children in need of care and protection, grants were given to voluntary organizations through the State Governments.

Human Resources Development being the major focus of the Eighth Five Year Plan (1992-97), policies and programmes relating to 'child survival, protection and development' were accorded high priority with emphasis on family and community based preventive services to combat high infant and Under-5 child mortality and morbidity. Following the ratification of the 'Convention on the Rights of the Child', in 1992 the Government of India formulated two National Plans of Action (NPA)-one for children and the other exclusively for the Girl-Child. While the NPA for Children sets out quantifiable goals to be achieved by 2000 AD in the priority areas of health, nutrition, education, water, sanitation and environment, the NPA for the Girl Child (1991-2000) aims at removal of gender bias and enhances the status of girl child in the society, so as to provide them the equal opportunities for their survival, protection and development. Both the Plans of Action have adopted an inter-sectoral approach in achieving sectoral goals laid down in the Action Plans in close uniformity with the major goals of 'Health For All', 'Education For All' etc.

NINTH FIVE YEAR PLAN (1997-2002): A CRITICAL REVIEW

The Ninth Five Year Plan (1997-2002) re-affirms its priority for the development of early childhood as an investment in the country's human resource development through the following inter-ministerial strategies:

i) To place the Young Child at the top of the Country's Developmental Agenda with a Special Focus on the Girl Child,

ii) To institute a National Charter for Children ensuring that no Child remains illiterate, hungry or lacks medical care;

iii) To ensure `Survival, Protection and Development' through the effective implementation of the two National Plans of Action-one for the Children and the other for the Girl Child;

iv) Acknowledge that the first six years as critical for the development of children, therefore, greater stress will be laid on reaching the younger children below 2 years;

v) To continue to lay a special thrust on the 3 major areas of child development viz. health, nutrition and education;

vi) To universalize ICDS as the main-stay of the Ninth Plan for promoting the over-all development of the young children, especially the Girl Child and the mothers all over the country;

vii) To arrest the declining sex ratio and curb its related problems of female foeticide and female infanticide;

viii) To bring down the IMR to less than 60 and the CMR to below 10 by 2002 AD through providing easy access to health care services including RCH services and 100% coverage of immunization in respect of all vaccine preventable diseases;

ix) To universalize the Nutrition Supplementary Feeding Programmes to fill the existing gaps in respect of both pre-school and school children and expectant and nursing mothers with a special focus on the Girl Child and the Adolescent Girl;

x) To promote the nutritional status of the mother and the child by improving the dietary intake through a change in the feeding practices and intra-family food distribution;

xi) To strengthen the early joyful period of play and learning in the young child's life and to ensure a harmonious transition from the family environment to the primary school;

xii) To view girl's education as a major intervention for breaking the vicious inter-generational cycle of gender and socio-economic disadvantages;

xiii) To expand the support services of crèche / day-care services and to develop linkages between the primary schools and of the child care services to promote educational opportunities for the Girl Child;

xiv) To expand the scheme of Adolescent Girls in preparation for their productive and re-productive roles as confident individuals not only in family building but also in nation building;

xv) To widen the scope and the spectrum of child development services with necessary interventions related to empowerment of women and children, families and communities through effective convergence and coordination of various sectoral efforts and services.

Towards fulfilling the above commitments/strategies, special efforts are being made during the Ninth Plan through various policy/programmatic interventions, in all child-related sectors through effective coordination and convergence of services and personnel. Details of various sectoral efforts and achievements are listed below:

Women and Child Development

Efforts are being made to strengthen the on-going approach of converging the basic services of health, nutrition and pre-school education towards promoting the holistic development of the young child through the programme of Integrated Child Development Service (ICDS) Scheme. ICDS continues to be the major intervention during the Ninth Plan for the overall development of children. It caters to the pre-school children below 6 years and expectant and nursing mothers with a package of services viz. immunization, health check-ups, referral services, supplementary nutrition, pre-school education and health and nutrition education.

In support of the universalisation of ICDS, the World Bank has been assisting the Government of India in the expansion of ICDS Programme since 1990-91. Apart from providing the normal ICDS package it extends World Bank assistance for a few additional inputs like construction of Anganwadi buildings and CDPOs office-cum-godowns on a selective basis, strengthening of training and communication, improved health facilities, income-generation activities etc. While the WB-ICDS Project-I (1991-97) covered 301 ICDS projects in the States of Andhra Pradesh (110) and Orissa (191), the WB-ICDS Project II (1997-2000) covers 454 projects in the States of Bihar (210) and Madhya Pradesh (244). The same got extended for another 2 years, i.e., till 2002. The WB-ICDS Project III (1998-2004) which was started in 1998-99 proposes to cover 461 projects in the States of Andhra Pradesh, Kerala, Madhya Pradesh, Maharashtra, Rajasthan and Uttar Pradesh. The World Bank ICDS programme in Andhra Pradesh is being implemented in 257 blocks as part of the total programme of Andhra Pradesh Economic Reconstruction Programme (APERP).

Though universalisation of ICDS was contemplated by the end of 1995-96 through expanding its services in all the 5652 Blocks all over the country, yet only 4200 could become operational at the beginning of Ninth Plan, before the ban on further operationalisation of ICDS projects was imposed by the Ministry of Finance w.e.f. 16.5.97. However, the ban was finally lifted and now the Government has decided to universalize ICDS all over the country by the end of the Ninth Plan.

The impact of ICDS, which completed 25 years of its implementation in October 2000, was evaluated by a number of individual experts and various research organisations. Of these, the National Evaluation of ICDS conducted by the National

Institute of Public Co-operation and Child Development (NIPCCD), New Delhi in 1992 and the Mid-term Evaluation of World Bank assisted ICDS need a special mention. The findings of the Study by NIPCCD indicated a very positive impact of ICDS on the health and nutrition status of pre-school children. The Mid-term evaluation of the World Bank assisted ICDS (Project-I) conducted in Andhra Pradesh during 1995-96 also revealed that the Project interventions had brought down the IMR to 62 per 1000 live births which was in consonance with the project objective of 60 per 1000 live births. The incidence of severe malnutrition amongst children of 0-3 years was reduced to about 5 per cent and that of 3-6 years to 3 per cent. The proportion of low birth weight babies also came down to 20 per cent as against the project goal of 24 per cent. Similarly, in Orissa, the IMR had come down to 93.6 and the incidence of low birth weight of babies to 23 per cent.

Yet another national level Evaluation Study conducted by the National Council of Applied Economic Research (NCAER), New Delhi during 1997 reveals some of the weaknesses. The weaknesses of the programme as depicted in the survey report are that only 36% of AWCs have pucca building, inadequacy of space for AWC activities, especially for cooking, nearly 75% of AWCs do not have toilet facilities. The various opportunities listed in the survey report include that AWCs have been playing an important role in the delivery of health services in remote regions by providing opportunity for increasing referral services. But, there is a need to increase the involvement of community in the programme. The threats as emerged from the findings of the survey are: inadequate in-service training, inadequate supply of learning kits, toys, poor quality and inadequate supply of medicine kits, irregular supply of nutrition, poor community participation, poor rapport with adolescent girls. In addition, it was observed that the support from Panchayati Raj Institutions and other community leaders is limited. Despite several gaps, findings clearly highlighted that the ICDS programme has been able to create the necessary awareness among the target population about the need of inadequate nutrition and proper health of women in overall development of child.

The ICDS experience since 1975 has taught several valuable lessons with a larger applicability to programmes for the human resource development, as follows-Community-based women workers can be effective and viable instruments of human resource development, if these workers are supported with training guidance and the necessary material inputs; an integrated approach, including a package of mutually supportive services, is more cost effective and efficient than individual services delivered separately; community ownership is fundamental to improved programme quality, impact and sustenance; flexibility in responding to local patterns of women's work and time is critical for reaching younger children more effectively; the ICDS type of network makes it feasible and easier to apply new, simple technology on a larger scale; the flow of human and material inputs has to be planned in detail and monitored very carefully, with community participation; collaboration of academic/research institutions is very useful in providing low cost objective feedback on the programme and continuing education to workers. The educational process in academic institutions is also enriched with the field experience of the programme; field experience needs to be continuously reviewed and utilised for strengthening training; need for continuous enrichment of training and development of standardised training modules with focus on core items; the experience of ICDS during these two and a half decades indicates that it has the potential of bringing about a silent revolution-a profound instrument of community and human resource development.

Kishori Shakti Yojana Adolescent Girls Scheme is a special intervention devised using the ICDS infrastructure. The Scheme is primarily aimed at breaking the inter-generational cycle of nutritional and gender disadvantage and providing supportive environment for selfdevelopment of the girl child in the age group 11-18 years. The Scheme is based on the recognition that programmes aimed at improving the nutritional and health status of adolescent girls and promoting self-development, awareness of health, hygiene, nutrition, family welfare and management could significantly improve the health and nutritional status of women and children and promote the decision making capabilities of women. Under the Scheme, emphasis is on improvement of nutritional and health status of adolescent girls. The options are regular supply of IFA and De-worming tablets, nutritional and health education, life education, which may include knowledge of physical and psychological developmental processes including the psychosexual development. Another option could be emphasis on education with particular attention on school dropouts and functional literacy among illiterate adolescent girls. Education activities should be conducted through non-formal education pattern. The adolescent girls may be congregated at Anganwadi centres and the education could be provided through experts, consultants, NGOs and specialized government functionaries. Alternatively, vocational training activities are to be undertaken for adolescent girls for their economic empowerment.

UDISHA is an effort to strengthen the on-going ICDS Training Programme into a dynamic, responsive and comprehensive training-cum-human resource development programme. For the implementation of UDISHA, World Bank has agreed to extend financial assistance to the extent of Rs.600.55 crore. The National Institute of Public Cooperation and Child Development, New Delhi with its nation-wide network of 3 Regional Centres, 18 Middle Level Training Centres (MLTCs) and 300 Anganwadi Workers Training Centres (AWTCs) is expected to implement UDISHA. By the end of the Ninth Plan, 2925 CDPOs/ACDPOs, 9756 Supervisors and 216000 Anganwadi workers are likely to be trained.

The Scheme of Balika Samriddhi Yojana (BSY) originated from the announcement of the Prime Minister on 15 August 1997 stating that 'the Government would extend financial help to the families to whom a girl child is born and if they are living Below Poverty Line (BPL). Later, scholarships would also be given when the girl child goes to school'. Accordingly, a programme of Balika Samriddhi Yojana was launched on 2 October 1997 to extend a postdelivery grant of Rs.500/-for the mother of the Girl Child belonging to the BPL Group. For this, the Government released an ad-hoc grant of Rs.60 crore to cover 12 lakh girl children in the financial year 1997-98.

To make the programme more effective, a Group of Ministers reviewed the implementation of the programme in 1999. Based on their recommendations, the programme was recast as a Centrally Sponsored Scheme with the following features:-

i) a post-delivery grant of Rs.500/-per girl child upto two girl children born on or after 15 August, 1997 will now, instead of being paid in cash, be deposited either in the Bank / Post Office in an interest-bearing account in the name of the girl child. Withdrawal of a portion of the post-birth grant of Rs.500/-or of the amount of the annual scholarships eligible for deposit, may be permitted towards the sole purpose of paying the premium of an insurance policy in the name of the girl child under the Bhagyashree Balika Kalyan Bima Yojana. Such a utilization may be permitted with due authorization of the mother/guardian of the girl;

ii) Annual scholarships would also be given to the girl child when she starts going to school. The rate of scholarships will be Rs.300 each in classes I-III, Rs.500 in class IV, Rs.600 in class V, Rs.700 each in classes VI and VII, Rs.800 in class VIII and Rs.1000 each in classes IX and X per annum. The scholarship amount can also be deposited in the same Account, at the option of the guardian of the Girl Child, in which the post-delivery grant of Rs.500/-was kept. These deposits will be paid to the girl child on attaining the age of 18 years and remaining unmarried till then. The amount of scholarships can also be paid in kind at the discretion of the guardian of the girl child. The programme of Recast BSY with the above revisions is being put into action during 1999-2000.

The scheme of Creches and Day Care Centres for children of working/ailing mothers, being a non-expanding scheme, maintained the same level of 12470 creches benefiting 3.12 lakh children. However, to meet the growing demand for more creches, a National Creche Fund (NCF) was set up in 1994 with a corpus of Rs.19.90 crore received under Social Safety Net. The NCF extended financial assistance for the opening of creches besides conversion of the existing Anganwadis into Anganwadi-cum-Creches. Under the NCF, 2,455 creches were added benefiting about 0.61 lakh more children. A wider expansion of Creche/ Day-care services under NCF is envisaged during the Ninth Plan.

A proposal to set up a National Commission for Children to safeguard the constitutional and legal rights of children, National

Commission for Children is under consideration of the Department. The proposal has been approved by the Parliamentary Standing Committee. Most of the State Governments, UT administrations/ Ministries/ Departments have agreed to setting up of the National Commission for Children on the lines of National Human Rights Commission. The draft bill is now under consideration of the Government. A draft National Charter for Children is also on the anvil, which delineates government commitments and resources for the child.

Health and Family Welfare

The Reproductive and Child Health (RCH) Programme, being operated by the Ministry of Health and Family Welfare since October 1997 aims at integration and expansion of family welfare services, upgradation of their quality and making them easily accessible to the people. The Scheme, inter-alia, focuses on maternal health and child survival issues with giving full attention to all the components. Efforts are made to improve the health status of women and children so that, decline in population growth is achieved. RCH has close convergence with the ICDS Programme as health check-up and nutrition education are the services being provided at the Anganwadi centres. Anganwadi Worker is also required to impart health and nutritional education to the woman beneficiary. It has been decided in consultation with the Department of Family Welfare that village health worker and Auxiliary Nurse Midwives (ANMs) have to work in close coordination with the Anganwadi Workers. Anganwadi Worker, as she comes from the grass-root level and normally from the same village, is better placed to drive home the points about reproductive and child health and nutrition etc. to the rural people, especially women. Besides the RCH Programme, various other related activities namely, immunisation, birth registration activity, pulse polio campaign are also undertaken by the ICDS functionaries, especially Anganwadi Worker at the grass-root level.

Nutrition

In line with the commitments of the National Nutrition Policy (NNP) of 1993, priority is being accorded to promote the nutrition status of the mother and the child by improving the dietary intake and through a change in the feeding practices and intra-family food distribution and preventing the deficiency diseases. Accordingly, every effort is being made to improve/ensure the quality of effectiveness of the nutrition feeding programmes, viz., Special Nutrition Programme for Children below 6 years and expectant and nursing mothers through ICDS and Mid-Day Meals Programme for school going children implemented by the State Governments. Further, the nutrition component of Prime Minister's Gramodaya Yojana (PMGY) has been specifically outlined with the objective of eradicating mal-nutrition amongst children under 3 years by increased nutritional coverage of supplementary feeding of these children through ICDS schemes. This Additional Central Assistance (ACA) for nutrition component under PMGY is an additionality over and above the provision for the number funded under the State Plan for ICDS scheme.

Also, CARE-India extends food aid for supplementary nutrition to children below six years of age and to pregnant and nursing mothers in the ICDS programme. In accordance with the List of Provisions (LOP) approved for 1999-2000, CARE-India has committed to supply food aid to 66.05 lakh beneficiaries distributed in the States of Andhra Pradesh, Bihar, Madhya Pradesh, Orissa, Rajasthan, Uttar Pradesh and West Bengal. In addition to that, World Food Programme (WFP), a United Nations agency, under its Project 2206 extends food aid for supplementary nutrition to children below six years of age and to expectant and nursing mothers under the ICDS Scheme. There is a Country Programme (CPI) for India for a five-year period from 1st April 1997 to 31st March 2001. In addition to this, 3500 MTs. of food is also available from Canadian International Development Agency (CIDA) assistance for the State of Rajasthan, which will cover an additional 2.30 lakh beneficiaries.

Education

Sarva Shiksha Abhiyan (SSA) aims at universalisation of elementary education in a mission mode. The Scheme is holistic and convergent in approach. The Scheme seeks to incorporate all existing programmes of elementary education in the central and centrally sponsored categories under its framework. Early childhood care and education constitutes an integral part of Sarva Shiksha Abhiyan. This component of SSA will be primarily implemented through the Anganwadi Centres of the ICDS. The ICDS Scheme is poised for universalisation during mid-Tenth Five Year Plan. Obviously, it would be most important to enrich and strengthen the early learning aspect of the ICDS Scheme since it is the foundation for the child's cumulative lifelong learning.

The Department of Women and Child Development has requested the Department of Elementary Education and Literacy to provide one part-time teacher in Anganwadi Centre for imparting pre-school education and providing for necessary teaching and learning materials and game kits for Anganwadi centres. This is critical for releasing the over-burdened AWW to focus on family and community based interventions for improved health, nutrition and development outcomes in younger children under 3 years, adolescent girls, pregnant and nursing mothers. The part-time preschool teacher would also improve the quality of early learning activities for 3-6 year olds at the AWC, strengthening the early development and learning continuum across the young child's life. Coordinated action between the Sarva Shiksha Abhiyan and ICDS Scheme will go a long way in achieving the goal of universal retention by 2010 under the Sarva Shiksha Abhiyan Scheme.

Welfare and Social Justice

The Ministry of Social Justice and Empowerment implements many welfare programmes for children in difficult circumstances, as detailed below:

(i) A Child Line Foundation was set up to extend child line services in major cities to protect children facing abuse, exploitation and neglect etc.;

(ii) Under the Schemes of Assistance to Homes for Infants and Young Children for promoting in-country adoption institutional care to children who have lost parental support at a very early age (0-6 years) is provided till the time they are placed in adoption. Under this scheme, grant-in-aid is given to voluntary agencies for setting up homes (Shishu Griha) for Infants for promoting in-country adoption;

(iii) the Programme for Juvenile Justice aims to strengthen the implementation of Juvenile Justice Act 1986 and to bring about a qualitative improvement in the services provided for both neglected as well as delinquent children. Under this Scheme, Children Homes, observation homes, juvenile homes, special homes and after-care institutions are established. Besides, juvenile courts and juvenile welfare boards are also operating in different parts of the country for implementation of the Juvenile Justice Act.

Similarly, under the Scheme of Pre-Matric Scholarships for Children of those engaged in unclean occupations, financial assistance is provided to enable the children of families involved in unclean occupation to pursue pre-matric education courses in recognised institutions. Central assistance is provided to the State Governments on a 50:50 basis and 100 UT administrations over and above their committed liabilities. The scheme has been extended to cover OBCs also;

(iv) the scheme of Rehabilitation of Children of Sex Workers implemented by voluntary organisations, aims to rehabilitate the children of the sex workers who are one of the most disadvantaged segment among the neglected children through imparting vocational training, non-formal education, health care and nutrition. Under this scheme, grants are also given for setting up of Day-Care Centre for children of fishermen, maintenance of orphan children etc.;

(v) the Integrated Programme for Street Children aims to prevent destitution of children and facilitate their withdrawal from life on the streets. The programme provides for shelter, nutrition, health care, education, recreation facilities to street children and seeks to protect them against abuse and exploitation. The target group of this programme is children without homes and families such as street children, children of sex workers and children of pavement dwellers. Under this scheme, grants are given to voluntary organisations, state governments, UT administrations, local bodies and educational institutions;

In pursuance of the directions of the Hon'ble Supreme Court of India, a Central Adoption Resource Agency (CARA) was set up as one of the sections of the Ministry in 1990 and was registered as an autonomous body in 1999 with the objective of providing a detailed framework for regulating and expediting adoptions in India. Various efforts have been initiated to ensure promotion of adoptions as well as to streamline adoption services. CARA has been closely networking and coordinating with State Governments in monitoring and evaluating adoption agencies, Voluntary Coordinating Agencies (VCAs) and NGOs that are receiving grants under the Shishu Griha Scheme. CARA has also initiated various steps in promotion of in-country adoptions. These include strengthening the VCAs by enhancing their grant-in-aid. In order to enhance the capacity building of various agencies involved in adoption, a series of 17 training programmes were organised all over the country under the National Initiative for Child Adoption in collaboration with the National Institute of Social Defence.

Youth Affairs

The view on Adolescent girls and boys has been varied and ridden with gender bias in the planning process hitherto. Universalisation of supplementary feeding with a special emphasis on adolescent girls is mentioned in the Ninth Plan "....... In preparation for their productive and reproductive roles as confident individuals not only in family building but also in nation building" (Planning Commission, Government of India 1998). The girl has been viewed primarily as a future mother whose health and nutritional care attain significance in the fulfillment of this role, reflecting a gender stereotyped attitude and perspective. The perception for boys is however as a potential workforce, as `human capital' in relation to their productive role alone. The Ninth Plan was limited in its perspective of opportunities and spaces for adolescents, and it is hoped that through a specific focus on this age group, the biases and limitations will be corrected and new thrust provided for the development of adolescents as individuals.

Policy perspectives on Adolescents in the period upto the Ninth Plan have been piecemeal, with various sectors referring to this age group as part of the overall approach, and no specific focus was given in most cases. The National Policy on Education (1986, modified in 1992) lays emphasis on the eradication of illiteracy especially for the 15 to 35 age group and universalisation of primary education and the Adolescent age group are considered as part of children to be provided primary education and adults who are participants of adult literacy activity. To some extent, the employment related educational needs are addressed through vocational education at the higher secondary level.

The policy also talks about meeting the nonformal and need-based vocational needs of youth (15-35 years). "Education for Women's Equality" has special relevance for education programmes for adolescents. Mahila Samakhya Programme which aims inter alia, at ensuring equal access to educational facilities for adolescent girls and young women has responded to a growing demand from adolescent girls for opportunities to complete formal education and also acquire leadership and vocational skills. Mahila Shikshan Kendras, Kishori Melas and other educational activities are organized to create opportunities for education and self-development of adolescent girls.

The National Population Policy (2000) recognized the earlier invisibility of adolescents and they are the subjects of one of its 12 strategic themes. They are specifically referred to in the sections on information, nutrition, contraceptive use, STDs and other population-related issues.

There is a special mention about developing a health package for adolescents and enforcing the legal age at marriage. The Draft Health Policy (1999) expresses concern for the health of special groups such as adolescent girls, with regard to their nutritional needs. Adolescent girls are clubbed with pregnant women and children instead of treating them as a distinct group and only the pregnancy and maternity related health needs of adolescents are referred to.

Draft National AIDS Policy (2000) recognizes adolescents as a significant portion of the sexually active population, and calls for them to be a special focus group under the Policy. The issue of AIDS however is dealt with in an alarmist way, instead of taking an educative approach to the adolescents needs for information and choices. National Nutrition Policy (1983) focused on adolescent girls and that too only in relation to the importance of their role as mothers and housewives. National Policy for the Empowerment of Women (2001) has recognized the girl child as a separate category and adolescent girls seem to be covered there under. The policy takes cognizance of their nutrition, education, adopts a holistic approach to health, violence, sexual abuse and the rights of the girl child.

The Draft National Youth Policy (2001) provides a comprehensive overview of youth issues and concerns and comes closest to a policy on adolescents. The current draft policy "Working with youth and not merely for youth" highlights several areas of concern for adolescents and youth in the country today and emphasizes an inter-sectoral approach. The policy lays stress on providing youth with `more access to the process of decision making and implementation of these decisions'. The Draft Youth Policy actually makes a distinction between the age of adolescence (13-19) and the age of attainment of maturity (20-30 years). By marking the age of adolescence, the policy facilitates advocacy efforts for focus on adolescents in government programmes.

Programmes for Adolescent Girls

Apart from the 2 schemes for Adolescent Girls implemented by the Department of Women & Child Development, Kishori Shakti Yojana and the Balika Samriddhi Yojana other departments are also implementing programmes for adolescent girls which have a bearing on their well-being and developmental opportunities. Nehru Yuva Kendras undertake activities for Health Awareness to educate and enable people to adopt health and family welfare programmes.

The Ministry of Social Justice and Empowerment implements a scheme for providing educational facilities including scholarships and hostels for tribal girls. The Department of Family Welfare provides for maternal care including safe motherhood and nutrition facilities, prevention of unwanted pregnancies, and safe abortion facilities to all women. Adolescents get subsumed under the general target group of women. An unwritten code is known to prevail that denies services to unmarried adolescents. Besides, the lack of privacy and confidentiality prevent adolescents from accessing these facilities. The Directorate General of Employment and Training, Ministry of Labour registration in employment exchanges for job placements and career counselling and vocational guidance for adolescents. While present policies address themselves to specific sectors like education, health, family welfare, nutrition, HIV/AIDS, sports etc. or address certain population groups like women, children and youth, the rights approach to adolescent issues seems to be missing in all these policies. There are a fairly large number of NGOs which address adolescent issues either in an integrated manner or sectorally and work on health, education, reproductive health, employment, gender, and/or vocational issues.

IMPACT OF POLICIES, PLANS AND PROGRAMMES

Crucial indicators like Infant Mortality Rate (IMR), Child Mortality Rate (CMR), School Enrolment Ratio, Drop-Out Rate and levels of malnutrition have shown significant improvement in the status of children as a result of the implementation of various developmental policies and programmes since 1950's, as indicated below:

Sex Ratio

Sex ratio in the age group of 0-6 years reduced from 945 in 1991 to 927 in 2001. The declining juvenile sex ratio, as already discussed 'Empowerment of Women' is a matter of concern. Between 1991 and 2001, the sex ratio in the 0-6 years declined in all States and Union Territories, except in Sikkim, Mizoram, Tripura, Lakshadweep and Kerala. In 2001, while Punjab recorded the lowest sex ratio of 793, declining from 875 in 1991, Sikkim recorded the highest at 986, rising from 965 in 1991. Reports have confirmed that the practice of the two social evils viz. Female Foeticide and Female Infanticide is mainly due to the strong preference for son and as such, these are responsible to a large extent for the ever declining sex ratio. Misuse of modern technique of Amniocentesis is an added dimension to the problem. Adding to this is the problem of ineffective implementation of the Act of Compulsory Registration of Births and Deaths, which fails to provide information on vital statistics.

PERSISTING PROBLEMS REQUIRING PRIORITY ATTENTION

No doubt, the children of India made good progress while responding to the special attention paid by the Government during the last fifty years, but they continue to face certain problems till today, which in fact are standing as major obstacles on their way to further progress, as discussed below:

Declining Juvenile Sex Ratio and Problems of Foeticide and Infanticide

As per 2001 Census, the juvenile sex ratio has declined from 945 in 1991 to 927 in 2001. The adverse sex ratio for females and its decline are attributed mainly to higher mortality among females, as compared to males. Also, the increasing problems of female foeticide and infanticide are presumably responsible for the present tend of declining sex ratio. Limited access to the health infrastructure and relative deprivation of the female child from nutrition, health and medical care have also been identified as some of the other contributory factors. The NCRB recorded a total of 61 cases of foeticide and 87 cases of infanticide in 1999, forming 1.2% and 1.8% respectively of the total number of crimes reported against children.

Health: Needs a Life Cycle Approach

Development has to have a life cycle approach. A young girl grows up under discrimination of various kinds-she works hard, takes care of the siblings, misses out on school, gets married early and is not able to achieve her full potential of growth-physical, psychological, mental etc. She becomes pregnant in her teens and in all probability will produce a low birth weight baby, who will grow and develop less well, will have a higher risk of mortality and in turn will give birth to a low birth weight baby, and the cycle goes on.

Problems of Malnutrition and Under Nutrition

Malnutrition and under-nutrition have been standing as obstacles in the improvement of health status of young children and adolescents. The major nutritional deficiencies in the country having important socio-economic and health consequences are protein energy malnutrition (PEM) and micro nutrient deficiencies like vitamin A deficiency and iron deficiency anaemia. PEM or under-nutrition among pre-school children assessed through weight deficit for age is the most sensitive indicator of nutritional status of the community. Chronic malnutrition among preschool children results in their stunted growth. Malnutrition is caused by inadequate and poor quality diet, female illiteracy, delayed complementary feeding, poor infant feeding practices, lack of nutritional awareness, poor hygiene and sanitation and low purchasing power.

Adding to these is the problem of under-weight children. The findings of National Family Health Survey (NFHS) 2 (1998-99) reveal that 47% of children under 3 years are underweight, which is a very high proportion as compared to other South Asian and African countries. 45.5% and 15.5% of children in the same age group are stunted and wasted, respectively. Even at birth, one in 3 children born in the country is of low birth weight. Malnutrition and anaemia of the mother result in the low birth weight of children which perpetuates an inter-generational cycle of malnutrition. Nutritional anaemia due to iron and folic acid deficiency is widely prevalent in the country, being highest among infants, young children, adolescent girls and pregnant women. As per NFHS 2 (1998-99) 74.3% of children under 3 years of age suffer from nutritional anaemia.

The National Nutrition Monitoring Bureau (NNMB) 1995 data reveals that the incidence of Bitot's spot in pre-school children due to Vitamin A deficiency was 1.1% in 1994-95. Vitamin A deficiency results in diarrhoeal diseases and respiratory infections, besides causing night blindness.

Low literacy and High Drop-Out Rates

Despite programmes like Universalisation of Elementary Education and girl specific education programmes, low literacy rate and low Gross Enrolment Ratio (GER) continue. The GER at the primary level has risen to 94.90 in 1999-2000 from 80.50 in 1980-81. Although, the Gross Enrolment Ratio at the middle level has increased from 41.90 to 58.79 over the same period, yet it is still very low. There is a positive trend of girls' enrolment. However, the enrolment for boys continues to be higher than that for girls.

In spite of the declining trend of drop-out rates at both primary and middle level, these still continue to be high. The drop-out rate at the middle level was as high as 54.6 and 40.3 at the primary level in 1999-2000.

The poor attendance and high drop-out rates in adolescents are a cause of concern. Lack of accessible middle schools in rural areas, early entry into the work force due to economic reasons, social attitudes and expectations are some of the factors which account for low enrolment and high drop out rates for adolescents. For adolescent girls the additional reasons are-the burden of sibling care, early assumption of domestic responsibilities, physical and sexual insecurity, early marriage, distance from schools and parental educational levels.

Pre School Education-Needs a Better Perspective

Early Childhood Care and Pre-school Education under ICDS-non formal pre-school education which is a crucial component of the package of services envisaged under ICDS Scheme, aims at universalisation and qualitative improvement of primary education in remote and socio-economically backward areas with primary attention being given to girl. The Early Childhood Care and Pre-school Education (ECCE) component of the ICDS may well be considered the backbone of the ICDS programme, since all its services essentially converge on the AW. This is also the most joyful play way daily activity, visibly sustained for 3 hours a day. It brings and keeps young children at the Anganwadi Centre-an activity that motivates parents and communities. ECCE, as envisaged in the ICDS, focuses on the total development of the child, in the age range of up to six years, from the underprivileged groups. It includes promotion of early stimulation of the children under 3 years of age through intervention with mothers/caregivers. Child-centred play way activities, which build on local culture and practices, using local support materials developed by Anganwadi workers, through enrichment training, are promoted. The early-childhood pre-school education programme, conducted through the medium of play, aims at providing a learning environment for the promotion of social, emotional, cognitive, physical and aesthetic development of the child.

As per Census 2001, we have approximately 593 lakh children in the age-group of 3-6 years. Through ICDS, nearly 153 lakh children (3-6 years of age), from disadvantaged groups, are participating in centre-based pre-school play-way activities. Thereby, leaving a last segment of 3-6 population unattended for pre-school activities. This again raises the issue of whether "all children from disadvantaged groups get covered or universal access to early childhood development services is provided only by ensuring coverage of all blocks under the ICDS. This issue will need to be addressed more so as the universal coverage of all children by early childhood development and learning interventions is critical as the foundation to achieve universal Elementary Education as outlined in the "Sarva Shiksha Abhiyan".

Inadequate Welfare Services

There are hardly any childcare centres for mothers working in the unorganized sector. They are not entitled to any leave and have to go back to work as soon as possible after birth of the baby. This certainly cannot and should not be left to the adolescent girl. The need is child care centres where a mother can leave her child in the care of a reasonably trained person and in a clean environment and she can come back to breastfeed the child as and when required or give complementary food. This can be done at the community level, through the Panchayats and various women's programmes. With minimum inputs and with support from the community, these could become active childcare centres. This will help child development and nutrition as well as free the adolescent girl from this responsibility. She can go to school and develop in a free environment. It is, therefore, suggested that the contractors should provide child care facilities for children of women labourers irrespective of number of labourers and children. This is essential because this group remains neglected in other schemes.

Discrimination against the Girl Child

Socially, a daughter is accepted as belonging to the family in which she is married. The parents of daughters are socially banned from thinking of their daughters as their own once she gets married. This belief that a married daughter belongs to the marital home also undermines her position as an individual since she is not supposed to belong to her parental home after marriage and in practice is not accepted as an equal member in marital home. This gives rise to the psychology of an exile. The result is that the parents even when they claim to love their daughters, identify with this sense of deprivation of their daughter, but are also helpless to do anything about it as per social norms. Having a daughter is therefore identified as a relationship that causes unhappiness in one way or another. Society, therefore, needs to be made aware that even when a girl is married, she continues to be her parents' daughter and the word "Paraya Dhan" should be completely banned in the Indian media. This exerts a powerful influence on the mind of a parent who considers it to be a dead investment to invest in the bringing up of a daughter. Therefore, it would be essential to amend inheritance laws in such a manner that daughters get an equal share in the parents property along with their brothers. This will reinforce their sense of belonging as daughters also.

In the end, what emerges is a problem which is neither economic nor related to educational levels. It involves the perception of a girl child as a life long liability. It is a problem of human relationships in the context of society responding to opposing pulls of tradition and modernity. The interventions of the Government in human relationships can at best be limited. What we need here is a reformist movement which originates in society and is granted an enabling atmosphere by the Government. We have to work towards a re-orientation where a girl child is perceived as an asset. She already is one-but is not perceived as such.

The Girl Child and Gender Issues

The girl child does not have adequate recognition as a major concern in the nation's vision of development with justice. She does not figure adequately in policies and measures for either child rights or development of women's rights and empowerment. The 2001 Census of India has starkly established how important it is for the country to realise that this neglect can seriously affect India's future viability. The provisional results of the decennial countrywide headcount reveal that the female/male ratio in the 0-6 age group has fallen from 945/1000 to 927/1000. It is this group, which shows this dramatic decline, while the upper age ranks show slightly improved ratios. The 11th April remarks of the National Population Commission show signs of a new perception of the challenge.

The fact that the Indian population is young, largely composed of people below the age of 25 years (58%), and significantly of people below the age of 20 (47.6%), means that it is the term 'female', rather than the term 'woman', that defines the half of India which is crying out for equal opportunity-and a substantial proportion of the investments and approaches aimed at achieving 'women's empowerment' should in fact be designed for girl children and female adolescents.

The Ninth Five Year Plan identifies the girl child's status and condition as a priority, but the February 2000 mid-term review of the Plan expresses grave concern at her continuing marginalisation and the failure to ensure the expected level and actual benefits to her. The Ninth Plan seems to imply that the girl child, or any child, passes out of childhood at the age of 14 years. The UN Convention on the Rights of the Child defines childhood as 0-18 years. India is party to the Convention. In placing the Plan action for the girl child under the section on 'child development' the Ninth Plan has also missed the chance to connect the childhood, adolescence and adult phases of a person's life.

The Tenth Plan exercise offers the opportunity to examine the rights and needs of the female Indian as they occur in every block of age and growth, beginning with conception, and in the case of the girl child extending to the completion of 18 years.

There is a very strong case for focusing the 'empowerment' lens on the youngest age groups among females. The 2001 Census is already showing that the sex ratio in the 0-6 year age group has worsened since 1991. What does this imply for the demographic viability of the Indian people? Demographers will probably predict that the age structure of the Indian population may have changed and 'aged' by the conclusion of the Fourteenth Five Year Plan, but the years from now to then are clearly a period in which gender justice must be achieved, disparities must be overcome, and needed change must occur. Demographers should even now make visible the implications of not redressing the female-male imbalance already apparent in the youngest age group. This risk goes beyond the considerations of equal rights for women.

It is insufficient to look at measures that would fall within the official portfolio and programme frame of the Department of Women and Child Development. The setting of the girl child extends into the sectors and ministries of Health, Secondary Education & Higher Education, Youth Affairs, Labour, Social Justice and Empowerment, Information & Broadcasting, and Law as well as Urban, Rural and Tribal Development, and even Home Affairs. It would be unjust to the issues and their gravity to limit either policy perspectives or programme interventions to the largely conventional measures that the Department of Women and Child Development oversees. Gender injustice and disparity affecting Indian females under 18 is a serious problem and a matter of national shame; it must be addressed as such. Early childhood is the best opportunity for breaking this intergenerational cycle of multiple disadvantage faced by girls and women sometimes even before conception.

Age-Group Specific Problems

Problems/Issues relating to girl child as differentiated in specific groups are discussed in details as below:

Age Group-Conception to 1 Year

One of the basic problems at this stage is female foeticide. As per 2001 census, there were 861 women per thousand males in Haryana. In general, the practice of female foeticide is more prevalent amongst that class of society which is both educated and financially secure.

Most approaches to the raising perception about a woman's position in society have hitherto focused on education and economic security. Therefore, it is a sad paradox that it is in education and economic security that female foeticide is flourishing. The enactment of laws to check this practice can have only limited effect without any social commitment to check it and would go the way of the Dowry Act. In tackling this problem, therefore, certain cultural, religious and social attitudes have to be identified as contributory to this preference for boys and the same then need to be addressed in a cultural, religious and social context. Obviously, this is not an easy subject to deal with, but it would be necessary to identify all such religious beliefs which place a premium on a son being crucial in certain stages in ones life and making the daughter an equal and alternative participant in the same. Religious leaders of all religions need to be persuaded to reinterpret ancient beliefs in a way which is more in tune with modern times in respect of giving women a fairer treatment in society.

Age Group-1-5 Years

In this age group, the parents sometimes have biased attitude in feeding practices/health care. Therefore, the need is to have awareness generation programmes which would educate parents about the equal health and nutrition needs of both the girl and the boy child.

Age Group-6-10 Years

Here one of the problems is enrolment and retention of the girl child in the educational main stream. One of the reasons why the girl child is not enrolled in school and drops out school is that she is required to help her mother in housework. What we need, therefore, is an equal distribution of household work and leisure between the son and the daughter. Therefore, we should have awareness generation programmes to educate both mothers and fathers that the sons should also share in the household duties.

Age Group-11-14 Years

At this age, the girl is saddled with household responsibility, collects fuel and water and perhaps also studies. In fact, one of the reasons for a higher drop out rate at this stage could be that an adolescent girl does not have sufficient energy to work full time at home to carry fuel and water and then to attend school and to do her home work. Therefore, there is need to train the boys to help sisters at home and also to participate in the work of fetching water and fuel and assist in housework. One of the major reasons for low self-stream can be a back breaking work load and to have no leisure. So along with reducing the work-load of an adolescent girl, we have to arrange leisure time for her and also leisure activities which help in building her personality. Therefore, in the Tenth Plan, there should be tournaments organised for girl only in which there should be flexibility in the choice of games, depending upon local interests as well as social sensibilities regarding girls.

Age Group-15-18 Years

In this age group, one of the major problems is early marriage at an age when the girl is not aware of what this would entail. In many cases, the girls do not want to have an early marriage, but are forced by the parents and society to do so. In this case, and in general too, the fathers of daughters should be educated on their special responsibilities. The fact remains that major decisions in a family are made by the father.

Negative Portrayal of Girl Child

Culturally, the depiction of women in the media reinforces the negative stereo types attributed to women. This should not detract from her role as a woman. Media should also not show her as inferior and servile. This is a delicate task and there should be a continuous interaction of the Ministry with the Advertising Standards Council of India regarding the representation of the girl child in the media. Perhaps, the advertisement for wheat flour should show the daughter studying and the son helping his mother in serving chapattis rather than viceversa.

CHILDREN WITH SPECIAL PROBLEMS

Children with Disability

Children with disabilities generally face asymmetric opportunity for survival and development. In most of the cases they do not enjoy personal or economical security and generally are deprived of proper health care, education and earning generating activities. These children also face difficulties in getting opportunity to participate in developmental programme and are often victims of deprivation alienation and neglect. Unfortunately, there is no systematic, scientific and statistical information of disability, particularly for children. However, Census 2001 (Report under review) has collected data on disability through the country, therefore, detailed information on number of disabled children with the type of disability will be available after the Census Report are analysed.

According to the India Human Development Report, the crude estimate of the size of the population from various forms of disabilities in India has been estimated to be 23 million in 0-12 years age group.

Special emphasis has been given to the children with disability in the various national policies. These include the National Policy on Children, 1974, which emphasise on providing facilities, special treatment, education and rehabilitation of children suffering from all types of disabilities; the National Policy on Education, 1986, which stresses on integrated education and the national Health Policy, 1983 which lays emphasis on care and rehabilitation of the disabled. One of the major steps taken to prevent discrimination against disabled persons was the enactment of the persons with disabilities (Equal Opportunities, Protection of Rights and Full Participation) Act, 1995. In order to effectively implement the provisions of the Actvarious measures have been initiated by the Government, however, most of these are in the stages of infancy and need regular review and strengthening. The National Programmes for Rehabilitation of Persons with Disabilities (NPRPD) needs a special focus on children and dovetailing with the ICDS.

Child Labour

The increasing problem of Child Labour demands immediate attention of the Government. According to the 1991 Census (Census data for 2001 is still not available), the estimated figure of working children was 11.28 million. This figure was 17.02 million according to the estimation of the 43rd round of the National Sample Survey conducted in 1987-88. While in rural areas working girl children are concentrated in agricultural and allied activities accounting for 84.9%, their concentration in urban areas is located in manufacturing, servicing and repairing following by services. Other occupations where the concentration of child labour is pronounced include the glass industry, brass ware, locks, carpet making, slate and tile making, match and fireworks, gem-cutting, agri/chemicals and beedi rolling etc. To abolish this social evil, the Ministry of Labour has enacted a legislation, viz., Child Labour (Prohibition and Regulation) Act, 1986 banning employment of children below the age of 14 years in factories, mines and hazardous employment and also adopted a National Policy on Child Labour (NPCL) in 1987.

In 1992, the Government launched a 'Child Labour Action and Support Programme (CLASP)' aided by the Government of Germany aiming at strengthening the country's capabilities for elimination of child labour. Another action programme established by ILO is International Programme for Elimination of Child Labour (IPEC) which would benefit 79,000 children through 101 projects in 14 States during the Eighth Plan. The National Child Labour Project which extends welfare and rehabilitative services through NGOs, has been expanded in 1984 to cover the entire country. The programme is benefiting 2.00 lakh children till the end of December 2000 through 96 projects located in the Child Labour Intensive Areas. A National Authority for Elimination of Child Labour headed by Labour Minister has been created in 1995. With all these measures, yet the problem of child labour still continues in its magnitude.

Child Prostitution

Child Prostitution is a bigger evil than child labour with dangerous consequences. According to a multi-centric study on Prostitution conducted by the CSWB in 1991, the estimated number of prostitutes in each metropolitan city of Bangalore, Bombay, Calcutta, Delhi, Hyderabad and Madras ranges between 70,000 to 1,00,000. Of this, the number of child prostitutes has been estimated to be around 12 to 15 per cent. With the ratification of Child's Rights, the country has an obligation to save the girl children from this exploitation and to preserve their dignity. All-out efforts should be made to curb this social evil at its bud. All-out efforts need to be put into action to eradicate the most dangerous social evil of child prostitution.

Street Children

A sample study conducted in 1993 in six cities, viz., Bangalore, Bombay, Calcutta, Delhi, Hyderabad and Madras, made a rough estimate of the existence of 4.15 lakh Street Children. An effective strategy to meet their needs may require skills, capabilities and expertise with a holistic approach including preventive health services, nutrition support, educational facilities, shelter and hygienic living, counselling, guidance and referral services, recreation etc.

The nodal Ministry of Welfare has released grants to a number of non-governmental organisations from 1993-94 onwards to implement a scheme for them. The voluntary organisations have benefited 140,000 children with the help of non-institutional basic services for their care, protection and education since its inception. Apart from this, the Ministry of Urban Affairs and Employment also takes care of the Street Children through its urban Basic Services (UBS) Scheme. The most transparent lacuna observed under these schemes is the weak line of rehabilitation component as a result of which the Street Children try to get back to their original way of living on streets. Alternative Models need to be developed not only to avert the problem but also for rehabilitating these children in the right perspective.

Juvenile Delinquents and Vagrants

As per the statistics available, there has been a rise from 7,909 Juvenile Crimes in 1997 to 9,352 Juvenile Crimes in 1998 (at the rate of 18.2%). The Juvenile Justice Act provides for the care, protection, treatment, development and rehabilitation of neglected/delinquent Juveniles and lays down a uniform legal framework. In the Ninth Plan, 618 Homes (Observation, Special, Juvenile, After-care Institutions etc.) were established. The Juvenile Justice Act must, therefore, be strengthened with the requisite infrastructural support of various statutory institutions in rehabilitating the children who come in conflict with law.

Another serious concern requiring attention is the declining sex ratio. As per the census data, the sex ratio has been declining over the years. The sex ratio which was 972 females per thousand males in 1901 has declined to 933 in 2001. The adverse sex ratio for females and its decline since 1901 is attributed mainly to higher mortality among females, as compared to males in all age-groups right from childhood through child-bearing ages. Also, the problems of female foeticide and infanticide, as revealed by some recent studies, are presumably responsible for the present trend of declining sex ratio. Limited access to the health infrastructure contributing to high maternal mortality and relative deprivation of the female child from nutrition, health and medical care have also been identified as some of the other contributory factors.

Violence against the Girl Child and the Adolescent Girl

Crimes against adolescent girls range from eve teasing and abduction to rape, incest, prostitution, battering, sexual harassment at the workplace etc. Social stigma often prevents the registration of police cases and convictions are even less. Girls grow up in circumstances in the majority of households in India unaware and silenced by the taboos related to menstruation and adolescence. The natural growth cycle itself becomes a burden and in turn causes the girl to be viewed as a liability to be sent off in marriage. The high rates of child marriage and incidence of child-birth to girls below 19 years of age bear testimony to this fact. Neglected since birth, anaemic and weak, large number of girls enter the role of motherhood even before they have had a chance to understand or deal with their own adolescence.

The incidence of crimes against women continues and more crimes are now being reported from within the arena of the `safe' spaces of the home and range of crimes against women also expanding with the application of technologies for sex selective abortions. While the NCRB data 1999 recorded a rise in the incidence of foeticide from 38 in 1995 to 61 in 1999, the incidence of infanticide reduced from 139 in 1995 to 87 in 1999. It also reveals that crimes committed against women as a proportion of the total crimes has increased from 6.4 per cent in 1997 to 7.0 per cent 1999 and crimes like kidnapping, abduction, dowry death, torture, molestation, sexual harassment, importation of girls, have increased both in absolute and relative terms. Most rape victims are in the age group of 10-16 years and a significant number are under 10 years of age. Reporting of cases of Importation of Girls and cases of sexual harassment increased significantly in 1998.

APPROACH TO THE TENTH PLAN (2002-07)

In the Tenth Five Year Plan (2002-07), Development of Children will be viewed not only as the most desirable societal investment for country's future, but as the right of every child to achieve full development potential. In fact, India's ratification of the Convention on the Rights of the Child in 1992 and the adoption of National Plans of Action for Children and for the Girl Child in 1992 makes it obligatory on the part of the Government to fulfil this universal rights of every child. Thus, the major challenge in the Tenth Plan will not only be reaching every young child in the country, but also to ensure their survival, protection and development. In other words, the Tenth Plan advocates a Rights-based approach to the development of children.

To ensure 'survival and protection' of children, especially that of the girl-child, the major strategy of the Tenth Plan will be to arrest the declining sex ratio and to curb its related problems of female foeticide and female infanticide. These problems will be attacked through a twopronged strategy of both direct and indirect measures. While the direct measures include effective implementation of the existing legislation, the indirect measures will be to change the mindset of the people in favour of the girl child, besides empowering women to exercise their reproductive rights and choices. Towards this, collaborative efforts of all concerned to prevent/control/eradicate these two social evils will be initiated. In these efforts, both medical and para-medical staff viz. doctors, auxiliary nurse midwives/trained dais and the front-line workers of ICDS and the local voluntary organizations are going to play a major role. The special efforts will include effective enforcement of the Pre-natal Diagnostic Techniques (Regulation and Prevention of Misuse) Act, 1994 and the Indian Penal Code, 1860 with a close and continuous vigil, surveillance and severe punishment for the guilty.

The next priority will be to fulfil the birth right of every child to 'development', especially those belonging to the disadvantaged and deprived groups with special needs and disabilities. In this regard, the present thrust will continue to be laid on the 3 major areas of child development viz., health, nutrition and education. While the most critical period, from conception to two years of age, will be addressed through key interventions to promote health, nutritional and psycho-social development of the mother and the young child through the programmes of Reproductive Child Health (RCH) and the Integrated Child Development Services (ICDS), the pre-school age will be taken care of exclusively by the ICDS through a sixservice package and the school going age through various health, nutrition and pre-school educational programmes.

12.4 The Tenth Plan also identifies the urgent need to review and synthesise all the existing policies and programmes, both child-specific and child-related. In this context, the National Policy for Children adopted in 1974 needs to be revised, in view of various developments that have taken place between 1974 and 1997, including the ratification of the UN Convention on the Rights of the Child and the adoption of the National Plans for Action for Children and the Girl Child (1992). Accordingly, action will also be initiated to reconstitute the National Children's Board which is expected to play the role of an advisory body to the Government in ensuring the well being and development of children. It is also time to consider instituting a mechanism both at the national and State levels to safeguard the rights and interests of children along with the services of a Public Defender to take up the cases on behalf of children and to investigate/redress the individual complaints and grievances.

Health and Nutrition

12.5 Efforts will continue in the Tenth Plan to bring down the IMR to less than 60 and the CMR to below 10 by 2002 A.D. through effective interventions of providing easy access to primary health care services and 100 per cent coverage of immunization in respect of vaccinepreventable diseases viz. Diptheria, Pertussis, Neo-natal Tetanus, Tuberculosis, Poliomyelitis and Measles. The special drives of Pulse Polio launched during 1995-96 will be continued till the complete elimination of the problem of Poliomyelitis. In all these efforts, special attention will be paid to improve the health and the nutritional status of the girl child and the adolescent girls as they both enjoy a lower status, when compared to their counterparts, due to vulnerability and discrimination.

Under the Reproductive and Child Health Care programme, attempts will be made to assess the health needs of children, adolescents and women belonging to all age groups at the PHC level and to undertake area-specific micro-planning to meet their needs through high quality integrated RCH services. The services for `Child Survival' under the RCH will include universal screening of women during pregnancy and identification and management of `at-risk' individuals to achieve reduction in the peri-natal and neo-natal mortality and morbidity.

In line with the commitments of the National Nutrition Policy (1993), priority will be accorded to promote the nutritional status of the mother and the child by improving the dietary intake through a change in the feeding practices and intra-family food distribution and preventing the deficiency diseases. The quality and effectiveness of health and nutrition interventions for mother and the child will be further strengthened with a special focus on early diagnosis and prevention of malnutrition during pregnancy and lactation for mothers and children before and after birth with a special focus on the most crucial age of 0-23 months.

In view of the continued importance accorded to nutrition adequacy in the Ninth Plan, all States/UTs will be encouraged to ensure provision of adequate funds for supplementary nutrition component of ICDS, by listing the same as one of the first 3 priorities under Basic Minimum Services, for which additional Central assistance is being extended to States/UTs. Decentralised funding, community contribution and procurement of local nutritious foods for the supplementary feeding programmes will be promoted to ensure that the food distributed is adaptable/ palatable for the young children and also rich in the micro-nutrients viz. Vitamin A, Iron and Iodine.

In this context, the role of the Food and Nutrition Board will be redefined and strengthened in view of the mother and child-related commitments of the National Nutrition Policy and its Plan of Action. Efforts are being made for the development of new tools for Nutrition Monitoring and Surveillance to assess the nutritional status of children and mothers from time to time facilitating early detection of deficiencies and diseases and necessary interventions are taken to that effect.

Education

In the Tenth Plan, the thrust will be on strengthening the early joyful period of play and learning in the young child's life to ensure a harmonious transition from the family environment to the primary school. Towards this, special efforts will be made to develop linkages between ICDS and primary education. These "operational linkages" will seek to reinforce coordination of timings and location based on community appraisal and micro-planning at grass-roots levels. Girls' education will be viewed as a major intervention for breaking the vicious inter-generational cycle of gender and socio-economic disadvantages. The effective expansion of day care services and linkages of child care services and primary schools will be a major input to promote developmental opportunities for the girl child for participation in primary education and support services for women.

Development

The scope and the spectrum of child development services will be further widened with necessary interventions related to empowerment of women and children, families and communities through effective convergence and co-ordination of all sectoral efforts and services. To this effect, the ongoing approach of converging the basic services of health, nutrition and pre-school education to promote holistic development of the young child, as embodied in ICDS, will be further strengthened with community participation and action to `Reach the Unreached' that is, children below 3 years. Thus, ICDS will continue to be the mainstay of the Ninth Plan promoting the overall development of the young children all over the country through its universalisation. In the expansion/universalisation of the outreach delivery systems of ICDS and RCH, emphasis will be on consolidation and enrichment of content to improve the quality sustenance of services. In this process, the role of an Anganwadi Worker will be that of a mobiliser of community participation and community contribution, apart from that of a service provider.

The Ninth Plan recognises the impending need for the support services of creches and day care centres for the children of working/ ailing mothers in the present day situation where more and more women are, coming out for employment/in search of employment both in the organised and unorganised sectors. In this context, there is an urgent need to strengthen the National Creche Fund to develop a network of creches all over the country.

The scheme for the adolescent girls will be expanded to promote their selfdevelopment, in preparation for their future productive and reproductive roles as confident individuals not only in family-building but also in nation-building. The programme for adolescent girls during the Ninth Plan will embrace the whole range of activities like health, nutrition, education, health and nutrition awareness and equip them with home-based entrepreneurial skills, vocational training and decision-making capabilities etc.

Capacity Building

In the field of child development, the major challenge in the Tenth Plan will be to achieve increased community ownership and qualitative improvement of child development programmes. Towards this, efforts will be made to re-orient the ongoing training/capacity building programmes. Priority will be accorded to strengthen the knowledge, skills and capabilities of front-line workers as mobilisers of convergent action. This entails a major change in the training process so as to equip the front-line workers to understand community perceptions, practices and emerging situations/demands. Thus, the major thrust would be to develop decentralised training strategies with innovative ground-based approaches. In consonance with the above, new approaches for mobilising assistance both in kind and cash for the sustenance of child development programmes will be experimented with community participation/contribution to ICDS. The principles enunciated above and the envisaged role of the Panchayati Raj Institutions and Urban Local Bodies will have major implications not only in planning but also in the control of the flow of funds for the programmes of child development.

Elimination of Discrimination Against the Girl Child

While taking note of the persistent discrimination against the girl child, concerted efforts will be put into action to eliminate all forms of discrimination and violation of the rights of the girl child by undertaking strong measures including punitive ones. These relate to strict enforcement of laws against pre-natal sex selection and the practice of harmful practices of female foeticide/female infanticide; child marriage; child abuse; child labour; child prostitution, etc. Long-term measures will also be initiated to put an end to all forms of discrimination against the Girl Child through providing special incentives to the mother and the Girl Child so that the birth of a Girl Child is welcomed and the family is assured of State's support for the future of the Girl Child. To this effect, a special package for the girl children belonging to the families living below the poverty line was launched on 2 October, 1997 with special incentives namely-Rs.500/-to the mother on the delivery of a Girl Child (limited to 2 girl children); an annual scholarship of Rs.500/-for a Girl Child in I-V Classes; and Rs.1000/-from VI-X Classes and special permits to enjoy the benefits under all development programmes till she becomes a confident and self-reliant individual. Lessons learnt from the implementation of this Special Package for the Girl Child and similar initiatives launched by some of the State Governments viz. Haryana, Tamil Nadu, Andhra Pradesh, Rajasthan, Punjab and Madhya Pradesh will be put to use in expanding/replicating these special packages throughout the country.

Child Labour

Towards fulfilling the national commitment of eliminating child labour, the Tenth Plan commits to enforce the on-going legal as well as remedial/rehabilitative measures to eliminate child labour not only by strengthening various instruments that prevent/combat the problem of child labour but also by ensuring their effective implementation. To this effect, strong regulatory and administrative measures to prevent exploitation of child labour will also be taken up. In the areas where child labour exists on a large scale, special preventive-cum-developmental measures will be put into action with the strength and support of legal/punitive measures. Simultaneously, efforts will also be made to organise suitable functional literacy/vocational training programmes and recreative facilities, after working hours for the overall development of these working children. The enforcement measures of Child Labour Prohibition and Regulation Act, 1986 will be further strengthened at all levels. Also, the enforcement of the National Policy on Child Labour (1987) will be given a fresh look to make it more effective. Public opinion against the social evil like child labour will also be mobilised through the print and electronic media and the support of the pressure/activist groups.

Child Prostitution

To contain the social evil of child prostitution, action will be initiated to make the Immoral Traffic (Prevention) Act, 1956 (as amended in 1986) more specific, through amendments, to the problem of child prostitution and also make the punishment more stringent. The Central Advisory Committee on Child Prostitution, set up in 1994 at the instance of the Supreme Court, will be activated to review the situation from time to time and suggest effective steps in eradicating this social evil. A rehabilitation package for those weaned out/ withdrawn from the profession will also be put into action not only to keep the children away from prostitution but also to keep them tied up with alternative education-cumincome generation programmes.

Legislation

A thorough review of all the existing child-specific and child-related legislations will be undertaken to plug the loopholes in their implementation. Every effort will be made to protect children from all forms of exploitation through strict enforcement of the existing legislations viz. the Immoral Traffic (Prevention) Act, 1956 to check child prostitution; the Juvenile Justice Act, 1986 to remove maladjustment and ensure rehabilitation of juvenile delinquents in the family and in the society; the Child Labour (Prohibition and Regulation) Act, 1986 to eliminate child labour; the Hindu Succession Act, 1956 as amended in 1993 to ensure equal rights to the girl child in the property of parents; Compulsory Registration of Marriages and Minimum Age of Marriage to avoid child marriages etc. Similarly, to promote breast-feeding and protect children from milk substitutes, the Infant Foods (Regulation of Production, Supply and Distribution) Act, 1992, will need to be enforced with a ban on the promotion of milk substitutes and baby foods through media. Enforcement of the Pre-natal Diagnostic Techniques (Regulation and Prevention of Misuse) Act, 1994 and the Indian Penal Code, 1860 will receive special thrust to arrest the increasing incidence of Female Foeticide and Female Infanticide.

Child care services constitute a crucial support service for women in their multiple roles of self development, care giver, mother, worker and household provider, enabling then to participate in development in the various spheres and pursue other goals. Women may thus be enabled to participate effectively in civic, political, institutional and collective life and action for development. The absence of such services discriminates against women in their reproductive roles.

The programmatic setting for the Girl Child extends into various ministries and it is imperative that the issues and their gravity are addressed in departmentalized conventional ways through the limited purview of the portfolio of the nodal Department of Women and Child Development. Gender injustice and disparity affecting women and girl children upto 18 years is a serious problem; and must be addressed as such. The problem of female foeticide and female infanticide continue to prevail. It is a sad paradox that it is in areas and sections of higher levels of educational attainment and economic security that female foeticide is flourishing. The enactment of laws can have only limited effect without any social commitment to check it. In tackling this problem, therefore cultural, religious and social attitudes that perpetuate preference for boys have to be addressed and challenged. Obviously, this is not an easy subject to deal with, but is an imperative that goes beyond religious beliefs and cultural sentiments. Leaders of all religions need to be persuaded to reinterpret ancient beliefs in a way which is more in time with modern times in respect of giving women a fairer treatment in society.

To sum-up, a life cycle approach to planning for the child would enable a focused strategy for interventions based on the following age-specific requirements: Age 1-5: Biases in attitude in feeding practices/health care would need to be addressed through awareness generation programmes which would educate parents about the equal health and nutrition needs of both the girl and boy child. Age 6-10: Enrolment and retention of the girl child in the educational main stream is a major problem. Reasons relate to the requirement of her help in housework, as well as the lack of perceived value of her education. On the other hand is the poor conditions of schools where they do exist. Concerted awareness programme to educate parents to change the traditional division of labour towards an equal distribution of household work and leisure between the son and the daughter. Age 11-14: Saddled with household responsibility, for collection of fuel and water and perhaps also studies, one of the reasons for a higher drop out rate among girls at this stage is the heavy demand on the girls time and energy for these chores. Girls also become more self-conscious and withdrawn as they attain adolescence. Therefore, it is necessary to engage them in confidence building activities namely group games.

Age15-19: Early marriage occurs for the girl at an age when the girl is not aware or physically or emotionally prepared for such a relationship and responsibility. In many cases, the girls do not want to have an early marriage, but are forced by the parents and society to do so. The Tenth Plan proposes to organize "Balika Pita Sammelan" where fathers of daughters are sensitized on their role as major caregivers to a girl child and are encouraged to empower their daughters to educate themselves, to learn to communicate with their fathers so that their fathers understand their needs.

At the end, what emerges is a problem which is neither economic nor social, but a problem of human relationships in the context of a patriarchal society in flux. The interventions of the Government in human relationships can at best be catalytic in bringing about a change in the environment for girls and women. Recognizing the unique contribution of the holistic approach of ICDS and to work towards its effective universalisation, emphasis will be on the consolidation and content enrichment to enhance program quality, impact and sustenance. The community base of ICDS will be strengthened through processes for women's empowerment to enable ICDS to emerge as the major convergent interface between the disadvantaged communities and Government systems, especially the health, nutrition and primary education systems as the core of State/District Plans of Action on

Survival, Protection and Development with special priority for the young child under 3 and the Girl Child.

RECOMMENDATIONS FOR THE DEVELOPMENT OF CHILDREN

Keeping in view the proposed approach as detailed in the previous chapter, the Steering Committee suggests the following Strategy and Recommendations for translating the same into action during the Tenth Plan:

Guiding Principles

Reaffirm that children's rights-economic, social, cultural, civil and political, are inalienable from human rights. These are achievable within the normative and ethical framework provided by the UN Convention on the Rights of the Child, within which interventions for the fulfilment of young child rights to survival, development, protection and participation will be designed, implemented and monitored.

Recognise that the early childhood years-especially the prenatal-first 3 years, are the most crucial and vulnerable period in life for the achievement of full human development potential and cumulative lifelong learning. This is when the foundations for physical, cognitive, emotional and social development are laid. Reiterate a belief in integrated approach to the "whole child"-a child centered approach which promotes a convergence of actions, in the areas of health, nutrition, early learning and better parenting and which is driven by the best interests of the child.

Reinforce the commitment to family focused and community based interventions, in addition to centre-based interventions. This is critical for changing their behaviours within the family and community, for enhanced survival, growth and development, of young children, adolescent girls and women, across the life cycle.

Highlight the role of both parents in shared parenting and caring responsibilities that enable the family to function as the primary institution for supporting the growth and development of young children. To promote affirmative action to raise the status of girls and women, support improved care of girls and women (including within the family) as well as the enhanced involvement of men and families in childcare. Emphasize the criticality of decentralised, locally responsive approaches to the care of young children, girls and women, which respect local cultural patterns and diversity.

Acknowledge that efforts need to be made to reach all children-within which special efforts need to be made to reach the most difficult to reach, the most disadvantaged community groups-the most "at risk" groups, contributing to cohesive and inclusive societies. Promote preventive approaches to malnutrition and disability-intervening as early as possible across the life cycle. Ensure the best possible start to, life of the young child-for the child's learning to learn, learning to do, learning to be and learning to live together. Foster new partnerships of parents, communities, civil societies and governments to meet their obligations to children-especially the very young children.

PROGRAMMATIC APPROACH ENSURING CHILD DEVELOPMENT: ICDS IN TENTH PLAN

Principles for Action

Emerging from 25 years of rich experience in the programmatic perspective, the task ahead is not only that of feeding and teaching the young child but of synergistic approach to strengthen the capacity of caregivers and communities for child care and development and to provide nurturing physical and social environment for the young child in the family/community and at the Anganwadi Centres. The ICDS programme has also now reached a stage, where it is essential to harmonize the expansion of the programme and its content enrichment. The spectrum of ICDS services has broadened with interventions related to the empowerment of women and communities and convergence of sectoral services. This emerging profile of ICDS should rededicate itself to promoting early childhood care for survival, development, protection and participation during the Tenth Five Year Plan. Accordingly, the thrust areas under ICDS during Tenth Five Year Plan have been identified as under:

Universalisation of ICDS-By the end of Ninth Five Year Plan, ICDS Projects would cover 5171 Blocks/Major Urban Slums, which means that about 90% of the Blocks would be covered. The priority of the Government during Tenth Five Year Plan should be thus to cover the remaining 481 Blocks during the first two years of the Plan. This would lead to reaching out to all young children/ pregnant and nursing women of the deprived sections of the society throughout the country.

Addressing the needs of urban poor-It is estimated that more than 40% of the poor children in the country would be residing in urban areas-mostly slums during the Tenth Five Year Plan. So far, the emphasis of ICDS has been on the development of children in tribal and rural areas. During the Tenth Five Year Plan, special efforts should be made to extend and strengthen the services of ICDS in Urban/Semi-Urban Slums.

Tackling malnutrition through ICDS-The ICDS Scheme has the infrastructure for direct intervention to fight rampant malnutrition among children and women. The Supplementary Nutrition Component under ICDS needs strengthening and rejuvenation and accordingly, one of the priority areas under ICDS during Tenth Five Year Plan should be comprehensively addressing the issue of supplementary nutrition component. Under this component, the issues like, linkages with PDS and Antodaya Anna Yojana, comprehensive review of guidelines, specific allocation of funds of non-transferable nature to the State Governments under BMS/ACA/PMGY, tapping of additional resources for this purpose etc. should be taken up.

Conversion of Anganwadi Centres into Anganwadi-cum-Creches-The Day Care services under ICDS is available only for a limited period i.e. up to 12 noon. Therefore, the working and ailing mothers have not been able to make full use of Day Care facilities at the Anganwadi Centres.

There is a strong demand and justification for having extended Day Care facilities at the Anganwadi Centres specially in areas where the women work force is in large number. Setting up of Anganwadi Centres-cum-creches and additional/mini-Anganwadi Centres-During the natural/man-made disasters like droughts, floods, cyclones, earthquakes, etc. the vital role of Anganwadi Centres for providing immediate relief to the people has been recognized. Accordingly, setting up of temporary Anganwadi Centres would be taken up during the Tenth Five

Year Plan. Setting up of additional/mini-Anganwadi Centres should be also continued and emphasized during the Tenth Five Year Plan.

Community involvement under ICDS-The basic philosophy under ICDS is to empower the community so that they ultimately share and take-over the issues of child development as well as adopt the Anganwadi Centre. Efforts should be made to actively involve the Panchayati Raj Institutions and NGOs in managing the ICDS Projects and Anganwadi Centres.

Universalisation of Kishori Shakti Yojana (Adolescent Girls' Scheme) as a component of ICDS Scheme-The Kishori Shakti Yojana aims at empowerment and self-development of adolescent girls. The Yojana is likely to be expanded in 2000 Blocks during the Tenth Five Year Plan. Efforts should be made to universalize the Kishori Shakti Yojana in all ICDS Projects.

Fostering innovation under ICDS-To tackle the area/locality specific bottlenecks and problems under ICDS Scheme, enhanced support for piloting and experimentation with new approaches to care for women and children should be undertaken/permitted during Tenth Five Year Plan. The innovations may also focus on the pre-natal and under 3 age group. Improving the quality in service delivery and management-The efforts for quality management under ICDS undertaken during the Ninth Five Year Plan would be continued during the Tenth Five Year Plan also. Synergistic approach involving the Education, Health, Family Welfare, Rural and Urban Development Sectors should be strengthened for the best quality in service delivery.

Strengthening of basic infrastructural facility-Various evaluation studies and long experience of the Department indicate that the Services under ICDS Scheme have delivered better quality and results in those Anganwadi Centres which are located in their own premises. It has been also established that the State Governments have not been able to channelise enough funds for construction of Anganwadi Centres through SJRY/State Funds. Efforts should be made to provide resources to the State Governments for construction of Anganwadi Centres during Tenth Five Year Plan.

Universalisation of ICDS

Universalisation should be linked with availability of services of all eligible children and not with the coverage of blocks / projects only. State/ District specific strategies would need to be evolved through a participatory process using community based self-surveys, social assessment and mapping.

Growth Monitoring and Promotion

New tools for Growth Monitoring and Promotion will have to be developed to improve community assessment of the nutrition status of its children, in order to act to improve the same. Assessment tools will also include development screening-achievement of development milestones and early intervention when developmental delays are detected.

It is recommended that both monitoring and promotion for children under 2 years of age be done monthly and for children 2-5 years of age, this may be done quarterly. This accords priority to younger children for prevention of malnutrition and early action. It also will help reduce and rationalise the workload of the anganwadi worker.

Strengthening NHED Component: The Nutrition and Health Education component under ICDS should be redesigned with a particular emphasis on Mahila Mandals to a more comprehensive parenting support initiative. This should cover both mothers and fathers and not mothers alone, for improved health, nutrition and psycho-socio development of young children. Mahila Mandals under ICDS should be restructured as parent groups so as to include men/fathers in child care.

Strengthening Pre-School Component: In the Tenth Plan, Pre-School Education will need to be given its due recognition as the first step in the education ladder, which should, therefore, in terms of its priority, get appropriate back-up of financial, material and human resources by all concerned sectors.

The Tenth Plan will need to emphasise strengthening of the early joyful play/learning continuum across the young child's life-ensuring a harmonious transition from the family environment to the primary school. This is the real ICDS/Primary education linkage. This 'operational linkage' will seek to reinforce coordination of timings and location, based on community appraisal and local micro-planning, in the context of district plans in a flexible mode in addition to programmatic linkage.

Training and Capacity Development

UDISHA is the nation training component of the World Bank assisted Women and Child Development Project. It envisages a key transformation in approaches to the training of Child care functionaries and caregiver education. This is through a holistic approach to the young child, reflected in a new child centered curriculum, that is structured along the life cycle and development continuum of the child. Greater emphasis is placed on addressing the developmental needs of the prenatal and the under 3-year old child. The emphasis is on locally responsive participatory learning and action processes.

Advocacy, Communication and Social Mobilization Community participation in ICDS programme, a hitherto ignored area in the State is now progressively being looked at as an essential component of the programme strategy. The Village Contact Drives are seen as the precursors of widespread and sustained community participation as a result of a better understanding and appreciation amongst the communities of the ICDS programme as well as nutrition and health issues. The IEC involves various approaches, builds linkages, strengthens capacities, and enhances capabilities and skills besides building the environment for a state wide people's movement of participation in the ICDS programme. The communication strategy, the strengthened training curricular for job training and refresher training, the PIS for new projects, women's empowerment initiative and monitoring and evaluation components, each reflect the focus on community participation under ICDS.

Decentralisation and linkages with Local Self-Governments, PRIs etc.

The 73rd and the 74th Constitutional amendments have created vibrant new partnerships-to reach the most disadvantaged and underserved-and the most vulnerable-the young child. In some States, devolution of powers to Panchayati Raj Institutions has also involved transfer of some functions for managing and monitoring ICDS to District Zila Parishads, Block Panchayat Samitis and Gram Panchayats. This constitutes a major opportunity for rooting development programmes, more firmly in the community, with the active participation of women. The Gram Panchayat will help create a supportive environment for childcare, by enlisting better teamwork form frontline workers, (ANMs, AWWs, school teachers) to ensure convergence of services. It will also help promote the participation of communities; to understand the needs of children and women and finding local ways to respond to the same. The department has initiated steps for the constitution of Bal Vikas Mahila Samitis at village, block, and district levels, with representation of women Panchayat members, NGOs and ICDS functionaries.

Improving the status of the Girl Child

Promote affirmative action on a large scale for women, through community action, involving both men and women, both parents and the family as a unit, to enhance value care and protection of the girl child-especially in early childhood e.g. Baal Mitra Committees for tracking and registering pregnancies, promoting antenatal care, safe delivery and care of the young girl child. Identification and mapping of the areas where foeticide and infanticide are in practice and monitoring and counseling for 'at-risk' pregnancies should be carried out. The Balika Samriddhi Yojana and Adolescent Girls' Scheme (Kishori Shakti Yojana) should be further strengthened and a comprehensive scheme under ICDS on girl children may be included.

- o Make a special design for young adolescent girls programmes, attach it to women's groups, self-help groups, NGOs with a livelihood component.
- o Set up villagers' committee to monitor clinics with sex determination facilities; media campaigns on equality of girl child. Also media campaign and contact persons of mother and father to say do not give dowry; give her education, livelihood, and inheritance.
- o Village Anti-Violence Committee should be set up. Mahila Samakhya member, Panchayat women member, friend,

neighbour, teacher, NGO member-should be visiting each girl child/mother and should be looking out for signs of verbal/physical abuse.

REACHING SPECIAL CHILD GROUPS

Child Labour

There should be a separate policy for providing social security and services of education, health, for the children of families below the poverty line. Existing poverty alleviation programmes and adult employment schemes have to be coordinated and linked up to efforts for the elimination of child labour.

Children under Sexual Exploitation

The problem is essentially linked to the trafficking issue. There is a further category of children of those women who are already in the flesh trade. Both categories-child prostitutes and children of prostitutes-need special attention in the Tenth Five Year Plan as a priority group. As the child prostitutes are deprived of their childhood (neglected childhood, no education, no proper food, no recreation etc.) and are outcast in the society, their rehabilitation and reintegrated involves great challenges.

Children in Conflict with Law

In the light of the present situation of the children in conflict with the law, the Group recommends the following provisions for action during the Tenth Plan. Establishment of Children's Homes in all districts without having observation home so far across the country (308) and Establishment of Special Home in those districts without such homes (258).

Children in need of Care and Protection

Children in need of Care and Protection include children who are denied their rights, especially street children, child labour, sexually exploited children including child victims of flesh-trade, children in drugs remands, children in conflict with the law, children in institutions, children with special needs (physically and mentally disabled children), children affected by HIV/AIDS, children of HIV/AIDS parents, children affected by national and international conflict-political refugees, war victims and internally displaced and children whose families are in crisis, economic, social (including children from broken homes). An in-depth study on national level is required for the knowledge of such children, their specific needs, identification of the geographical areas of high concentration and other related subjects; creation of essential infrastructure-shelter home, children home and after care home for proper implementation of Juvenile Justice Act, 2000.

Policy and Legislation

Review and harmonize different existing legislations for the child, in the light of the CRC; Set up an inter-sectoral National Task Force on Child Development, which will also review comprehensively the resource allocations for children in different sectors/ Ministries to ensure that children have the first call on resources; all major developmental schemes especially for disadvantaged community groups and women will be reviewed by a sub-group of the National Task Force on Child Development to ensure that they are "child friendly" in concept and practice; Integrate a focus on early childhood care for survival, growth and development in the upcoming National Charter for Children; revisit and update the National Policy for Children in a rights perspective and with emphasis on the very young child.

Formulate state specific policies for the young child; Revisit and update State Plans of Action for Children and emphasis on the very young child; children not to be excluded under 6 years of age from the "right to development" and Article 45, if and when legislation for education is proposed; to ensure the fulfilment of the rights of all young children, there is a need to regulate the private sector and strengthen the autonomous sector to improve the access and quality of childcare services; strengthen the protection of the basic rights of women, especially those working in the unorganized sector-including their children's right to early childhood care; facilitate clear articulation of national/state guidelines for DPEP, to promote early childhood care for survival, growth and development (especially the very young child under 3 years); and accelerate decentralization and foster autonomy of implementation at local levels.

FINANCIAL REQUIREMENTS

Allocation of Plan Resources exclusively for the Women and Child Development (WCD) Sector had started, when a separate Department of WCD was constituted under the newly-set up Ministry of Human Resource Development in 1985. The increasing allocations for WCD Sector from Plan to Plan confirm the fact that they have been responding not only to the existing needs but also to the emerging situations, as shown below:

OFFICE MEMORANDUM

Sub: Tenth Five Year Plan (2002-07)-Setting up of a Steering Committee on the ' Empowerment of Women and Development of Children '.

In the context of the formulation of the Tenth Five Year Plan (2002-07), it has been decided to set up a Steering Committee on the ' Empowerment of Women and Development of Children ' with the following Composition:

1. Member,

In-charge of WCD

Planning Commission,

New Delhi. Chairperson

2. Secretary

Department of Women & Child Development,

Shastri Bhavan

New Delhi. Member

3. Secretary,

Department of Health

Nirman Bhavan

New Delhi. Member

4. Secretary,

Department of Family Welfare

Nirman Bhavan

New Delhi. Member

5. Secretary
Department of Elementary Education & Literacy,
Shastri Bhavan,
New Delhi. Member

6. Secretary
Department of Secondary Education
& Higher Education,
Shastri Bhavan
New Delhi. Member

7. Secretary,
Ministry of Labour
Shram-shakti Bhavan
New Delhi. Member

8. Secretary
Ministry of Urban Employment
& Poverty Alleviation,
Nirman Bhavan
New Delhi. Member

9. Secretary,
Ministry of Rural Development
Krishi Bhavan
New Delhi. Member

10. Secretary,
Deptt. of Agriculture & Co-operation
Krishi Bhavan
New Delhi. Member

11. Secretary,
Ministry of Social Justice and Empowerment
Shastri Bhavan
New Delhi. Member

12. Secretary,
Deptt. of Science & Technology
Technology Bhavan,
New Mahrauli Road.
New Delhi. Member

13. Secretary,
Ministry of Information & Broadcasting
Shastri Bhawan,
New Delhi. Member

14. Secretary,
Women & Child Development
Government of Andhra Pradesh
Hyderabad-(500022). Member

15. Secretary,
Women and Child Development
Government of Karnataka,
Secretariat, Multi-Storey Building,
Bangalore-(560001). Member

16. Secretary,
Women and Child Development
Government of Gujarat
Gandhi Nagar-(382010) Member

17. Secretary,
Women and Child Development
Government of Rajasthan
Jaipur-(302001). Member

18. Secretary
Women and Child Development
Government of Uttar Pradesh,
Sachivalaya Bhavan,
Lucknow-(226001). Member

19. Secretary
Women and Child Development
Government of Sikkim
Gangtok-(737101). Member

20. Chairperson,
National Commission for Women
ICCW Building
4, Deen Dayal Upadhaya Marg
New Delhi-(110002). Member

21. Chairperson,
Central Social Welfare Board
12, Tara Crescent Road
Institutional Area
New Delhi-(110016). Member

22. Director,
National Institute of Public Cooperation
and Child Development.
5, Siri Fort Institutional Area,
New Delhi-(110016). Member

23. Executive Director,
Rashtriya Mahila Kosh
1, Abul Fazal Road
Bengali Market
New Delhi-(110001). Member

24. Chairman
All India Women's Conference
6, Bhagwan Das Road
New Delhi-(110 001). Member

25. Smt. Ela R. Bhatt
SEWA
Opposite Victoria Garden, Bhadra
Ahmedabad-(380001). Member

26. Smt. Mohini Giri
Chairperson, Guild of Service
C-25, Qutab Institutional Area,
Behind Qutab Hotal,
New Delhi-(110016). Member

27. Smt. Viji Srinivasan
ADITHI,
2/30, State Bank Colony II
Bailey Road,
Patna-(800014). Member

28. President
Mahila Dakshita Samithi
19, Fire Brigade Lane,
Connaught Place,
New Delhi-(110001). Member

29. Smt. Prema Purao
Annapurana Mahila Mandal
Navnit, Block No.4
Rammurti Road, Dadar
Mumbai-(400 028). Member

30. Dr. Kamala Krishnaswamy
Director
National Institute of Nutrition,
Jamia Osmania
Tarnaka
Hyderabad-(500007). Member

31. President
Indian Council for Child Welfare,
4, Deen Dayal Upadhyay Marg
New Delhi-((110002). Member

32. Shri J.N. Kaul
SOS Children's Village of India
Kailash Colony
New Delhi. Member
33. Smt. Mridula Bajaj
Mobile Creches
DIZ Area, Raja Bazar
Sector IV, Near Gol Market
New Delhi. Member
34. Smt. Devaki Jain
Tharang, 10th Cross
RMV Extension
Bangalore. Member
35. Smt. Nirmala Buch
Mahila Chetna Munch
E-4/17, Arera Colony
Bhopal. Member
36. Dr. Sarala Gopalan
138-Vasant Enclave,
New Delhi-(110057). Member
37. Dr. Susheela Kaushik
Director,
Women's Studies Centre,
Chhatra Marg, University of Delhi,
New Delhi-(110007). Member
38. Smt. Nirmala Banerjee
Centre for Studies in Social Sciences
10, Lake Terrace
Calcutta. Member
39. Smt. Padma Seth
Legal Consultant
13, Mahadev Road
New Delhi. Member

40. Shri Amod Kanth
Secretary
PRAYAS
Juvenile Aid Centre
F-IX, 4 X Jhangirpuri
Delhi-110023. Member

41. Representative
The Congregation of the Sisters of the Cross
Chavanad
Tirucharapally
Tamil Nadu Member

42. Adviser
SD & WP Division
Planning Commission
New Delhi. Member-Secretary

2. The Terms of References of the Steering Committee will be as follows:

i) to review the existing approach, strategies and priorities; the on-going policies and programmes of empowering women and development of children in the Ninth Five Year Plan; and suggest, if necessary, alternative strategies, priorities, policies and programmes to accelerate the empowering process;

ii) to assess the effectiveness of the implementation of ' Women's Component Plan ' and suggest specific measures and mechanisms to ensure that the funds / benefits flow to women from other development sectors;

iii) to assess the impact of the on-going economic reforms and progressive globalisation/ liberalization of economy on the conditions of women and children and suggest effective strategies to cope up with the situation;

iv) to review the effectiveness of the existing women & child-specific and women & child-related legislations and their enforcement and suggest corrective measures;

v) to review the effectiveness of the existing Institutional Arrangements for implementation of policies and programmes relating to women and children, both at Central and State levels and suggest improvements, if necessary;

vi) to assess the role of NGOs and the status of devolution of Powers and resources to Panchayati Raj Institutions and Local Self Government Bodies, as per the 73 rd and 74 th Constitutional Amendments and suggest specific measures for their involvement in the planning policies; and

vii) to suggest an approach and necessary strategies, priorities, policies and programmes along with physical and financial targets, in pursuing the commitment of Empowering Women and Development of Children during the Tenth Five Year Plan (2002-07).

3. The Chairman of the Steering Committee, if necessary, may constitute Sub-Group on any specific area / problem and also co-opt additional Members.

4. The Steering Committee shall submit its Report positively by 31 May, 2001.

5. The expenditure on TA/DA in connection with the meetings of the Steering Committee will be borne by the parent Department/ Ministry Organization to which the officers belong. Non-official members will be entitled to TA / DA as admissible to Grade-I Officers of the Government of India and this will be paid by the Planning Commission.

Sd/-

(T. R. Meena)

Deputy Secretary (Admn)

To

Chairman and all Members of the Steering Committee

Copy to:-

1. PS to Deputy Chairman

2. PS to Member (KVS)

3. Sr. PPS to Secretary
4. All Heads of Divisions
5. Adviser (PC & Admn.)
6. Adviser (SD&WP)
7. PS to Deputy Secretary (Admn)
8. Administration I Branch / Accounts I Branch
9. Guard File

Sd/-

(T. R. Meena)

Deputy Secretary (Admn)

OFFICE MEMORANDUM

Sub: Tenth Five Year Plan (2002-07)-Setting of a Working Group on ' Empowerment of Women'

In the context of the formulation of the Tenth Five Year Plan (2002-07), the Chairman of the Steering Committee on Empowerment of Women and Development of Children has decided to set up a Working Group on ' Empowerment of Women'. The Composition of the Working Group will be as follows:

1. Secretary

Department of Women & Child Development,

Shastri Bhavan

New Delhi. Chairperson

2. Representative

Department of Health

Nirman Bhavan

New Delhi. Member

3. Representative

Department of Family Welfare

Nirman Bhavan

New Delhi. Member

4. Representative
Department of Elementary Education & Literacy,
Shastri Bhavan,
New Delhi. Member

5. Representative
Department of Secondary Education
& Higher Education,
Shastri Bhavan
New Delhi. Member

6. Representative
Ministry of Labour
Shram-shakti Bhavan
New Delhi. Member

7. Representative
Ministry of Urban Employment & Poverty Alleviation
Nirman Bhavan
New Delhi. Member

8. Representative
Ministry of Rural Development
Krishi Bhavan
New Delhi. Member

9. Representative
Deptt. of Agriculture & Co-operation
Krishi Bhavan
New Delhi. Member

10. Representative
Ministry of Social Justice and Empowerment
Shastri Bhavan
New Delhi. Member

11. Representative
Deptt. of Science & Technology
Technology Bhavan,
New Mahrauli Road.
New Delhi. Member

12. Representative
Ministry of Information & Broadcasting
Shastri Bhawan,
New Delhi. Member

13. Representative
Ministry of Tribal Affairs
Shastri Bhavan
New Delhi. Member

14. Secretary
Department of Women and Child Development
Government of Kerala
Vikas Bhavan
Thiruvananthapuram-(695 001). Member

15. Secretary
Department of Women and Child Development
Government of Himachal Pradesh
Shimla-(171 001). Member

16. Secretary
Department of Women and Child Development
Government of Gujarat
Gandhi Nagar-(382 010). Member

17. Secretary
Department of Women and Child Development
Government of Jammu & Kashmir
Jammu-(190 001). Member

18. Secretary
Department of Women and Child Development
Government of Bihar
New Secretariat
Patna-(800 015). Member

19. Member-Secretary
National Commission for Women
ICCW Building
4, Deen Dayal Upadhaya Marg
New Delhi-(110002) Member

20. Executive Director
Central Social Welfare Board
12, Tara Crescent Road
Institutional Area
New Delhi-(110016). Member

21. Executive Director
Rashtriya Mahila Kosh
1, Abul Fazal Road
Bengali Market
New Delhi. Member

22. Dr. Usha Nayyar
Director (Women's Division)
NCERT
Aurobindo Marg
New Delhi. Member

23. Director
National Crime Records Bureau
East Block 7, R K Puram
New Delhi-(110 066). Member

24. Dr. Banerjee
Director
Centre for Women's Development Studies
25, Bhai Virs Singh Marg
New Delhi. Member

25. Vice-Chancellor
SNDT Women's University
1, Nathibai, Thackersay Road
Mumbai. Member

26. Dr. Vidya Rao
Tata Institute of Social Sciences
P.B. 8313, Zion-Trombay Road, Deonar
Mumbai. Member

27. Prof. B. Vijyalakshmi
Department of Social Work
Arts College, Andhra University
Vishaka Patnam. Member

28. Chairman
All India Women's Conference
6, Bhagwan Das Road
New Delhi-(11000!) Member

29. Shri Subhash Medhapurkar
Director
Social Upliftment Through Rural Action (SUTRA)
Jagjit Nagar via Garkhal
Solan Distt. (H.P.) Member

30. Smt. Radha Rajan
Vigil Public Opinion Forum
12/3, Park Street
Kalakshetra Colony, Besant Nagar
Madras-(600 090). Member

31. Smt. Ruth Manorama
President
National Alliance of Women
8/10, Naina Shetty Palaya
Dannerghatta Main Road
Bangalore-(560 076). Member

32. Smt. Renana Jhabvala
SEWA
Opposite Victoria Garden, Bhadra
Ahmedabad-(380001). Member

33. Smt. Vasudha Dhagamwar
MARG
113-A, Shahapur Jat
New Delhi. Member

34. President
Mahila Dakshita Samithi
19, Fire Brigade Lane,
Connaught Place,
New Delhi-(110001). Member

35. Joint Secretary
Dept. of Women & Child Development
Shastri Bhavan
New Delhi. Convener

2. The Terms of Reference of the Working Group will be as follows:

i) to review the existing approach, strategies, priorities; the on-going policies and programmes and their implementation for the welfare, development and empowerment of women, both within the women-specific and women-related Sectors and suggest rationalization / minimization of the on-going programmes and effective inter-sectoral convergence;

ii) to identify neglected areas and groups; gaps, weaknesses and bottlenecks in the implementation; and take note of the emerging problems / situations related to welfare, protection, development and empowerment of women in the changing scenario and suggest necessary interventions;

iii) to review the progress of the implementation of Women's Component Plan-a strategy introduced in the Ninth Plan to ensure flow of benefits / funds from other developmental sectors to women and suggest necessary measures to improve its effectiveness;

iv) to review the implementation of the existing women-specific and women-related legislations and mechanisms for their enforcement and suggest corrective measures;

v) to review the functioning of the existing institutional arrangements, both at the Central and State levels for implementation of policies and programmes for empowering women and suggest measures to make them more effective;

vi) to review and assess the involvement of Panchayati Raj Institutions / Local Self Government Bodies and NGOs in the implementation of programmes for empowering women, and suggest measures for their effective involvement in the planning process; and

vii) to review the physical and financial achievements in relation to the targets fixed under various programmes for women during the Ninth Plan and project programme-wise requirements, both physical and financial for empowering women during the Tenth Five Year Plan (2002-07);

3. The Chairman of the Working Group, if necessary, may constitute Sub-Groups on any specific area / problem and also co-opt additional Members.

4. The Working Group shall submit its Report positively by 28 February, 2001.

5. The expenditure on TA/DA in connection with the meetings of the Working Group will be borne by the parent Department / Ministry Organization to which the officers belong. Nonofficial

members will be entitled to TA / DA as admissible to Grade-I Officers of the Government of India and this will be paid by the Planning Commission.

Sd/-

(T. R. Meena)

Deputy Secretary (Admn).

To

Chairman and all Members of the Working Group.

Copy to:-

1. PS to Deputy Chairman
2. PS to Member (KVS)
3. Sr. PPS to Secretary
4. All Heads of Divisions
5. Adviser (PC & Admn.)
6. Adviser (SD&WP)
7. PS to Deputy Secretary (Admn.)
8. Administration I Branch / Accounts I Branch
9. Guard File

Sd/-

(T. R. Meena)

Deputy Secretary (Admn)

OFFICE MEMORANDUM

Sub: Tenth Five Year Plan (2002-07)-Setting up of a Working Group on 'Development of Children'

In the context of the formulation of the Tenth Five Year Plan (2002-07), the Chairman of the Steering Committee on Empowerment of Women and Development of Children has decided to set up a Working Group for the ' Development of Children '. The Composition of the Working Group is as follows:

1. Secretary

Department of Women & Child Development,

Shastri Bhavan

New Delhi. Chairperson

2. Representative
Department of Health
Nirman Bhavan
New Delhi. Member

3. Representative
Department of Family Welfare
Nirman Bhavan
New Delhi. Member

4. Representative
Department of Elementary Education & Literacy,
Shastri Bhavan,
New Delhi. Member

5. Representative
Department of Secondary Education
& Higher Education,
Shastri Bhavan
New Delhi. Member

6. Representative
Ministry of Labour
Shram-shakti Bhavan
New Delhi. Member

7. Representative
Ministry of Urban Employment & Poverty Alleviation
Nirman Bhavan
New Delhi. Member

8. Representative
Ministry of Rural Development
Krishi Bhavan
New Delhi. Member

9. Representative
Deptt. of Agriculture & Co-operation
Krishi Bhavan
New Delhi. Member

10. Representative
Ministry of Social Justice and Empowerment
Shastri Bhavan
New Delhi. Member

11. Representative
Deptt. of Science & Technology
Technology Bhavan,
New Mahrauli Road.
New Delhi. Member

12. Representative
Ministry of Information & Broadcasting
Shastri Bhawan,
New Delhi. Member

13. Representative
Ministry of Tribal Affairs
Shastri Bhavan
New Delhi. Member

14. Secretary
Department of Women and Child Development
Government of Tamil Nadu
Fort St. George
Chennai-(600 009). Member

15. Secretary
Department of Women and Child Development
Government of Maharashtra, Sachivalaya
Mumbai-(400 032). Member

16. Secretary
Department of Women and Child Development
Government of Haryana
Chandigarh-(160 001). Member

17. Secretary
Department of Women and Child Development
Government of Tripura
Agartala-(799 001). Member

18. Secretary
Department of Women and Child Development
Government of Manipur, S Block, Secretariat
Imphal-(795 001). Member

19. Secretary
Department of Women and Child Development
Government of Orissa
Bhubaneshwar-(751 001). Member

20. Director
National Institute of Public Co-operation
and Child Development
5, Siri Institutional Area, Hauz Khas
New Delhi-(110 016). Member

21. Executive Director
Central Social Welfare Board
12, Tara Crescent Road
Institutional Area
New Delhi-(110016). Member

22. Smt. Vinita Kaul
Department of Elementary & Pre-School Education
National Council for Educational
Research & Training, Sri Aurobindo Marg
New Delhi. Member

23. Director
National Insitute of Educational
Planning & Administration
Sri Aurobindo Marg
New Delhi. Member

24. Prof. D. B. Gupta
National Council of Economic
& Applied Research (NCEAR)
Parasheera Bhavan, Indraprastha Estate
New Delhi-(110 002). Member

25. Dr. Umesh Kapil
Associate Professor
All India Institute of Medical Sciences
New Delhi. Member

26. Representative
National Insitute of Nutrition
Jamia Osmania, Tarnaka
Hyderabad-(500 007). Member

27. Dr.(Mrs) Rajammal P. Devadas
Chancellor
Avinashlingam Institute of Home Science
and Higher Education for Women
Coimbatore. Member

28. President
Indian Council for Child Welfare
4, Deendayal Upadhaya Marg
New Delhi-(110 002). Member

29. Smt. Farida Meer
Vice-President
SOS Children's Village (Balgram Association)
Chenniram
Jammu. Member

30. President
Guild of Service
3, Casa Road, Egmore
Chennai. Member

31. Dr. Samir Roy Choudhary
Child-in-Need Institute
Village Daulatpur,(P.O. Amgachi)
24-Parganas
West Bengal. Member

32. Shri Amod K. Kanth
Secretary,PRAYAS
Juvenile Aid Centre
F-IX, 4 X Jhangir Puri
Delhi-(110 023). Member

33. Dr. Shanti Ghosh
5, Aurobindo Marg
New Delhi-(110 016). Member

34. Smt. Padma Seth
Legal Consultant (Child Rights)
13, Mahadev Road
New Delhi. Member

35. Joint Secretary
In-charge of Child Development
D / Women & Child Development
Shastri Bhavan,
New Delhi. Convener

2. The Terms of Reference of the Working Group will be as follows:

i) to review the existing approach, strategies, priorities; the on-going policies and programmes and their implementation for the survival, protection, welfare and development of children, both within the child-specific and child-related Sectors and suggest rationalization / minimization of the on-going programmes and effective intersectoral convergence;

ii) to identify the neglected areas and groups; gaps, weaknesses and bottlenecks in the implementation; and take note of the emerging problems / situations related to survival, protectin, welfare and development of children in the changing scenario and suggest necessary interventions;

iii) to review the implementation of the existing child-specific and child-related legislations and mechanism for their enforcement and suggest corrective measures;

iv) to review the functioning of the existing Institutional arrangements, both in the Central and State levels for implementation of policies and programmes relating to children and suggest measures to make their more effective;

v) to review and assess the involvement of Panchayati Raj Institutions/Local Self Govt. Bodies and NGOs in the implementation of the programmes relating to children and suggest measures for their effective involvement in the planning process; and

vi) to review the physical and financial achievements in relation to the targets fixed under various programmes for children during the Ninth Plan and project programme-wise requirements, both physical and financial for Survival, Protection, Welfare and Development of Children during the Tenth Five Year Plan (2002-07);

3. The Chairman of the Working Group, if necessary may constitute Sub-Groups on any specific area/problem and also co-opt additional Members

4. The Working Group shall submit its Report positively by 28 February, 2001.

5. The expenditure on TA/DA in connection with the meetings of the Working Group will be borne by the parent Department/ Ministry Organization to which the officers belong. Nonofficial members will be entitled to TA / DA as admissible to Grade-I

Officers of the Government of India and this will be paid by the Planning Commission.

Sd/-

(T. R. Meena)

Deputy Secretary (Admn).

5/6

To

Chairman and all Members of the Working Group.

Copy to:

1. PS to Deputy Chairman
2. PS to Member (KVS)
3. Sr. PPS to Secretary
4. All Heads of Divisions
5. Adviser (PC & Admn.)
6. Adviser (SD&WP)
7. Administration I Branch / Accounts I Branch
8. Guard File

Sd/-

(T. R. Meena)

Deputy Secretary (Admn)

6/6

Annexure-IV

Sub-Group on the Welfare and Development of Adolescents

No PC/SW/1-23(1)/2001

Government of India

Planning Commission

(SD & WP Division)

......

Yojana Bhavan, Sansad Marg,

New Delhi-110 001.

Date 2 November, 2001

OFFICE ORDER

Sub: Tenth Five Year Plan (2002-07)-Setting up of a Sub-Group on the

'Welfare and Development of Adolescents'.

In the context of the formulation of the Tenth Five Year Plan (2002-07), it has been

decided to set up a Sub-Group on the 'Welfare and Development of Adolescents' with the

following composition:

1. Shri N.C. Saxena

Secretary

Planning Commission

New Delhi Chairperson

2. Secretary

Department of Women & Child Development

Shastri Bhavan

New Delhi Member

3. Secretary

Department of Elementary Education & Literacy

Shastri Bhavan

New Delhi. Member

4. Secretary

Department of Secondary Education &

Higher Education

Shastri Bhavan

New Delhi. Member

5. Secretary

Department of Family Welfare

Nirman Bhavan

New Delhi Member

6. Secretary
Department of Youth & Sports
Shastri Bhavan
New Delhi. Member

7. Secretary
Department of Education
Government of Andhra Pradesh
Hyderabad Member

8. Shri Anil Bordia
Foundation for Education & Development
72, Devi Path, Kanota Bagh
Jaipur-(302004) Member

9. Dr. Pravin Visaria
Institute of Economic Growth
University Enclave
Delhi-110007. Member

10. Ms. Vimala Ramachandran
Health Watch Trust
X-C-1, Sah Vikas (CGHS)
68, I.P. Extension
New Delhi-(110092) Member

11. Ms. Nandana Reddy
The Concerned for Working Children
303/2, L.B. Shastri Nagar, Vimanpura Post
Bangalore-(560017) Member

12. Dr. Razia Patel
Indian Institute of Education
128/2, J.P. Naik Marg, Kothrud
Pune-(411029) Member

13. Prof. Denzil Saldanha
Tata Institute of Social Sciences
Sion-Trombay Road, Deonar
Mumbai-(400088) Member

14. Ms. K.K. Lathika
President
Kunnummal Gram Panchayat
P.O. Kakkodi
Calicut Member

15. Dr.Anita Rampal
National Literacy Resource Centre
L.B.S. National Academy of Administration
Mussoorie (Uttaranchal) Member

16. Ms. Sushma Iyengar
Kutch Nav Nirman Abhiyan
47, Vijaynagar (Near Kalpataru)
Bhuj, Kutch (370001) Member

17. Dr. N.H. Antia
Foundation for Research in Community Health
3-4, Trimurty Apartments
85, Anand Park, Aundh
Pune-(411007) Member

18. Dr. Susheela Kaushik
70, Dakshina Puram
New Campus, JNU
New Delhi-(110067) Member

19. Shri U.N.V. Rao (I.P.S.)
Chairman
Urivi Vikram Charitable Trust
2 Floor, Community Facility
Complex, Raghubir Nagar
New Delhi-110 027 Member

20. Shri Subba Rao

Director

National Youth Project

Department of Youth & Sports

Shastri Bhavan

New Delhi-110 001 Member

21. Adviser

SD & WP Division

Planning Commission

New Delhi-110 001 Member-Secretary

2. The Terms of Reference of the Sub-Group will be as follows:

i) to review the existing on-going policies and programmes meant for the welfare and development of Adolescent Girls and Boys, both in the governmental and non-governmental sectors and assess their impact on improving the status of the Target Groups, especially that of the Adolescent Girls;

ii) to identify the priority areas and groups; existing gaps, weaknesses and bottlenecks in the implementation of on-going programmes; and take note of the emerging problems/situations in the changing socio-economic scenario like juvenile delinquency/vagrancy, drug addiction, prostitution etc., and suggest necessary interventions for the welfare and development of the Target Group with a special focus on the Adolescent Girls.

iii) to review the functioning of the existing administrative structures and mechanisms both at the Central and State levels and suggest changes, if necessary;

iv) to review the physical and financial achievements in relation to the target set under various programmes for the welfare and development of Adolescent Girls and Boys during the Ninth Plan and project programmes-wise requirements, both physical and financial, in the Tenth Five Year Plan (2002-07).

3. The Sub-Group shall submit its Report positively by 31 March, 2001.

4. The expenditure on TA/DA of the Government Officials for attending the Meetings of the above said Sub-Group will be borne by the Department / Ministry Organisation to which the Officers belong to. Non-official members will be entitled to TA/DA as admissible to Grade-I Officers of the Government of India and the same will be paid by the Planning Commission.

Sd/-

(T.R. Meena)

Deputy Secretary (Admn.)

Tele. No. 3714078

To

Chairman and all Members of the Steering Committee.

27 Beneficiary Oriented Schemes for Women Monitored identified by WCD

(i) Ministry of Rural Development

1. Swarnjayanti Gram Swarozgar Yojana (SGSY)

The scheme of Swarnjayanti Gram Swarozgar Yojana (SGSY) came into force with effect from 1.4.1999. Under this programme, the erstwhile programmes viz. Integrated Rural Development Programme(IRDP), Training of Rural Youth for Self Employment (TRYSEM), Development of Women and Children in Rural Areas (DWCRA), Supply of Improved Toolkits to Rural Artisans(SITRA), Ganga Kalyan Yojana(GKY) and Millions Well Scheme(MWS) were integrated. This is a holistic programme covering all aspects of self-employment such as organisation of the poor into self-help groups, training, credit, technology and infrastructure.

SGSY has a provision of covering 40% women beneficiaries as Swamrojgaries. The scheme mainly aims to bring the assisted poor families (Swarozgaris) above the poverty line in three years by providing them income generating assets through a mix of bank credit and government subsidy. This programme is implemented through DRDA and with the active involvement of Panchayati Raj institutions, banks, and the line departments and the NGOs.

(ii) Ministry of Human Resource Development

a. Department of Education

2. Non-Formal Education Centers Exclusively for Girls

This scheme was launched during 1983-84 for children in the age group of 6-14 years.

The main aim of the scheme is to develop programmes of non formal education to meet the educational needs of children who are not able to attend formal schools.

(iii) Ministry of Health and Family Welfare

(Department of Family Welfare)

Reproductive & Child Health Programme (RCH)

The RCH Programme is an integrated approach aims at improving the health status of young women and children, which has been going on in the country. The RCH programme incorporate the components relating to child survival and safe motherhood and include two additional components, one relating to sexually transmitted diseases (STD) and other relating to reproductive tract infection (RTI). The RCH programme is a composite programme incorporating the inputs of the Government of India as well as funding support from external donor agencies. The main objectives of the scheme are:

integrate all interventions of fertility regulation, maternal and child health with reproductive health of both men and women;

provide services which will be client centred, demand driven, high quality and based on the needs of the community

upgrade the level of facilities for providing various interventions and quality of care.

improving the outreach of services primarily for the vulnerable groups of population who have till now been effectively left out of the planning process.

The scheme of RCH has following programmes:

Universal Immunisation against tetanus for mothers, Measles, DPT, Polio and BCG for children

Prophylaxis against Nutritional Anemia under which Iron Folic Acid Tablets are provided to women and children.

Training of Dais caters to the needs of trained Birth Attendants pregnant and nursing mothers and for safe delivery of the babies

(iv) Ministry of Social Justice and Empowerment

6. Schemes for Hostels for Scheduled Caste/Scheduled Tribe Girls Both the schemes are in operation since 1961. Details of these schemes are as under:

a. Hostels for SC Girls

To provide hostel facilities to Scheduled Caste Girls studying in middle school, higher secondary school, colleges and Universities, construction of Hostels is one of the means to enable and encourage girl students belonging to SC community to strive towards attainment of quality education. Such hostels are immensely beneficial to students of SC communities hailing from rural and remote areas as such students can avail of best of the educational facilities available mainly in urban areas. The scheme ensures adequate enrolment of Scheduled Caste girls in educational institutions, particularly, at the school stage.

b. Hostel for Scheduled Tribe Girls

This programme also plans to ensure adequate enrolment of Tribal girls in the educational institutions. The scheme ensures adequate enrolment of Scheduled Tribes girls in educational institutions, particularly, at the school stage.

v) Ministry of Labour

7. Women's Vocational Training Programme Launched in 1977, three Institutes namely, National Vocational Training Institute (NVTI) for Women at NOIDA; and Regional Vocational Training Institutes (RVTIs) for Women at Mumbai and Bangalore have been set up for offering skill training facilities to women so as to enable them find employment in industry as semi-skilled / skilled labourers; or instructors in vocational institutes; or engage in income generating activities / self-employment. Women candidates pass in matriculation or 10th class examination of 10+2 system (class XIIth pass in selected cases) or equivalent are eligible for admission to the basic skill programme.

8. Diversification/Expansion of Vocational Training Programme RVTI, Trivandrum (1983)

Vocational training facilities have been established under this scheme by setting up of an Regional Vocational Training Institute (RVTI) at Trivandrum. In this Institute, 5 units of basic level courses and 3 units of advanced level courses are being conducted to impart vocational training to girls/women. Women candidates passed matriculation or 10 th class of 10+2 system or equivalent are eligible for basic training scheme.

9. Establishment of RVTI at Hissar (Haryana) (1986-87)

A regional Vocational Training Institute was set up at Hissar and the institute is running courses of Secretarial Practice and Electronics.

10. Establishment of Placement Cells at NVTI/RVTIs.

The scheme envisages setting up of Placement Cells in the existing institutions in order to perform functions which will assist in placing trained women in the jobs/self-employment and to take follow-up activities for evaluation of occupational abilities of the ex-trainees. Women trainees who successfully undertake training in any of the regular training courses at NVTI/RVTI.

11. a) Establishment of Additional Regional Vocational Training Institutes (RVTIs) for Women at Calcutta, Tura and Munnar

The scheme envisaged expanding vocational training activities by setting up of three Regional Vocational Training Institutes (RVTIs) at Calcutta, Tura and Munnar to establish training facilities for basic skill and advanced and post advanced skills. While The RVTIs at Calcutta and Tura have been established, RVTI at Munnar (Kerala) is to be set up. Women candidates passed matriculation or 10 th class of 10+2 system (class XIIth pass in selected cases) or equivalent are eligible for basic skill programme.

Under this scheme grant-in-aid is extended for taking up action oriented projects for the benefit of child and women labour.

b) Setting up of new Regional Vocational Training Institutes:

The scheme aims at expanding vocational training facilities for basic, advanced & post advanced skill by setting up of 4 new Regional Vocational Training Institutes for Women with Work Bank assistance at Indore, Vadodara, Jaipur and Allahabad.

12. a) Strengthening of NVTI/RVTIs(Mumbai and Banglore)

The scheme envisages strengthening the training activities of the NVTI/RVTIs by extending facilities for training in non-conventional courses under women's Vocational Training Programme in the existing institutes at national Vocational Training Institute (NVTI) at Mumbai and Banglore.

b) Strengthening of NVTI/RVTIs

The scheme envisages strengthening the training activities of the NVTI/RVTIs by extending facilities for training in non-conventional courses under women's Vocational Training Programme in the existing institutes at National Vocational Training Institute (NVTI), Noida and Regional Vocational Training Institutes at Mumbai, Bangalore, Trivandrum, Hissar, Calcutta & Tura and also strengthening of method & development wing at NVTI.

13. Strengthening of Women Cell at DGE&T Headquarters/ Creation of Directorate at New Delhi The scheme envisages strengthening of the existing Women's Cell in DGE&T headquarters and monitoring the progress of implementation of plan schemes relating to women training. Further the scheme aims to strengthen the system of implementation of monitoring of the training schemes and to create additional posts as required.

14. Grant-in-aid to the State Government

(i) Establishment of new ITIs for Women and Strengthening of new women's ITIs/Wings

The scheme aims to expand the Women's Vocational Training Programme both quantitatively and qualitatively, to meet the growing skilled and semi-skilled man power requirement for Industry/Service sector/domestic income generating industries and self employment. The scheme targets to expand the skill training facilities for women and to make the women employable in the industry as semi-skilled worker

15. Vocational Rehabilitation of Women with Disabilities:

The scheme aims to coordinate with various Government and non-government organisations to promote speedy rehabilitation of the disabled women by providing training, job and self-employment services. Vocational Rehabilitation Centres for Handicapped, under the Government of India, Ministry of Labour are at 17 places. VRC at Vadodara is exclusively for women and the other Centres assist both men and women with disabilities. Department of Women and Child Development

16. Hostels for Working Women

Under the scheme of construction/expansion of hostel building for working women with a Day Care Centre financial assistance is given to voluntary organisations, local bodies and cooperative institutions engaged in the field of women's/social welfare/ women's education. The objective of the Scheme is to provide cheap and safe hostel accommodation to employed working living out of their homes. The target beneficiaries are single working women, widows, and divorcee, separated and working women whose husbands are out of town. Women getting training for employment and girl students studying in post-school professional courses are also eligible to stay in the hostel.

17. Setting up of Employment-cum-Income Generation-cum-Production Units (NORAD)

The programme launched in 1982-83 with assistance from NORAD (Norwegian Agency for Development Cooperation). The programme promotes training of women in mostly nontraditional trades and seeks to ensures their employment towards improving the lives of poor women. Under this programme, financial assistance is given to Women's Development Corporations, public sector/autonomous bodies and Social Organisations to organise training programmes.

18. Condensed Courses of Education for Adult Women

With the objective of providing basic education and skills to needy women to benefit widows, destitute, deserted and women belonging to economically backward classes, the scheme was launched by the Central Social Welfare Board during the year 1958. Under the scheme, grant is given to conduct courses of two year duration for passing primary/middle/ matric level examinations and one year course for matric failed candidates (women) of 15+ age group.

19. Socio-economic Programme

The Socio-Economic Programme endeavours to provide employment opportunities on full/ part time basis to women who are destitute, widows, deserted or with physical disabilities to supplement their family income. The scheme has two types of components for assistance under this programme as follows:

Agro-based Units: Assists voluntary organisations for setting up agro-based units like dairy, poultry and piggery etc..

Production Units: Setting up of production units which can provide part time jobs to women, particularly of marginalised sections.

20. Awareness Generation Projects for Rural & Poor Women

This programme aims to identify the needs of rural and poor women and generate awareness among them about their rights and handling of social issues. Since 1993-94, special emphasis has been given under this scheme to encourage participation of women in Panchayati Raj institutions and learn their role in the National Integration & Communal Harmony.

21. Short Stay Homes

This scheme was launched in 1969 to provide temporary shelter to women and girls who are under physical and moral danger; are without any means of subsistence; facing exploitation and/or litigation on account of marital disputes; victims of mental maladjustment, emotional disturbances and social ostracism etc.

22. Mahila Samriddhi Yojana (MSY)

The scheme has been merged with the recast IMY known as Integrated Women's Empowerment Programme (IWEP).

23. Support to Training and Employment Programme for Women(STEP) This scheme was launched in 1987 to train poor and assetless women with new skills and techniques in the traditional sectors, such as, agriculture, animal husbandry, dairying, fisheries, handlooms, handicrafts, khadi and village industries etc. towards enhancing their productivity and income levels. Women beneficiaries are organised into viable and cohesive groups or cooperatives.

A comprehensive package of services is provided to help women become economically empowered.

Since the inception of the programme, about 4,91,795 women have been covered under 95 projects launched in the States of Andhra Pradesh, Bihar, Gujrat, Haryana, Himachal Pradesh, Kerala, Karnataka, Orissa, Madhya Pradesh, Maharashtra, Manipur, Nagaland, Tamil Nadu, Tripura, Uttar Pradesh and West Bengal.

24. Rashtriya Mahila Kosh (RMK)

The Rashtriya Mahila Kosh (RMK) was set up as a Registered Society under the Societies Registration Act,1860, sponsored by the Department. of Women & Child Development on 30 th March, 1993. The main objective of RMK is to facilitate credit support or micro-finance to poor women, as an instrument of socio-economic change and development. RMK mainly channelises its support through Non-Governmental Organisations, Women Development Corporations, Women Cooperative Societies, Indira Mahila Block Samities under the Indira Mahila Yojana and suitable State Government agencies.

Since its creation in 1993, RMK has established itself as the premier micro-credit agency of the country and its success can be gauged by the geographical spread of its credit delivery system and its partnership with about 800 NGO in the country. 5/10

25. Crèche/Day Care Centers for Children of Working and Ailing Mothers This programme has been in operation since 1975. The scheme provides day care services, including nutrition, to children in the age group of 0-5 years. The facilities are extended to the children of working women belonging to economically backward sections working as casual, agricultural and construction labour in remote, rural and urban slums. Children of sick women also get the benefit of this programme.

26. Integrated Child Development Services (ICDS) Scheme

Launched in 1975, the Integrated Child Development Services (ICDS) scheme, country's largest programme, aims to improve the nutritional and health status of pre-school children, pregnant women and nursing mothers through providing a package of services including Supplementary Nutrition, Pre-school education,

Immunization, Health Check-up, Referral Services and Nutrition & Health Education. In addition, the Scheme envisages effective convergence of inter-sectoral services in the anganwadi centres.

The ICDS Scheme has now come to be regarded as the most viable vehicle for achieving the goals set for in the National Plan of Action for Children. These, inter-alia, include reduction of Infant Mortality Rate (IMR) to less than 60 per thousand, reduction in Child Mortality Rate (CMR) to less than 10 per thousand, reduction in Maternal Mortality Rate by at least 50 percent, reduction in severe and moderate malnutrition among children under 5 by at least 50% and universal enrolment and retention in primary schools.

The Scheme targets the most vulnerable groups of population including children upto 6 years of age belonging to poorest of the poor families and those living in disadvantaged areas including backward rural areas, tribal areas and urban slums. In addition to children below six years of age, ICDS also takes care of the essential needs of pregnant women and nursing mothers residing in socially and economically backward villages and urban slums. The identification of beneficiaries is done through surveying the community and identifying the families living below the poverty line.

(vi) Ministry of Science & Technology

Department of Science and Technology

27. Science and Technology for Women

Recognizing that Science and Technology have an important role to play in balanced development and it can contribute to a higher standard of living with improved opportunities for health care, education and employment, a scheme of Science and Technology for Women was started in Sixth Five Year Plan(1981). The main objectives of the scheme are to promote research, development and adaptation of technology to improve the life, working conditions and opportunities for gainful employment of women, especially in rural areas, and to increase the contribution of women to science and technology and development.

B. Schemes of Department of Women and Child Development

1. Education Work for Prevention of Atrocities on Women

The programme of Assistance to Voluntary Organisations for Education Work for Prevention of Atrocities on Women which was started in 1982, extends financial assistance to research and academic institutions like Universities, Colleges, Women's study centres and institutions of higher learning etc. and Voluntary Organisations conducting legal literacy camps and para-legal workers training and for various items of education work, propoganda, publicity and research work such as production of publicity materials, research studies on particular aspects of violence/atrocities on women, award for best films, short stories, poems and other creative efforts etc.

2. Women Empowerment Project (WEP)

Women Empowerment Project (WEP) has been launched in September, 1998 for training for women empowerment in Maharashtra with the financial assistance of UNFPA. This project is undergoing with a total cost of Rs.2.20 crore for a period of two years. This project is fully funded by external aid.

3. General Grants-in Aid to Voluntary Organisations through C.S.W.B and for Strengthening its field organisations.

This multifaceted programme provides for financial assistance to Voluntary Organisations for rendering welfare services to women, children, aged and infirm, handicapped and other special groups through various programmes such as Mahila Mandal, W.E.P.(CD), W.W. Hostel, Border Area Project, Demonstration Project (Balwadi), Voluntary Action Bureau/FCC, Innovative Schemes etc. In addition, expenditure on activities like Field Counselling & Inspections, Evaluation & Statistics/Data Bank and Admn. Expenditure of Central and State boards are also covered.

4. Balika Samriddhi Yojana (BSY)

The Balika Samriddhi Yojana (BSY) is a scheme to raise the status of the girl child and to bring about a positive change in the society's attitude towards her. The first component of the BSY was launched on 2 October, 1997. Under this, the mother of a girl child born on or after 15 August, 1997 in a family living below the poverty line was given a grant of Rs. 500/-. The benefits and means of delivery have been redesigned in the current financial year. The postdelivery grant of Rs.500/-per girl child (up to two girls born in a family living below the poverty line) will now be deposited in an interest-bearing account in a bank or post office in the name of the girl child. In the same account will be deposited annual scholarships ranging from Rs.300/-for Class I to Rs.1000/-for Class X when the girl starts going to school. The matured value of the deposits (along with interest) will be payable to the girl child on her attaining the age of 18 years and having remained unmarried till then.

The scheme was implemented in 1997-98 and 1998-99 as a Central Sector Scheme and grants were released to district-level implementing agencies such as DRDAs and DUDAs. The scheme has been converted into a Centrally Sponsored Scheme with effect from the current financial year (1999-2000). Grants for implementation of the scheme revised as above are being released to the State Governments/ Union Territory Administrations.

5. Distance Education Programme and Functionaries Working in the field of Women's Development and Empowerment

The Department has launched a project called "Empowering Women's Self Help Groups-A Certificate Programme for Development Practitioners" through Indira Gandhi National Open University (IGNOU). The main objective of the Project is to introduce a certificate course through 268 study centers of IGNOU and creation of awareness among rural women about various programmes being run by the Central Government as well as the State Government so that they could get benefit from these welfare programmes.

IGNOU has designed the basis software, including the training module, and has started enrolling participants to the Course. The programme will be initially in English and Hindi languages. There would be 7 training cycles in English and 5 cycles in Hindi during the next 5 years. ISRO is providing satellite linkage for at least 80 hours per year for this programme and is arranging some of the Hardware-related support. The Department of Women & Child

Development is to provide the required funds for the programme and also extend its existing expertise in this area to IGNOU. The nominees of this Department will be inducted in the programme without any fee. The programme will be open to employees of various Government bodies, NGOs and Students. The project also covers the installation of 150 units of receiving terminals with TV facilities and 250 new telephone connections at the identified centres.

6. Indira Mahila Yojana (IMY)-now recast as Integrated Women's Empowerment Project (IWEP)

The Indira Mahila Yojana (IMY) is a programme launched by the Government of India in August 1995 as a central sector project for the holistic empowerment of women. The vision of IMY is to develop empowered women who will:

Demand their rights from family, community and government;

Have increased access to and control over material, social and political resources;

Have enhanced awareness and improved skills; and

Be able to raise issues of common concern through mobilisation and networking.

It is premised on recognition of the fact that empowerment is a multifaceted process. It seeks to achieve this by the following objectives:

To generate awareness among women by disseminating information and knowledge, so as to bring about an attitudinal change;

To help women achieve economic strength through micro-level income generating activities; and

To establish convergence of various services such as literacy, health, non-formal education, rural development, water supply, entrepreneurship etc.

The IMY is based on the idea of the strength of the Self-Help Group. The development of Indira Mahila Kendras (IMKs) at the Anganwadi level and also recognising other groups under the adult literacy programmes, health programme and integrating them with or associating them with the IMKs at the Anganwadi level would provide the grassroots level organisations for women for various interaction. It has been proved by several experiments in different parts of the country that women's groups become a very strong medium for accessing various information and also for bringing about attitudinal changes on various matters. The groups become a very strong mechanism for empowering women with information, knowledge and resources. It is proposed to expand Indira Mahila Yojana (IMY) to 650 blocks during the Ninth Five Year Plan and to also merge MSY with recast IMY. A joint evaluation of IMY scheme was conducted during 1997-98. Based on the study, the IMY is being re-cast and expanded to 650 blocks during Ninth Plan.

7. National Resource Centre for Women (NRCW)

Based upon the recommendations made in the National Perspective Plan for Women 1988-2000 A.D. and the report of the National Commission on Self Employed Women and Women in Informal Sector, the Department has been considering the proposal of setting up of a National Resource Centre for Women as an autonomous body. The objectives of the Centre will be to:

9. orient and sensitize elected representatives, policy planners, administrators, members of the judiciary, police, bankers etc. towards gender issues;

10. facilitate leadership training for grass root level workers, newly elected panchayat leaders, members, of NGOs etc;

11. create an information base and disseminate information in the fields of women's development and also facilitate generation of data on contemporary issues of women in development;

12. facilitate and coordinate the monitoring and evaluation of existing Government programmes relating to women development;

13. undertake and coordinate policy and programme related research on women's development; i) provide networking facilities to institutions and individuals actively engaged in the field of women's development;

14. Strengthen institutional capacity of Department of Women and Child Development in relation to planning and

implementation processes, which are gender sensitive and participatory;

15. assimilate the gender perspective in policies, planning, implementation and monitoring in selected sectors;

16. undertake advocacy and provide policy support on women's issues; and

17. take up all or any other activity for the holistic development of women.

18. National Commission for Women (NCW)

The National Commission for a Women (NCW), set up in 1992, has initiated multifarious activities during the year in accordance with the functions laid down in the National Commission for Women Act, 1990. The major objectives of NCW are (i) to investigate, examine and review all matters relating to the safeguards provided for women under the Constitution (ii) review of the implementation of both women-specific and women related legislations and suggest amendments wherever needed and (iii) to function as an agency to keep surveillance and facilitate redressal of grievances of women.

The Constitution is reviewing the constitutional provisions and the Acts which has direct bearing on women and discriminate women. Expert committees have been set up to examine and review the provisions of various legislative measures affecting women.

The main function of the Commission, according to the NCW Act, is to safeguard the rights of women in the country. The Commission noted with great concern that the women were increasingly being denied their rights, as evinced by the rising trend of crimes against women, reported by the National Crimes Records Bureau. According to the report of the Bureau for year 1996, there was an increase of 5.9 per cent over 1995 in the number of crimes reported against women. Highest rise was reported in the percentage of "sexual harassment" i.e. 17.7 percent. Next in order was "torture" i.e. 13.2 percent, followed by dowry deaths 8.3 percent.

With a view to combating the rising wave of crimes against women, the NCW has initiated a multipronged strategy consisting of:

Generation of legal awareness among women (and masses in general), thus equipping them with the knowledge of their legal rights;

Assisting women in redressal of their grievances through a Complaints, Pre-litigation and Counselling Cell, set up in the Commission;

Facilitating speedy delivery of justice to women by organizing Parivarik Mahila Lok Adalats in different parts of the country;

Review of the existing provisions of the Constitution and other laws affecting women and recommending amendments thereto, suggesting remedial legislative measures to plug any lacunae and make up for inadequacies or shortcomings in such legislations.

9. Rural Women's Development and Empowerment Project-Swa-shakti The Rural Women's Development and Empowerment Project-SWA-Shakti has been sanctioned on 16.10.1998 as a Centrally-sponsored project for a period of 5 years and an estimated outlay of Rs.186.21 crore. In addition, an amount of Rs.5 crore is being provided, over the project period but outside the project outlay, for facilitating setting up, in the project states, of Revolving Funds for giving interest-bearing loans to beneficiary groups primarily during their initial formative stage.

The overall objective of the project is to strengthen the processes, and create an environment, for empowerment of women. Its specific objectives are:

i) Establishment of between 7400 and 12000 self-reliant women's self-help-groups (SHGs) having 15-20 members each, which will improve the quality of their lives, through greater access to, and control over, resources.

ii) Sensitizing and strengthening the institutional capacity of support agencies to proactively address women's needs.

iii) Developing linkages between SHGs and lending institutions to ensure women's continued access to credit facilities for income generation activities.

iv) Enhancing women's access to resources for better quality of life, including those for drudgery reduction and time-saving devices;

v) Increased control of women, particularly poor women, over income and spending, through their involvement in income generation activities which will indirectly help in poverty alleviation.

The project covers parts of 6 states viz. Bihar, Gujarat, Haryana, Karnataka, M.P. and U.P. The implementing agencies are the Women Development Corporation of the concerned states in Bihar, Haryana and Karnataka, Gujarat Women's Economic Development Corporation in Gujarat, Mahila Arthik Vikas Nigam in Madhya Pradesh and Mahila Kalyan Nigam in Uttar Pradesh, who actively associate NGOs in the implementation tasks. The Government of India in the form of grants-in-aid provides funds needed by the implementing agencies.

A substantial part of the outlay for the project will become available as soft-term loan/credit to the Government of India from IFAD and World Bank. The entire credit needs ofthe beneficiaries will be met from institutional sources. Funds needed for setting up of the Revolving Funds in project states will be provided by the Govt.of India itself.

7

NATIONAL POLICY FOR THE EMPOWERMENT OF WOMEN

INTRODUCTION

The principle of gender equality is enshrined in the Indian Constitution in its Preamble, Fundamental Rights, Fundamental Duties and Directive Principles. The Constitution not only grants equality to women, but also empowers the State to adopt measures of positive discrimination in favour of women.

Within the framework of a democratic polity, our laws, development policies, Plans and programmes have aimed at women's advancement in different spheres. From the Fifth Five Year Plan (1974-78) onwards, there has been a marked shift in the approach to women's issues from welfare to development. In recent years, the empowerment of women has been recognized as the central issue in determining the status of women. The National Commission for Women was set up by an Act of Parliament in 1990 to safeguard the rights and legal entitlements of women. The 73rd and 74th Amendments (1993) to the Constitution of India have provided for reservation of seats in the local bodies of Panchayats and Municipalities for women, laying a strong foundation for their participation in decision making at the local levels.

India has also ratified various international conventions and human rights instruments committing to secure equal rights of women. Key among them is the ratification of the Convention on Elimination of All Forms of Discrimination Against Women (CEDAW) in 1993.

The Mexico Plan of Action (1975), the Nairobi Forward Looking Strategies (1985), the Beijing Declaration as well as the Platform for Action (1995) and the Outcome Document adopted by the UNGA Session on Gender Equality and Development & Peace for the 21 st century, titled "Further actions and initiatives to implement the Beijing Declaration and the Platform for Action" have been unreservedly endorsed by India for appropriate follow up.

The Policy also takes note of the commitments of the Ninth Five Year Plan and the other Sectoral Policies relating to empowerment of Women.

The women's movement and a wide-spread network of non-Government Organisations which have strong grassroots presence and deep insight into women's concerns have contributed in inspiring initiatives for the empowerment of women.

However, there still exists a wide gap between the goals enunciated in the Constitution, legislation, policies, plans, programmes and related mechanisms on the one hand and the situational reality of the status of women in India, on the other.

This has been analyzed extensively in the Report of the Committee on the Status of Women in India, "Towards Equality", 1974 and highlighted in the National Perspective Plan for Women, 1988-2000, the Shramshakti Report, 1988 and the "Platform for Action, Five Years After-An assessment".

Gender disparity manifests itself in various forms, the most obvious being the trend of continuously declining female ratio in the population in the last few decades. Social stereotyping and violence at the domestic and societal levels are some of the other manifestations. Discrimination against girl children, adolescent girls and women persists in parts of the country.

The underlying causes of gender inequality are related to social and economic structure, which is based on informal and formal norms, and practices.

Consequently, the access of women particularly those belonging to weaker sections including Scheduled Castes/ Scheduled Tribes/Other backward Classes and minorities, majority of whom are in the rural areas and in the informal, unorganized sector-to education, health and productive resources, among others, is inadequate. Therefore, they remain largely marginalized, poor and socially excluded.

GOAL AND OBJECTIVES

The goal of this Policy is to bring about the advancement, development and empowerment of women. The Policy will be widely disseminated so as to encourage active participation of all stakeholders for achieving its goals. Specifically, the objectives of this Policy include:

i) Creating an environment through positive economic and social policies for full development of women to enable them to realize their full potential;

ii) The de-jure and de-facto enjoyment of all human rights and fundamental freedom by women on equal basis with men in all spheres-political, economic, social, cultural and civil;

iii) Equal access to participation and decision making of women in social, political and economic life of the nation;

iv) Equal access to women to health care, quality education at all levels, career and vocational guidance, employment, equal remuneration, occupational health and safety, social security and public office etc.;

v) Strengthening legal systems aimed at elimination of all forms of discrimination against women;

vi) Changing societal attitudes and community practices by active participation and involvement of both men and women;

vi) Mainstreaming a gender perspective in the development process;

vii) Elimination of discrimination and all forms of violence against women and the girl child; and

viii) Building and strengthening partnerships with civil society, particularly women's organisations.

POLICY PRESCRIPTIONS

Judicial Legal Systems

Legal-judicial system will be made more responsive and gender sensitive to women's needs, especially in cases of domestic violence and personal assault. New laws will be enacted and existing laws reviewed to ensure that justice is quick and the punishment meted out to the culprits is commensurate with the severity of the offence.

At the initiative of and with the full participation of all stakeholders including community and religious leaders, the Policy would aim to encourage changes in personal laws such as those related to marriage, divorce, maintenance and guardianship so as to eliminate discrimination against women.

The evolution of property rights in a patriarchal system has contributed to the subordinate status of women. The Policy would aim to encourage changes in laws relating to ownership of property and inheritance by evolving consensus in order to make them gender just.

Decision Making

Women's equality in power sharing and active participation in decision making, including decision making in political process at all levels will be ensured for the achievement of the goals of empowerment. All measures will be taken to guarantee women equal access to and full participation in decision making bodies at every level, including the legislative, executive, judicial, corporate, statutory bodies, as also the advisory Commissions, Committees, Boards, Trusts etc. Affirmative action such as reservations/quotas, including in higher legislative bodies, will be considered whenever necessary on a time bound basis. Women-friendly personnel policies will also be drawn up to encourage women to participate effectively in the developmental process.

Mainstreaming a Gender Perspective in the Development Process

Policies, programmes, and systems will be established to ensure mainstreaming of women's perspectives in all developmental processes, as catalysts, participants and recipients. Wherever there are gaps in policies and programmes, women specific interventions would be undertaken to bridge these. Coordinating and monitoring mechanisms will also be devised to assess from time to time the progress of such mainstreaming mechanisms. Women's issues and concerns as a result will specially be addressed and reflected in all concerned laws, Sectoral policies, plans and programmes of action.

ECONOMIC EMPOWERMENT OF WOMEN

Poverty Eradication

Since women comprise the majority of the population below the poverty line and are very often in situations of extreme poverty, given the harsh realities of intra-household and social discrimination, macro economic policies and poverty eradication progammes will specifically address the needs and problems of such women. There will be improved implementation of programmes which are already women oriented with special targets for women. Steps will be taken for mobilization of poor women and convergence of services, by offering them a range of economic and social options, along with necessary support measures to enhance their capabilities.

Micro Credit

In order to enhance women's access to credit for consumption and production, the establishment of new, and strengthening of existing micro-credit mechanisms and micro-finance institution will be undertaken so that the outreach of credit is enhanced. Other supportive measures would be taken to ensure adequate flow of credit through extant financial institutions and banks, so that all women below poverty line have easy access to credit.

Women and Economy

Women's perspectives will be included in designing and implementing macro-economic and social policies by institutionalizing their participation in such processes. Their contribution to socio-economic development as producers and workers will be recognized in the formal and informal sectors (including home based workers) and appropriate policies relating to employment and to her working conditions will be drawn up. Such measures could include:

a) Reinterpretation and redefinition of conventional concepts of work wherever necessary e.g. in the Census records, to reflect women's contribution as producers and workers.

b) Preparation of satellite and national accounts.

c) Development of appropriate methodologies for undertaking (i) and (ii) above.

Globalization

Globalization has presented new challenges for the realization of the goal of women's equality, the gender impact of which has not been systematically evaluated fully. However, from the micro-level studies that were commissioned by the Department of Women and Child Development, it is evident that there is a need for re-framing policies for access to employment and quality of employment. Benefits of the growing global economy have been unevenly distributed leading to wider economic disparities, the feminization of poverty, increased gender inequality through often deteriorating working conditions and unsafe working environment especially in the informal economy and rural areas. Strategies will be designed to enhance the capacity of women and empower them to meet the negative social and economic impacts, which may flow from the globalization process.

Women and Agriculture

In view of the critical role of women in the agriculture and allied sectors, as producers, concentrated efforts will be made to ensure that benefits of training, extension and various programmes will reach them in proportion to their numbers. The programmes for training women in soil conservation, social forestry, dairy development and other occupations allied to agriculture like horticulture, livestock including small animal husbandry, poultry, fisheries etc. will be expanded to benefit women workers in the agriculture sector.

Women and Industry

The important role played by women in electronics, information technology and food processing and agro industry and textiles has been crucial to the development of these sectors.

They would be given comprehensive support in terms of labour legislation, social security and other support services to participate in various industrial sectors. Women at present cannot work in night shift in factories even if they wish to. Suitable measures will be taken to enable women to work in night shift in factories. This will be accompanied with support services for security, transportation etc.

Support Services

The provision of support services for women, like child care facilities, including crèches at work places and educational institutions, homes for the aged and the disabled will be expanded and improved to create an enabling environment and to ensure their full cooperation in social, political and economic life. Women-friendly personnel policies will also be drawn up to encourage women to participate effectively in the development process.

SOCIAL EMPOWERMENT OF WOMEN

Education

Equal access to education for women and girls will be ensured. Special measures will be taken to eliminate discrimination, universalize education, eradicate illiteracy, create a gendersensitive educational system, increase enrolment and retention rates of girls and improve the quality of education to facilitate life-long learning as well as development of vocational / technical skills by women. Reducing the gender gap in secondary and higher education would be a focus area. Sectoral time targets in existing policies will be achieved, with a special focus on girls and women, particularly those belonging to weaker sections including the Scheduled Castes/Scheduled Tribes/Other Backward Classes/ Minorities. Gender sensitive curricula would be developed at all levels of educational system in order to address sex stereotyping as one of the causes of gender discrimination.

Health

A holistic approach to women's health which includes both nutrition and health services will be adopted and special attention will be given to the needs of women and the girl at all stages of the life cycle. The reduction of infant morality and maternal mortality, which are sensitive indicators of human development, is a priority concern. This policy reiterates the national demographic goals for infant Mortality Rate (IMR), Maternal Mortality Rate (MMR) that are set out in the National Population Policy 2000. Women should have access to comprehensive, affordable and quality health care. Measures will be adopted that take into account the reproductive rights of women to enable them to exercise informed choices, their vulnerability to sexual and health problems together with endemic, infectious and communicable diseases such as malaria, TB and water borne diseases as well as hypertension and cardiopulmonary diseases. The social, developmental and health consequences of HIV/AIDS and other sexually transmitted diseases will be tackled from a gender perspective.

To effectively meet problems of infant and maternal mortality, and early marriage, the availability of good and accurate data at micro level on deaths, birth and marriages is required. Strict implementation of registration of births and deaths would be ensured and registration of marriages would be made compulsory.

In accordance with the commitment of the National Population Policy (2000) to population stabilization, this Policy recognizes the critical need of men and women to have access to safe, effective and affordable methods of family planning of their choice and the need to suitably address the issues of early marriage and spacing of children. Interventions such as spread of education, compulsory registration of marriage and special programmes like Balika Samridhi Yjana should impact on delaying the age of marriage so that by 2010 child marriages are eliminated.

Women's traditional knowledge about health care and nutrition will be recognized through proper documentation and its use will be encouraged. The use of Indian and alternative systems of medicine will be enhanced within the framework of overall health infrastructure available for women.

Nutrition

In view of the high risk of malnutrition and disease that women face at all the three critical stages viz, infancy and childhood, adolescent and reproductive phase, focused attention would be paid to meeting the nutritional needs of women at all stages of the life cycle.This is also important in view of the critical link between the health of adolescent girls, pregnant and lactating women with the health of infant and young children. Special efforts will be made to tackle the problem of macro and micro nutrient deficiencies especially amongst pregnant and lactating women as it leads to various diseases and disabilities. Intra-household discrimination in nutritional matters vis-à-vis girls and women will be sought to be ended through appropriate strategies. Widespread use of nutrition education would be made to address the issues of intra-household imbalances in nutrition and the special needs of pregnant and lactating women. Women's participation will also be ensured in the planning, superintendence and delivery of the system.

Drinking Water and Sanitation

Special attention will be given to the needs of women in the provision of safe drinking water, sewage disposal, toilet facilities and sanitation within accessible reach of households, especially in rural area and urban slums. Women's participation will be ensured in the planning, delivery and maintenance of such services.

Housing and Shelter

Women's perspectives will be included in housing policies, planning of housing colonies and provision of shelter both in rural and urban areas. Special attention will be given for providing adequate and safe housing and accommodation for women including single women, heads of households, working women, students, apprentices and trainees.

Environment

Women will be involved and their perspectives reflected in the policies and programmes for environment, conservation and restoration. Considering the impact of environmental factors on their livelihoods, women's participation will be ensured in the conservation of the environment and control of environmental degradation. The vast majority of rural women still depend on the locally available non-commercial sources of energy such as animal dung, crop waste and fuel wood. In order to ensure the efficient use of these energy resources in an environmental friendly manner, the Policy will aim at promoting the programmes of nonconventional energy resources. Women will be involved in spreading the use of solar energy, biogas, smokeless chulahs and other rural application so as to have a visible impact of these measures in influencing eco system and in changing the life styles of rural women.

Science and Technology

Programmes will be strengthened to bring about a greater involvement of women in science and technology. These will include measures to motivate girls to take up science and technology for higher education and also ensure that development projects with scientific and technical inputs involve women fully. Efforts to develop a scientific temper and awareness will also be stepped up. Special measures would be taken for their training in areas where they have special skills like communication and information technology. Efforts to develop appropriate technologies suited to women's needs as well as to reduce their drudgery will be given a special focus too.

Women in Difficult Circumstances

In recognition of the diversity of women's situations and in acknowledgement of the needs of specially disadvantaged groups, measures and programmes will be undertaken to provide them with special assistance. These groups include women in extreme poverty, destitute women, women in conflict situations, women affected by natural calamities, women in less developed regions, the disabled widows, elderly women, single women in difficult circumstances, women heading households, those displaced from employment, migrants, women who are victims of marital violence, deserted women and prostitutes etc.

Violence against Women

All forms of violence against women, physical and mental, whether at domestic or societal levels, including those arising from customs, traditions or accepted practices shall be dealt with effectively with a view to eliminate its incidence. Institutions and mechanisms/schemes for assistance will be created and strengthened for prevention of such violence, including sexual harassment at work place and customs like dowry; for the rehabilitation of the victims of violence and for taking effective action against the perpetrators of such violence. A special emphasis will also be laid on programmes and measures to deal with trafficking in women and girls.

Rights of the Girl Child

All forms of discrimination against the girl child and violation of her rights shall be eliminated by undertaking strong measures both preventive and punitive within and outside the family. These would relate specifically to strict enforcement of laws against prenatal sex selection and the practices of female foeticide, female infanticide, child marriage, child abuse and child prostitution etc. Removal of discrimination in the treatment of the girl child within the family and outside and projection of a positive image of the girl child will be actively fostered. There will be special emphasis on the needs of the girl child and earmarking of substantial investments in the areas relating to food and nutrition, health and education, and in vocational education. In implementing programmes for eliminating child labour, there will be a special focus on girl children.

Mass Media

Media will be used to portray images consistent with human dignity of girls and women. The Policy will specifically strive to remove demeaning, degrading and negative conventional stereotypical images of women and violence against women. Private sector partners and media networks will be involved at all levels to ensure equal access for women particularly in the area of information and communication technologies. The media would be encouraged to develop codes of conduct, professional guidelines and other self regulatory mechanisms to remove gender stereotypes and promote balanced portrayals of women and men.

OPERATIONAL STRATEGIES

Action Plans

All Central and State Ministries will draw up time bound Action Plans for translating the Policy into a set of concrete actions, through a participatory process of consultation with Centre/State Departments of Women and Child Development and National/ State Commissions for Women. The Plans will specifically including the following:-

i) Measurable goals to be achieved by 2010.

ii) Identification and commitment of resources.

iii) Responsibilities for implementation of action points.

iv) Structures and mechanism to ensure efficient monitoring, review and gender impact assessment of action points and policies.

v) Introduction of a gender perspective in the budgeting process.

In order to support better planning and programme formulation and adequate allocation of resources. Gender Development Indices (GDI) will be developed by networking with specialized agencies. These could be analyzed and studied in depth. Gender auditing and development of evaluation mechanisms will also be undertaken along side.

Collection of gender disaggregated data by all primary data collecting agencies of the Central and State Governments as well as Research and Academic Institutions in the Public and Private Sectors will be undertaken. Data and information gaps in vital areas reflecting the status of women will be sought to be filled in by these immediately. All Ministries/ Corporations/Banks and financial institutions etc. will be advised to collect, collate, disseminate and maintain/publish data related to programmes and benefits on a gender disaggregated basis. This will help in meaningful planning and evaluation of policies.

INSTITUTIONAL MECHNISMS

Institutional mechanisms, to promote the advancement of women, which exist at the Central and State levels, will be strengthened. These will be through interventions as may be appropriate and will relate to, among others, provision of adequate resources, training and advocacy skills to effectively influence macro-policies, legislation, programmes etc. to achieve the empowerment of women.

National and State Councils will be formed to oversee the operationalisation of the Policy on a regular basis.

The National Council will be headed by the Prime Minister and the State Councils by the Chief Ministers and will be broad in composition having representatives from the concerned Departments/Ministries, National and State Commissions for Women, Social Welfare Boards, representatives of Non-Government Organizations, Women's Organisations, Corporate Sector, Trade Unions, financing institutions, academics, experts and social activists etc.

These bodies will review the progress made in implementing the Policy twice a year. The National Development Council will also be informed of the progress of the programme undertaken under the policy from time to time for advice and comments.

National and State Resource Centres on women will be established with mandates for collection and dissemination of information, undertaking research work, conducting surveys, implementing training and awareness generation programmes, etc. These Centres will link up with Women's Studies Centres and other research and academic institutions through suitable information networking systems.

While institutions at the district level will be strengthened, at the grassroots, women will be helped by Government through its programmes to organize and strengthen into Self-Help Groups (SHGs) at the Anganwadi/Village/Town level. The women's groups will be helped to institutionalize themselves into registered societies and to federate at the Panchayat/Municipal level. These societies will bring about synergistic implementation of all the social and economic development programmes by drawing resources made available through Government and Non-Government channels, including banks and financial institutions and by establishing a close interface with the Panchayats/ Municipalities.

Resource Management

Availability of adequate financial, human and market resources to implement the Policy will be managed by concerned Departments, financial credit institutions and banks, private sector, civil society and other connected institutions. This process will include:

a) Assessment of benefits flowing to women and resource allocation to the programmes relating to them through an exercise of gender budgeting. Appropriate changes in policies will be made to optimize benefits to women under these schemes;

b) Adequate resource allocation to develop and promote the policy outlined earlier based on (a) above by concerned Departments.

c) Developing synergy between personnel of Health, Rural Development, Education and Women & Child Development Department at field level and other village level functionaries'

d) Meeting credit needs by banks and financial credit institutions through suitable policy initiatives and development of new institutions in coordination with the Department of Women & Child Development.

The strategy of Women's Component Plan adopted in the Ninth Plan of ensuring that not less than 30% of benefits/funds flow to women from all Ministries and Departments will be implemented effectively so that the needs and interests of women and girls are addressed by all concerned sectors.

The Department of Women and Child Development being the nodal Ministry will monitor and review the progress of the implementation of the Component Plan from time to time, in terms of both quality and quantity in collaboration with the Planning Commission.

Efforts will be made to channelise private sector investments too, to support programmes and projects for advancement of women.

Legislation

The existing legislative structure will be reviewed and additional legislative measures taken by identified departments to implement the Policy. This will also involve a review of all existing laws including personal, customary and tribal laws, subordinate legislation, related rules as well as executive and administrative regulations to eliminate all gender discriminatory references.

The process will be planned over a time period 2000-2003. The specific measures required would be evolved through a consultation process involving civil society, National Commission for Women and Department of Women and Child Development. In appropriate cases the consultation process would be widened to include other stakeholders too.

Effective implementation of legislation would be promoted by involving civil society and community. Appropriate changes in legislation will be undertaken, if necessary.

In addition, following other specific measures will be taken to implement the legislation effectively:-

a) Strict enforcement of all relevant legal provisions and speedy redressal of grievances will be ensured, with a special focus on violence and gender related atrocities.

b) Measures to prevent and punish sexual harassment at the place of work, protection for women workers in the organized/unorganized sector and strict enforcement of relevant laws such as Equal Remuneration Act and Minimum Wages Act will be undertaken;

c) Crimes against women, their incidence, prevention, investigation, detection and prosecution will be regularly reviewed at all Crime Review fora and Conferences at the Central, State and District levels. Recognized, local, voluntary organizations will be authorized to lodge complaints and facilitate registration, investigations and legal proceedings related to violence and atrocities against girls and women;

d) Women's Cells in Police Stations, Women Police Stations, family Courts, Mahila Courts, Counselling Centres, Legal Aid Centres and Nyaya Panchayats will be strengthened and expanded to eliminate violence and atrocities against women;

e) Widespread dissemination of information on all aspects of legal rights, human rights and other entitlements of women, through specially designed legal literacy programmes and rights information programmes will be done.

GENDER SENSITIZATION

Training of personnel of executive, legislative and judicial wings of the State, with a special focus on policy and programmes framers, implementation and development agencies, law enforcement machinery and the judiciary, as well as non-governmental organizations will be undertaken. Other measures will include:

a) Promoting societal awareness to gender issues and women's human rights;
b) Review of curriculum and educational materials to include gender education and human rights issues;
c) Removal of all references derogatory to the dignity of women from all public documents and legal instruments;
d) Use of different forms of mass media to communicate social messages relating to women's equality and empowerment.

Panchayati Raj Institutions

The 73rd and 74th Amendments (1993) to the Indian Constitution have served as a breakthrough towards ensuring equal access and increased participation in political power structure for women. The PRIs will play a central role in the process of enhancing women's participation in public life. The PRIs and the local self Governments will be actively involved in the implementation and execution of the National Policy for Women at the grassroots level.

Partnership with the voluntary sector organizations

The involvement of voluntary organizations, associations, federations, trade unions, non-governmental organizations, women's organizations, as well as institutions dealing with education, training and research will be ensured in the formulation, implementation, monitoring and review of all policies and programmes affecting women.

Towards this end, they will be provided with appropriate support related to resources and capacity building and facilitated to participate actively in the process of the empowerment of women.

International Cooperation

The Policy will aim at implementation of international obligations/commitments in all sectors on empowerment of women such as the Convention on All Forms of Discrimination Against Women (CEDAW), Convention on the Rights of the Child (CRC), International Conference on Population and Development (ICDD+5) and other such instruments. International, regional and sub-regional cooperation towards the empowerment of women will continue to be encouraged through sharing of experiences, exchange of ideas and technology, networking with institutions and organisations and through bilateral and multi-lateral partnerships.

Salient Features of the UN Convention on the Rights of the Child (1990)

ARTICLE 1: A child means every human being below the age of 18 years.

ARTICLE 2: State shall respect and ensure the rights set forth in the present Convention to each child within their jurisdiction and without discrimination of any kind.

ARTICLE 3: The best interests of the child shall be of primary consideration. State shall take all appropriate legislative and administrative measures to ensure the protection and care of the child.

ARTICLE 4: State shall undertake all appropriate legislative, administrative, and other measures for the implementation of the rights recognised in the CRC.

ARTICLE 5: State shall respect the responsibilities, rights and duties of parents.

ARTICLE 6: State shall recognise that every child has the inherent right to life. State shall ensure survival and development of the child.

ARTICLE 7: The child shall be registered immediately after birth and shall have the right from birth to a name, nationality and as far as possible right to know and be cared for by his or her parents.

ARTICLE 8: Right to preserve his or her identity, nationality, name and family relations.

ARTICLE 9: A child shall not be separated from his parents.

ARTICLE 10: Re-unification of a child and his parents, if separated.

ARTICLE 11: State to take measures to combat the illicit transfer and non return of children abroad.

ARTICLE 12&13: Right to freedom of expression, subject to certain restrictions.

ARTICLE 14: Right to freedom of thought, conscience and religion.

ARTICLE 15: Right to freedom of association and to freedom of peaceful assembly.

ARTICLE 16: No child shall be subjected to arbitrary or unlawful interference.

ARTICLE 17: Child should have access to information and material from a diversity of national and international sources.

ARTICLE 18: Both parents shall have common responsibilities for the upbringing and development of the child.

ARTICLE 19: State Parties shall: Protect the child from all forms of physical and mental violence, injury or abuse, neglect, maltreatment or exploitation.

ARTICLE 20: Give special protection and assistance to a child deprived of family environment.

ARTICLE 21: Ensure the best interest of child in respect of adoption.

ARTICLE 22: Ensure protection and humanitarian treatment of refugee children.

ARTICLE 23: Right of a mentally or physically disable child to enjoy a full and decent life, to special care and special needs.

ARTICLES 24&25: Right of the child to the enjoyment of the highest attainable standard of health and to facilities for the treatment of illness and rehabilitation of health. Right to care, protection or treatment of his physical or mental health.

ARTICLE 26: Right to benefit from social security.

ARTICLE 27: Right to a standard of living.

ARTICLES 28&29: Right to education viz., compulsory and free primary education for all and opportunity to access higher education, and vocational information aimed at developing the child's personality, talents and abilities.

ARTICLE 30: State shall not deny the rights of the child belonging to minorities to enjoy his culture, profess and practice his own religion or use his language.

ARTILCE 31: Right to rest and leisure, play, recreational activities and to participate freely in cultural life and arts.

ARTICLE 32: Right to be protected from economic exploitation and from performing hazardous work.

ARTICLE 33: State to take all appropriate measures to protect children from illicit use of narcotic drugs and psychotropic substances.

ARTICLE 34: Right to protection from all forms of sexual exploitation and sexual abuse.

ARTICLE 35: State to take measures to prevent the abduction of, the sale or traffic in children.

ARTICLE 36: Right to protection against all other forms of exploitation prejudicial to any aspects of the child's welfare.

ARTICLE 37: No child should be subjected to torture, inhuman or degrading treatment or deprived of his liberty.

ARTICLE 38: State shall ensure that persons who have not attained the age of 15 years do not take a direct part in hostilities, and ensure protection and care of children who are affected by armed conflict.

ARTICLE 39: State to take appropriate measures to promote physical and psychological recovery of a child victim of exploitation, abuse, torture or armed conflicts.

ARTICLE 40: Children in conflict with the law should be treated with due regard to their human rights and fundamental freedoms with the objective of promoting the child's reintegration as a constructive member of society.

Rs. 13,758.04 crore suggested by the Steering Committee is less than 2 times.

The proposed increase in the outlay for the Tenth Plan include- i) expansion of the On-going Schemes viz. National Creche Fund; ICDS; ICDS Training; enhancement of honorarium to Anganwadi Workes and Helpers; consequential expenditure due to Universalisation of ICDS; Hostels for Working Women, STEP, NORAD, Rashtriya Mahila Kosh, Integrated Women's Empowerment Programme; and ii) for the New Starts viz. National Children's Commission, Women in Difficult Circumstances and Action Plan for the implementation of the National Policy.

As the priorities of the Department stand today, programmes for children alone take away 88.70% of the total resources, while the rest of the 11.30% resources get distributed amongst the Women's Development, Food and Nutrition Board and Other Grant-in-Aid Programmes.

This was already pointed in the Mid-Term Appraisal of Ninth Five Year Plan. But, it appears from the figures above that the Department did not make any efforts even to maintain the level of the Ninth Plan outlay for empowering women.

In fact, this is the most appropriate time for the Department to make some earnest efforts in rectifying the present imbalance in the internal resource allocation between the Empowerment of Women and Development of Children.

However, the only possible way for the Department to reduce the burden of the Centre in respect of Development of

Children is to consider the suggestion of the Planning Commission and to initiate action to transfer the programme of ICDS to the State Sector, in a phased way, as the commitment of Universalisation is expected to be completed by the end of the Ninth Plan.

To start with i.e. right from the Tenth Plan itself, it would be better to consider the transfer of 1037 projects which was the level achieved by the end of the Sixth Five Year Plan (1984-85).

In fact, ICDS has already over-stayed at the Centre for more than 5 Plan periods starting from the Fifth Plan onwards, while the original decision at the time of launching ICDS refers to only for 2 or 3 Plan periods.

BIBLIOGRAPHY

Alam, Bilquis: 1981, *Women Members of Union Parishad, A Few Statistics*, NILG, Dhaka.

Alamgir, Mohiuddin Khan: 1988, *Development Strategies for Bangladesh*, Dhaka, Bangladesh.

Ali, Tariq: *An Indian Dynasty: The Story of the Nehru-Gandhi Family*, New York, Putnam, 1985.

Arvind, Sharma : *Women in World Religion*, New York Press, New York, 1990.

Baker, Christopher J.: *An Indian Rural Economy: The Tamiland Countryside*, Oxford, Clarendon Press, 1984.

Benjamin, J.: *Socio-religious Status of Girl Child in India*, New Delhi, Ashish Publishing, 1991.

Bhai, N.: *Harijan Women in Independent India*, Delhi, BR Publishing 1986

Burton, Antoinette: *Burdens of History: British Feminists, Indian Women, and Imperial Culture, 1865-1915*, Chapel Hill, University of North Carolina, 1994.

Calman, J.: *Toward Empowerment: Women and Politics in India*, Colorado, Westview Press, 1992.

Chandra Mowli, V.: *'Jogin'. Girl-Child Labour Studies*, New Delhi, Sterling 1992

Dak, T.M.: *Women and Work in Indian Society*, Delhi, Discovery, 1988.

Datta, V.N.: *Sati: Widow Burning in India*, New Delhi, Manohar, 1990.

Dikshit, D.P.: *Political History of the Chalukyas of Badami*, New Delhi, Abhinav, 1980.

Erikson, E. H.: *Childhood and Society*, New York, W. W. Norton, 1993.

Fine, M.: *Women with Disabilities: Essays in Psychology, Culture, and Politics*, Philadelphia, Temple University Press, 1988.

Gilligan, C.: *In a Different Voice: Psychological Theory and Women's Development*, Cambridge, Harvard University Press, 1993.

Heinsath, Charles: *Indian Nationalism and Hindu Social Reform*, Princeton, Princeton University Press, 1964.

Jain, D.: *Women's Quest for Power*, Sahibabad, Vikas, 1980.

Jordan, J. V.: *Women's Growth in Diversity*, New York, Guilford Press, 1997.

Karl Marilee: 1995, *Women and Empowerment: Participation and Decision-Making*, Zed Books Limited, London.

Kelles-Viitanen, A.: *Invisible Hands. Women in Home-based Production*, New Delhi, Sage, 1987.

Mathur, B.B.: *Women and Depressed Class Population in India*, Allahabad, Chugh, 1994.

Minakshi, C.: *Administration and Social Life under the Pallavas*, Madras, University of Madras, 1977.

Mueller, R.: *Women's Work in Third World Agriculture*, Geneva, ILO, 1985.

Nair, Janaki: *Women and Law in Colonial India*, New Delhi, Kali, 1996.

Palriwala, R.: *Structures and Strategies. Women, Work and Family*, New Delhi, Sage 1990.

Panini, M.N.: *From the Female Eye. Accounts of Women Fieldworkers Studying their Own Communities*, Delhi, Hindustan, 1991.

Selliah, S.: *The Self-Employed Women's Association, Ahmedabad*, Geneva, ILO, 1989.

Stern, R.: *Changing India*, Cambridge University Press, Cambridge, 1993.

Tinker, I.: *Persistent Inequalities: Women and World Development*, New York, OUP, 1990.

Viitanen, A.: *Invisible Hands. Women in Home-based Production*, New Delhi, Sage, 1987.

Vyas, A. & Singh, S.: *Women's Studies in India. Information Sources, Services and Programmes*, New Delhi, Sage, 1993.

INDEX

A

Approach, 24, 33, 43, 48, 56, 57, 60, 61, 64, 153, 155, 156, 157, 159, 160, 161, 172, 183, 184, 192, 193, 195, 196, 197, 198, 199, 200, 201, 202, 207, 212, 219, 220, 222, 225, 229, 232, 233, 234, 235, 236, 247, 249, 252, 256, 257, 258, 259, 261, 263, 273, 274, 280, 287, 295, 310, 316.

C

Castes, 4, 5, 6, 7, 11, 12, 24, 87, 90, 96, 125, 196, 212, 311, 316.

Committee, 6, 24, 92, 93, 105, 123, 155, 156, 157, 159, 162, 163, 175, 198, 210, 228, 255, 258, 264, 267, 273, 274, 275, 282, 294, 311, 329.

Communication, 45, 52, 64, 144, 166, 223, 263, 319, 320.

Constitution, 2, 4, 5, 11, 14, 25, 31, 34, 36, 37, 57, 65, 72, 83, 84, 85, 86, 87, 110, 112, 115, 119, 120, 124, 125, 126, 158, 209, 217, 218, 264, 307, 308, 310, 311, 325.

Corporations, 2, 164, 210, 299, 301, 321.

Councils, 85, 86, 88, 91, 92, 93, 94, 99, 103, 110, 122, 125, 133, 322.

D

Democracy, 1, 2, 3, 4, 6, 16, 20, 24, 25, 27, 30, 34, 35, 36, 37, 43, 56, 57, 65, 82, 85, 97, 109, 110, 111, 114, 118, 149, 169, 180.

Development, 1, 2, 5, 6, 7, 8, 9, 10, 15, 23, 24, 27, 28, 33, 34, 35, 36, 37, 38, 39, 41, 43, 44, 46, 47, 48, 49, 50, 53, 57, 58, 60, 61, 62, 63, 64, 67, 69, 78, 80, 82, 83, 85, 86, 87, 88, 89, 100, 102, 103, 105, 106, 107, 109, 110, 111, 112, 114, 117, 118, 119, 120, 121, 123, 129, 132, 133, 134, 135, 136, 138, 140, 141, 142, 144, 145, 146, 147, 148, 149, 150, 151, 152, 154, 155, 156, 157, 158, 159, 160, 162, 163, 164, 167, 168, 170, 171, 173, 174, 179, 182, 183, 186, 188, 190, 191, 193, 194, 195, 196, 198, 199, 200, 206,

208, 210, 211, 212, 213, 215, 216, 217, 218, 219, 220, 221, 222, 223, 224, 225, 226, 229, 230, 232, 233, 234, 236, 238, 239, 240, 242, 244, 245, 247, 249, 250, 251, 252, 253, 254, 256, 258, 259, 260, 261, 262, 263, 264, 266, 267, 268, 269, 270, 273, 274, 275, 276, 277, 278, 279, 280, 281, 282, 283, 284, 285, 287, 288, 289, 290, 291, 293, 294, 295, 298, 299, 301, 302, 303, 304, 305, 306, 307, 308, 309, 310, 311, 312, 313, 314, 315, 316, 317, 319, 321, 322, 323, 324, 325, 326, 327, 329.

Devolution, 37, 38, 43, 64, 83, 84, 105, 109, 114, 116, 123, 127, 156, 263, 274.

E

Economic Empowerment, 31, 37, 131, 194, 205, 214, 226, 314.

Elections, 2, 7, 9, 11, 15, 17, 19, 20, 21, 22, 23, 24, 28, 29, 34, 36, 38, 41, 62, 67, 84, 85, 86, 87, 91, 92, 93, 96, 112, 118, 120, 121, 122, 126, 128, 132, 133, 138, 139, 143, 150, 152, 153, 180.

Empowerment, 30, 31, 33, 34, 35, 36, 37, 38, 39, 41, 42, 43, 44, 45, 49, 51, 53, 54, 56, 60, 61, 62, 64, 65, 70, 83, 84, 85, 93, 94, 95, 101, 102, 106, 108, 109, 112, 113, 115, 123, 125, 131, 132, 135, 137, 149, 153, 156, 157, 160, 161, 162, 163, 164, 173, 181, 184, 191, 192, 193, 194, 195, 197, 198, 199, 201, 205, 207, 210, 211, 214, 216, 222, 226, 230, 234, 240, 242, 252, 257, 259, 261, 263, 267, 268, 275, 276, 280, 281, 282, 284, 296, 300, 303, 304, 305, 308, 310, 311, 312, 313, 314, 316, 321, 325, 326, 329.

Evaluation, 43, 44, 45, 56, 63, 69, 72, 137, 166, 198, 215, 216, 223, 224, 261, 263, 297, 303, 306, 321.

G

Governance, 1, 3, 6, 9, 30, 37, 43, 64, 82, 83, 89, 92, 97, 100, 102, 105, 106, 107, 108, 109, 111, 112, 115, 116, 118, 119, 120, 121, 122, 123, 134, 148, 150, 191.

Government, 3, 5, 6, 7, 8, 10, 11, 14, 15, 16, 21, 22, 24, 26, 27, 31, 35, 43, 45, 46, 47, 48, 50, 54, 60, 62, 63, 64, 65, 66, 70, 72, 81, 83, 84, 85, 86, 87, 91, 92, 97, 99, 100, 101, 102, 104, 105, 107, 108, 109, 110, 111, 112, 113, 114, 115, 116, 118, 119, 120, 121, 122, 123, 124, 125, 126, 127, 128, 129, 132, 133, 137, 140, 142, 146, 147, 148, 149, 150, 151, 154, 156, 159, 167, 171, 179, 183,

184, 186, 187, 191, 193, 200, 201, 208, 209, 213, 215, 217, 220, 223, 226, 228, 232, 234, 236, 240, 245, 246, 249, 250, 257, 260, 269, 270, 274, 277, 278, 281, 282, 284, 285, 289, 291, 294, 295, 298, 299, 301, 304, 305, 306, 309, 311, 322.

I

Institutional Mechnisms, 321.
Institutions, 1, 2, 7, 21, 24, 25, 28, 30, 31, 33, 35, 36, 37, 40, 43, 44, 54, 56, 57, 61, 64, 81, 83, 84, 85, 86, 101, 108, 109, 110, 112, 113, 114, 115, 116, 120, 121, 123, 126, 132, 134, 136, 156, 170, 179, 180, 189, 191, 195, 200, 207, 210, 211, 214, 215, 216, 224, 225, 231, 247, 253, 261, 263, 265, 274, 281, 288, 294, 296, 297, 299, 300, 303, 306, 308, 314, 316, 319, 321, 322, 323, 325, 326.
Interventions, 44, 45, 46, 47, 48, 49, 53, 54, 55, 60, 63, 88, 118, 147, 158, 179, 182, 194, 202, 206, 222, 224, 230, 239, 240, 242, 250, 251, 252, 256, 257, 258, 259, 281, 288, 293, 295, 313, 317, 321.

L

Laws, 1, 3, 5, 71, 107, 108, 126, 141, 166, 168, 186, 189, 194, 196, 204, 207, 209, 210, 217, 240, 242, 254, 256, 308, 310, 313, 314, 320, 323, 324.
Leadership, 16, 27, 28, 29, 55, 62, 85, 87, 88, 89, 91, 97, 99, 101, 102, 104, 105, 112, 113, 115, 127, 128, 135, 136, 137, 148, 151, 153, 191, 200, 233, 306.
Legislatures, 1, 84, 125, 191.

M

Methodology, 8, 32, 50, 60, 62, 116, 118.

N

National Policy, 161, 184, 193, 194, 197, 198, 201, 218, 219, 220, 233, 234, 245, 246, 250, 255, 266, 310, 325, 329.

O

Observations, 47, 54, 63, 64.

P

Panchayati Raj, 2, 7, 8, 10, 12, 13, 15, 16, 22, 24, 29, 31, 32, 33, 35, 36, 38, 40, 44, 45, 54, 55, 65, 81, 82, 83, 84, 85, 106, 112, 117, 125, 126, 156, 170, 179, 180, 210, 224, 253, 261, 274, 287, 294, 297, 301, 306, 330.
Panchayats, 2, 4, 5, 14, 15, 21, 25, 26, 31, 32, 36, 37, 38, 39, 41, 42, 43, 44, 45, 46, 47, 48, 50, 51, 52, 53, 55, 56, 59, 61, 63, 64, 65, 66, 67, 68, 69, 70, 71, 73, 82, 83, 84, 85, 87, 93, 94, 98,

99, 112, 113, 114, 118, 120, 121, 125, 126, 127, 128, 139, 140, 143, 147, 148, 154, 191, 210, 239, 264, 310, 322, 324.
Powers, 4, 5, 18, 37, 38, 40, 43, 46, 65, 66, 70, 83, 87, 105, 109, 156, 263, 274.

R

Religions, 7, 35, 243, 256.
Research, 15, 38, 49, 50, 51, 61, 62, 69, 70, 89, 98, 103, 116, 148, 208, 215, 216, 223, 224, 225, 285, 286, 292, 302, 303, 306, 321, 322, 325.
Revolution, 31, 102, 104, 107, 118, 126, 225.

S

Social Empowerment, 34, 195, 201, 214, 316.

W

Women, 1, 2, 3, 4, 6, 7, 8, 9, 11, 12, 13, 14, 15, 16, 17, 18, 19, 20, 21, 22, 23, 24, 25, 26, 27, 28, 29, 30, 31, 32, 33, 34, 35, 36, 37, 38, 39, 40, 41, 42, 43, 44, 45, 46, 47, 48, 49, 50, 51, 52, 53, 54, 55, 56, 57, 60, 61, 62, 64, 65, 66, 67, 68, 69, 70, 71, 72, 73, 74, 76, 81, 82, 83, 84, 85, 86, 87, 88, 89, 90, 91, 92, 93, 94, 95, 96, 97, 98, 99, 100, 101, 102, 103, 104, 105, 106, 107, 108, 110, 111, 112, 113, 114, 115, 116, 117, 118, 119, 120, 121, 122, 123, 124, 125, 126, 127, 128, 129, 130, 131, 132, 133, 134, 135, 136, 137, 138, 139, 140, 141, 142, 143, 144, 145, 146, 147, 148, 149, 150, 151, 152, 153, 154, 155, 156, 157, 158, 159, 160, 161, 162, 163, 164, 165, 166, 167, 168, 169, 170, 171, 172, 173, 174, 175, 176, 177, 178, 179, 180, 181, 182, 183, 184, 185, 186, 187, 188, 189, 190, 191, 192, 193, 194, 195, 196, 197, 198, 199, 200, 201, 202, 203, 204, 205, 206, 207, 208, 209, 210, 211, 212, 213, 214, 215, 216, 219, 222, 224, 225, 228, 230, 233, 234, 235, 237, 239, 242, 243, 244, 248, 249, 251, 252, 253, 256, 257, 258, 259, 260, 261, 263, 264, 265, 266, 267, 269, 270, 273, 274, 275, 277, 278, 280, 281, 282, 284, 285, 286, 287, 290, 294, 295, 296, 297, 298, 299, 300, 301, 302, 303, 304, 305, 306, 307, 308, 309, 310, 311, 312, 313, 314, 315, 316, 317, 318, 319, 320, 321, 322, 323, 324, 325, 326, 329, 330.